BREACH OF TRUST

How Washington Turns Outsiders into Insiders

TOM A. COBURN, M.D.

with

JOHN HART

WND BOOKS
Nashville
www.WNDBooks.com

Published in Nashville, Tennessee, by WND Books.

Published in association with Yates & Yates, LLP, Attorneys and Counselors, Orange, California.

Library of Congress Cataloging-in-Publication Data

Coburn, Tom A.
    Breach of trust : how Washington turns outsiders into insiders / Tom A. Coburn with John Hart.
        p.   cm.

    ISBN 0-7852-6220-2

1. Bureaucracy—United States.   2. Public administration—United States.
I. Title.
    JK421.C583   2003
    328.73'092—dc21   2003013214
                                                                                    CIP

Printed in the United States of America
03 04 05 06 07   BVG   5 4 3

To all of our children and grandchildren whose futures have been mortgaged by Congresses that have forsaken the Constitution and its design for limited government. Their future, and the future of this nation, hinges upon our ability to regain the wisdom of our founders—a wisdom informed by history and rooted in Truths beyond party and ideology.

To the true public servants in Congress who have honored their oath of office by defending the Constitution and its ideals of limited government.

To my staff who worked tirelessly while I served in Congress. I thank you immensely and dedicate this work to you as a reflection of the purpose of your service.

To John Shadegg, Mark Sanford, Mark Souder, Matt Salmon, Walter Jones, Lindsey Graham, Sue Myrick, and Gil Gutknecht for their consistent courage as well as their friendship.

To Zack Wamp, Bart Stupak, Mike Doyle, Steve Largent, and John Baldacci who became some of the best friends I have ever known. Your loyal friendship and accountability made it possible for me to serve in a way in which I could be proud.

To my father, O. W. Coburn, who, with an eighth-grade education, worked hard and enjoyed the benefits of the American free enterprise system. His chances of success in today's government-regulated and controlled environment would have been several orders of magnitude less likely. It was his example that has led me at every level to challenge the infringement of our rights as free people by a government that is increasingly straying from our founders' vision.

Lastly, to my loving wife Carolyn who has put up with six years of Congress and the completion of this book. I say an eternal thank you!

CONTENTS

FOREWORD

by Robert D. Novak

I N THE NEARLY HALF CENTURY that I have been observing the Washington scene and writing and talking about it, I doubt anything has delighted me more than Dr. Tom Coburn of Muskogee, Okla., telling the Congressional establishment to go stuff it.

It happened early in 1998, as Coburn was beginning his third year as a member of the House of Representatives. He had always intended to maintain his medical practice while serving in Congress. From the start, he had returned home every weekend to Muskogee to deliver babies— 200 of them in the first three years.

Since 1997, however, the House Ethics Committee had been pondering a complaint, filed by colleagues, that Coburn was violating House rules. After a year's procrastination, the committee ruled that delivering babies was a "fiduciary" relationship—akin to practicing law or selling insurance and real estate. Thus, his colleagues ruled, Coburn was in violation of a 1989 law restricting outside income by members of Congress.

That decision did not faze Dr. Coburn in the slightest. "I'm not going to abide by what they've said," he said. "If I can't resolve it I won't be here, period." He went on to declare: "I'm going to continue practicing medicine regardless of what they say." Faced with that determination, the House ethicists backed down.

It would not have broken Coburn's heart if he had returned home to Oklahoma in 1998. That would have advanced his timetable by three years. He had pledged to serve only three two-year terms, which meant 2000 would be his last year in Congress. That pledge and his refusal to abandon his medical practice makes Coburn the purest citizen legislator that I have ever seen in a Congress dominated by long-serving professional politicians.

That is why this revealing book is so important for Americans, who should understand the corruption of their national legislative branch. Tom Coburn's story is the modern version of *Mr. Smith Goes to Washington*. In the melodramatic climax of the Frank Capra movie, the idealistic young "Sen. Smith" (played by Jimmy Stewart) appears to have won an ill-defined victory over corrupt special interests. Real life is more complicated. Coburn left Washington, intrepid and vindicated but unable to really change the status quo on Capitol Hill.

Coburn came to Congress as part of the big and boisterous Republican class of 1994 that won the party control of the House of Representatives for the first time in 40 years. These new legislators were ready to march behind fiery Speaker Newt Gingrich to effect a revolution in government. They were now in Washington, but did not want to be part of Washington.

Few of the rookie House members showed any inclination to settle in by moving their families to the capital. Most had campaigned on what was then the very popular issue of term limits. Several winning Republicans—Coburn among them—had promised to serve only three terms (some pledged four terms). Supposedly, the trend toward domination of the professional politician had ended, and the road back to citizen legislators had begun.

Supposedly, but not really. Even before the 104th Congress convened in January 1995, House Majority Leader-designate Dick Armey mused that term limits might no longer be necessary now that Republicans had miraculously won the Congressional majority. The House roll call votes in 1995 subsequently were rigged so that every Republican had a chance to vote for one version of term limits while no version actually received enough votes to pass. Hypocrisy was the watchword.

As for House members who were self-term-limited, some blatantly ignored their campaign promises. Most notorious was George Nethercutt, who in the state of Washington had defeated Democratic House Speaker Thomas Foley (the first incumbent speaker to be defeated for re-election to the House since before the Civil War) by attacking Foley's law suit against the voters in his state for approving term limits in a referendum.

Some House members who kept their term-limiting promises quickly moved on to a new political venue. Mark Sanford was elected governor of South Carolina. Lindsey Graham was elected to the U.S. Senate from South Carolina. Matt Salmon was defeated for governor of Arizona. Tom Coburn was among the few who returned to his pre-Congressional profession. He was a genuine citizen legislator.

I suppose the most extreme form of citizen legislator I have encountered was a retired farmer from Norfolk, Nebraska named William Purdy, who served in the 1957 session of the Nebraska unicameral legislature (which I covered for the Associated Press in my first taste of legislative reporting). In his campaign, Purdy had promised to make no speeches on the floor of the legislature, to introduce no bills, to vote against any new expenditure or extension of government-and to serve only one two-year term. He fulfilled each pledge to the letter. I then thought of Purdy as an eccentric, but over the years I have come to regard him as a wise man.

To be sure, by virtue of his non-participation, Bill Purdy was a cipher in the Nebraska legislature. Tom Coburn was far from a cipher in

Congress. From his first day in the House, he violated legendary Speaker Sam Rayburn's advice to new members to spend their first few years with their mouths clamped shut before daring to say anything or attempt anything on their own. Coburn had only six years, and he meant to make use of them.

The 104th Congress contained many freshman Republicans who were outside the political stereotype, but none more unusual than Coburn. After working in his family's optical business, he became a doctor at age 35 and—"disgusted with Congress," he said—was elected to the House at 46 in his first attempt at public office from a district that had not been represented by a Republican since 1922 and was thought to be unwinnable.

Coburn made his presence felt immediately. It became clear to him that Speaker Gingrich, House Majority Leader Armey and the rest of the Republican leadership were not what they pretended to be. They were revolutionaries in name only, content to take possession from the Democrats of the machinery of government and then run it virtually unchanged. That froze in place the system of pork barrel spending that young Woodrow Wilson described in *Congressional Government* more than 130 years ago.

So, the obstetrician from Muskogee, new to government, on his own began analyzing the contents of appropriations bills and exposing the heavy infusions of pork. That created the curious situation where this freshman congressman knew more about what was contained in these spending measures than the "appropriators"—members of the appropriations committees of the House and Senate who considered themselves an elite corps in Congress.

The appropriators had long since delegated these details to career staff members, but they are hardly unique among today's lawmakers. As part of their evolution as professional politicians, current House members are far less knowledgeable about legislative issues than their predecessors of 1957 when I first began covering Congress. Increasingly, their time is spent raising campaign money—a far lower priority for Coburn and his term-limited colleagues.

Coburn, along with other rookie Republicans, totally violated the Rayburn doctrine in 1997 by planning a coup to remove Gingrich as speaker. Coburn, as a plainspoken Oklahoman, killed whatever chance the effort had of succeeding. Armey had joined the plotters in hopes of becoming speaker. When Coburn blurted out that they did not want Armey either, Armey abandoned the enterprise and resumed his place at Gingrich's side.

No wonder that after two years of trouble making by Coburn, senior Republicans suddenly took notice of his weekly excursions to Muskogee to deliver babies. The 1989 act was passed to prevent members of Congress from using their office to fatten their bank accounts as lawyers, real estate agents, and insurance brokers. Behind the legislation was an unsavory history of immigration bills sold by well-placed Congressmen, acting under the guise of attorneys. Until it was decided to punish Coburn, nobody dreamed that the relationship of a doctor and a mother giving birth was "fiduciary."

When Coburn refused to bow to the Ethics Committee, the Republican leadership capitulated (just as they had surrendered to President Bill Clinton on many issues). After all, Coburn would be gone in another three years anyway.

He has been gone since the end of 2000, and he has been badly missed. So have the other term-limited House members. There is an unmistakable difference between the term-limited lawmaker and the rest of Congress. The fate of some pork barrel project is everything to the latter and nothing to the former. The member who is not making a career of politics looks quite differently at the world. A Congress that is fully term-limited would open the way to limitation of government and badly needed reform of federal taxation, Social Security, tort law, and much else.

Without question, life on Capitol Hill corrodes the most principled of legislators. As the years go by, they are no longer the persons they were when they arrived in Washington. It is the very rare member of Congress who improves with time, and most lose their focus and indeed their principles as the years go by. Nobody better exemplifies this phenomenon than Dick Armey, as Dr. Coburn makes clear in these pages.

Armey, a 44-year old professor at the University of North Texas with a Ph.D. in economics, came to Congress in 1984 as a conservative with a libertarian flavor and as a citizen legislator with no taste for the ways of Washington. To save money and in the process show his contempt for capital society, he slept on a couch in his office and showered in the members gym. After eight years in Congress, he was elected chairman of the Republican conference and two years later was tapped by Gingrich to be majority leader. By then, he was no longer the anti-establishment professor who had come to Washington.

Coburn's interaction with Armey is one of the most fascinating parts of this book. It shows Armey turning from being an idol of the Class of '94 to its anathema. When Gingrich resigned under pressure following the disappointing 1998 election a year and a half after the aborted coup against him, there was no support for Armey as speaker. Indeed, he barely was retained as majority leader after three ballots of voting by his colleagues. Yet, when he decided not to run for a tenth Congressional term in 2002, he soon seemed more like the old Dick Armey, concerned with big government and civil liberties. Here was the therapeutic value of being a civilian again.

Unfortunately, the term limits movement is in retreat. The Supreme Court dealt it a devastating blow by finding invisible writing in the U.S. Constitution that, according to a 5 to 4 decision of the justices, prohibited states from limiting terms of their representatives in Congress. The Republican party in effect has abandoned the issue. Successive biennial elections since 1994 have produced fewer and fewer advocates of term limits. The bulk of freshman Republicans entering Congress tend toward the professional politician rather than the citizen legislator model.

Typical of the newcomers is the bright and ambitious Evin Nunes, elected in 2002 from the Central Valley of California at age 29—making him the second youngest member of Congress. He probably never heard of Tom Coburn, and would not look to him as a role model if he had. Nunes's mentor and patron is 13-term Rep. Bill Thomas, the imperious chairman of the House Ways and Means Committee who runs a mini-political machine in California that is responsible for Nunes being in Congress. Nunes frankly asserts that he wants to be like Bill Thomas, that he wants to provide as much government spending as possible to his district and that he wants to stay in Congress for a very long time so that he can be a committee chairman and bring still more aid back to his constituents in Tulare and Fresno counties.

Although most voters still prefer term limits, that goal is not high on their wish list, and public support is slowly but steadily falling. Tom Foley predicted to me years ago that while support for term limits by ordinary people was superficial, the determination by politicians to defeat it was firm and would prove decisive. It looks as though as he was correct.

Since Coburn returned to Oklahoma, one deplorable development has accelerated the degeneration of Congress as a democratic institution. The decennial reapportionment mandated by the 2000 census produced what is arguably the most gerrymandered Congressional districting in the nation's history. Thanks to the introduction of computers, the distortion of districts that used to be accomplished crudely with pen and ink now has been brought to a fine art.

Gerrymanders originally were intended to provide an unfair advantage for one party or another, but that is not their primary purpose in the 21st Century. It is to protect incumbents. A post-2000 re-map of New York's delegation nearing approval would have given Republicans a slight advantage in two incumbent Democratic districts, but incumbent Republican House members blocked that change because it would have narrowed the very comfortable margins some of them enjoyed. So, no additional Republican seats were gained, and the delegation is controlled by Democrats, 19 to 10.

In California the same year, Republican leaders passed up a chance to challenge incumbent Democrats and settled for a new map where no incumbent is in danger. The nation's largest Congressional delegation (controlled by Democrats, 33 to 20) offers the voters no contests. (To his credit, young Rep. Nunes was embarrassed that his district was so badly loaded in favor of the Republicans that—as an unknown new candidate—he received 72 percent of the vote. Nunes is pushing for a referendum to force a fairer redistricting, but his party's leaders are not enthusiastic about it.)

Indeed, there are not many contests nationwide. In a perversion of democracy, only 35 to 40 out of the current 435 House districts can be called competitive. Coburn's 2nd Congressional District of Oklahoma is not considered one of them. It is doubtful that any Republican other than the doctor could win this district. When Coburn made clear he would stick to his promise and not run for a fourth term in 2000, Republican leaders were conflicted. They were delighted to be rid of so principled and troublesome a member but saddened by the loss of one seat (captured in 2000 by a Democrat, who was re-elected easily in 2002).

The absence of statutory term limits leads to a dilemma. Members of Congress serving under self-imposed term limits are those most willing to reform and restrain the government. Not only Coburn and the other warriors from the Class of '94 have departed, but members who were elected in later years and try to follow in Coburn's footsteps are going as well. Patrick Toomey of Pennsylvania, elected in 1998, will not seek re-election in 2004. Jeff Flake of Arizona, elected in 2000, will not run in

2006. The professional politicians, of course, stick around. Much as I admire the integrity of the term-limited members of Congress, I also miss them.

To hear again from Dr. Coburn not only dramatizes how much he has been missed but sends an important message from the belly of the Congressional beast to the rest of America. This book provides a rare, invaluable portrait of life as it really is on Capitol Hill that should open the eyes of ordinary citizens.

In a book published early in 2000 *(Completing the Revolution)*, I pondered the abandonment of genuine reform by Congressional Republicans and came to this conclusion: "What we need is to have a whole succession of Tom Coburns. A proliferation of Tom Coburns. Who knows? Maybe Tom Coburn should run for president."

It still seems like a good idea.

Robert D. Novak
Washington, D.C.

INTRODUCTION

Remember democracy never lasts long. It soon wastes, exhausts, and
murders itself. There never was a democracy yet that
did not commit suicide.

—JOHN ADAMS,
letter to John Taylor, April 15, 1814

IN THE SPRING OF 1999 I made my way through the corridors of the
Capitol for a meeting with Speaker of the House J. Dennis Hastert
(R-Illinois). I had made this walk many times before, usually on my way
to the "woodshed" where a member of leadership would chastise me for
not falling in line with the vast majority of other Republicans who had
"grown" and abandoned the zeal of the 1994 Republican revolution.
Hastert, who watched the downfall of former Speaker of the House
Newt Gingrich in 1998, preferred to talk with members before a revolt
broke out and was looking for ways to work with restless conservatives to
avoid another end-of-the-year budget train wreck that was becoming an
annual event in Congress.

While I was not particularly hopeful that a renewed commitment to
restrain spending would result from our meeting, I had to try. My days in
Congress were numbered. I had signed a term limits pledge and had just
started my third and final term. Soon I would leave Washington and
return full-time to my permanent job as a family physician in Muskogee,
Oklahoma. I was looking forward to going back to the real world, but I

was not going to leave Congress quietly. I intended to do everything I could to restart the revolution that brought me and seventy-two other newcomers to Washington.

My specific mission that day was to perform a procedure my colleagues called a "spinal transplant," intended to give another member the fortitude necessary to keep a commitment. In this instance, my goal was to convince Speaker Hastert to force members of the Appropriations Committee to abide by spending caps outlined in the 1997 Balanced Budget Agreement—an agreement that was a law, not a suggestion. The only way Hastert could enforce discipline among the appropriators, I believed, was to risk his position as Speaker.

"Denny, you have got to lead the appropriators. Only you can do that, and you know it. The only way we'll ever keep the budget caps is if you force their hand," I said bluntly.

Hastert listened to my argument carefully. As our new Speaker he was doing a good job of truly listening to the concerns of his fellow Republicans, a strength that few Republicans saw in Gingrich. Before Hastert could respond, however, Senate Majority Leader Trent Lott (R-Mississippi) slipped in and interrupted our meeting. As Hastert and Lott discussed what to do about funding for the F-22 fighter plane, I knew this was the perfect opportunity to press my case for spending restraint before the two most powerful members of Congress.

Sensing the conversation between Hastert and Lott was about to conclude, I interjected to turn the conversation back to how leadership could prevent another budget disaster. Hastert continued to listen attentively, as he was well aware of how the previous year's omnibus train wreck set in motion the series of events that led to Newt Gingrich's resignation.

Lott, however, now seated across from me, was less interested. After I finished my speech, before Hastert could respond, Lott looked at me, rested his chin on his hand, and said in his Mississippi baritone drawl,

"Well, I've got an election coming up in 2000. After that we can have good government."

It made me sick. Here was one of the most powerful men in the country brazenly admitting, in effect, "Yes, the government we have now is not good, but I don't really care as long as I keep getting elected." I was not so naïve as to not understand the importance of reelection in the minds of many members, but to have one of the leaders of my party declare that careerism would control the Senate agenda was frightening.

Sadly, the sentiment expressed by Lott that day was the norm, not the exception, during my six years in Congress. No single moment better illustrated the problem that derailed the Republican revolution and is still preventing Congress from making the tough choices necessary to preserve our freedoms in these perilous times: *careerism,* the self-centered philosophy of governing to win the next election above all else.

Although the events of September 11, 2001 have focused the public's attention on the threat of international terrorism, the greatest threat to the continuity of our form of government is our government itself. Throughout history, great powers have collapsed not so much under foreign threat, but from benign neglect and complacency at home. We have no choice but to fight the war that has been thrust upon us, but we can no longer ignore the other battlefront where our freedom is being eroded day by day by an out-of-control federal government that is threatening to bankrupt our nation. As one commentator observed, "A democracy cannot exist as a permanent form of government. It can only exist until the voters discover that they can vote themselves money from the public treasure. From that moment on the majority always votes for the candidates promising the most money from the public treasury, with the result that a democracy always collapses over loose fiscal policy followed by a dictatorship. The average age of the world's great civilizations has been two hundred years. These nations have progressed through the following sequence: from bondage to spiritual faith, from spiritual faith to liberty, from liberty to abundance, from abundance to selfishness, from selfishness to complacency, from complacency to apathy, from apathy to dependency, from dependency back to bondage."[1]

In the next decade or two, the convergence of three trends will create a day of reckoning for the federal government as we know it today: 1) the impending bankruptcy of Social Security and Medicare; 2) unsustainable annual increases in overall federal spending combined with exploding deficits; and 3) the ever-increasing costs of prosecuting the war on terrorism, rebuilding and developing shattered nations, and securing the homeland.

The convergence of these three trends will force our country to make a stark choice between massive tax increases and massive spending cuts. In either case, the result will be a political and economic earthquake unlike any since the Great Depression.

Prior to September 11, the dual challenges of entitlement reform and reducing the scope and size of government seemed nearly insurmountable. Now the task is that much more difficult—yet more important than ever. In 1994, I was one of seventy-three new members of Congress elected to fight on what, at the time, seemed to be the main battlefront where our freedoms were being eroded by an out-of-control federal government. Big government was causing profound insecurity in the homeland. Of course, in our post-September 11 world the battle for homeland security looks quite different, but the front that existed in 1994 is no less critical now. The battle for homeland security truly is a two-front war: one enemy—the nexus of terrorism and evil states—threatens us from abroad, while the other enemy—an ever-expanding federal government—threatens to undermine us from within.

---

[1] Author unknown, often attributed to historians Arnold Toynbee and Alexander Tytler.

INTRODUCTION

For me and my colleagues from the "Class of 1994," our intent was nothing less than to halt and reverse the federal government's reckless course toward unsustainable expansion by restoring the revolutionary ideals of limited government as established by our founders. In 1994, I was one of many members who believed that without a major course correction our nation would follow the path of other great nations that collapsed because of their own excesses.

We believed we could retake our government from the career politicians in Washington who had transformed a government "for the people" into a government for themselves and for special interests. If we accomplished that objective I was confident our majority status would take care of itself. The worst course of action we could take would be to behave like the career politicians we were sent to Washington to replace and to resume business as usual, Republican style.

> WE BELIEVED WE COULD RETAKE OUR GOVERNMENT FROM THE CAREER POLITICIANS IN WASHINGTON WHO HAD TRANSFORMED A GOVERNMENT "FOR THE PEOPLE" INTO A GOVERNMENT FOR THEMSELVES AND FOR SPECIAL INTERESTS.

For at least those first "100 days" in 1995, the vast majority of Republicans, not just the seventy-three freshmen from the "Class of 1994," seemed to be united in this purpose and vision. The early days of work implementing the "Contract with America" truly were revolutionary. On our very first day in the majority we passed more substantial reforms than had been passed in more than a decade. Yet when the Republican party faced withering criticism during the government shutdown of 1995 to 1996, our leaders folded instead of standing their ground. Rather than doing the hard work of explaining to the public, or even to rank-and-file Republicans, what was necessary to reduce the size of government, our leaders retreated. When our own generals called a halt to the revolution, many of our troops defected to the ranks of the career politicians we wanted to displace, and the members who wanted to keep fighting the fight the voters elected us to fight became known as the "rebels."

The conventional wisdom among the media—and many senior Republicans—nearly ten years after the inception of the 1994 "Republican revolution" is that it was a brief season in which the new Republican majority got carried away with its enthusiasm, lurched to the right, overplayed its hand, and nearly squandered its new power. The heady first hundred days of the 104th Congress and the Contract with America are a faint memory some Republicans seem embarrassed by and are eager to forget. In fact, among leadership circles running the trifecta of Republican power in the House, Senate, and White House, the early days of the revolution are cited as an example of how *not* to handle power in a narrow majority. Conservative members and activists today are lectured against wanting too much change too quickly.

Another key event that shaped the conventional wisdom about the revolution, at least among the media, was the defection of Republican Senator Jim Jeffords of Vermont to the Independent ranks in 2001, which put the Democrats back in charge of the Senate until the 2002 elections. Marjorie Williams of the *Washington Post* summed up the view of many pundits and talk-show hosts when she called Jeffords' decision "a dire referendum on the GOP's march to the right." Jeffords played up the notion that he no longer felt at home in a Republican party that was kowtowing to hard-line conservatives.

However, if the Republican party was marching anywhere before Jeffords' defection, it was to the left, not the right. For instance, the decision of Republicans to annually blow away the budget caps agreed to in the 1997 budget deal was hardly a conservative move. Nor was increasing government spending between 1996 and 2001 at a faster rate than the Democrats in the five years prior to the Republican takeover. Passing a highway bill in

1998 that contained more than fourteen hundred pork projects—ten times the number in a bill President Reagan vetoed a decade earlier—was not particularly "conservative" either. And, in 2001, the year the Republican party had become too conservative for Jeffords, the Republican-led House asked for a record nineteen thousand special projects at a cost of $279 billion—almost the size of that year's Pentagon budget. The real motives driving Jeffords' decision, I believe, had little to do with ideas and more to do with what he believed would advance his career.

From the perspective of a soldier who was fighting in the trenches, the Republican revolution stalled not because we were too bold, but because we were not bold enough. The narrow Republican majority that was briefly erased in the Senate by Jeffords' defection is the consequence of political cowardice, not courage. Whenever our leadership played it safe so we could build on our majority, our majority shrank. Had we kept fighting for the agenda that swept us into office, our majority would have grown. In the shutdown battle, for example, we were on the brink of victory but lost when our leaders gave up the will to fight. We had gained control of Congress, but we weren't willing to risk that position to truly regain control of the runaway federal government. We had started a revolution but failed to carry it through.

Once the Republicans lost the government shutdown battle of 1995 to 1996, winning the next election became more important than risking our majority to fight for the principles that propelled us into power. Lott's argument about waiting to work toward good government after his political position was more secure was the line of reasoning career politicians have always used to justify the cowardice of political expediency. When good government is something to

> WHEN GOOD GOVERNMENT IS SOMETHING TO BE PURSUIED TOMORROW, THAT TOMORROW NEVER ARRIVES; IT IS ALWAYS AFTER THE NEXT ELECTION CYCLE.

be pursued tomorrow, that tomorrow never arrives; it is always after the next election cycle. In the eyes of career politicians, the perfect political moment for change is a mirage that is always just over the horizon.

Contrary to today's conventional wisdom, the real drift in the Republican party since 1994 has been toward *careerism*, not conservatism. The visible distinction in Congress is a conflict between two competing political parties and ideologies. However, unless a person is within the institution itself, it is difficult to see how the invisible force of careerism is influencing events. The public's intuition that most partisan debate is nothing more than political posturing is largely correct. In the back rooms of Congress and meetings of the Republican and Democratic conferences, career politicians are more often preoccupied with how their decisions will influence the next election than whether they are taking principled, or ideologically consistent, positions. Careerism is to politics what "dark matter" is to physics—a force directing movements that seem to defy logic and common sense.

An honest understanding of how and why the Republican revolutionaries were co-opted by the system they hoped to reform is critical to the task of completing the unfinished business of the Contract with America. This agreement at its core was a commitment to the American people to restore our founding principle of limited government and to address the long-term challenges that are threatening our future prosperity and strength.

While the Republican revolution did produce some significant changes—chiefly welfare reform—much of the work of the Contract has been undone, and the long-term challenges that helped inspire the public to call for a changing of the guard in 1994 have grown worse.

- Government spending has grown at a faster rate in the years since the Republican takeover than in the eight years preceding the takeover (**see graph on facing page**).

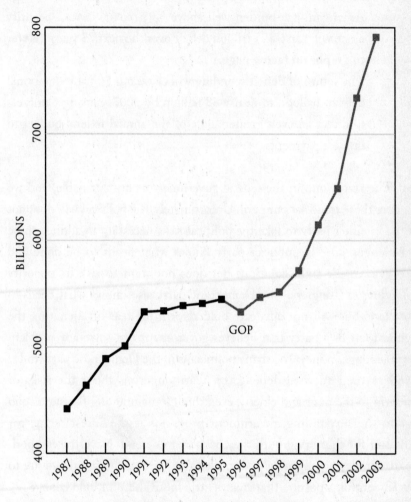

Figure 1. Government Spending

- Social Security and Medicare are going bankrupt. Without major reforms, these programs can only be sustained by massive benefit cuts or tax increases that would push the average American's tax burden well above 50 percent. Social Security alone will run a $25 trillion deficit over the next 75 years. (**Refer to graphs on facing page.**)
- The return of deficit spending will cause our $6 trillion national debt to balloon to nearly $8 trillion by 2007, causing Congress to direct an even greater share of the annual federal budget to interest payments.

The status quo in the federal government is unsustainable, and we ignore these trends at our peril. Unfortunately, the political will does not exist in either party to take the political risks necessary to address these challenges. The Republican party knows what needs to be done and believes in the right solutions but does not want to risk its majority standing in Congress. The Democratic party also knows what needs to be done but will not advocate bold reform for fear of alienating the radical left in a party that believes government can solve any problem with enough money. Too many politicians in the Democratic party today believe their survival depends on fearmongering about the risks of reform to the poor and elderly, even though maintaining the status quo or further expanding government programs is the surest recipe for disaster for the very groups they purport to defend. Nevertheless, both parties today are ultimately controlled not by ideas, but by the desire to be in control, a posture that creates little motivation for bold change.

President Bush, to his credit, recognized when he took office that careerism in the Republican party had undermined the Republican agenda and would pose as serious a threat to his plans for change as Democratic careerism. While traveling across the country to rally support for his tax cut plan, Bush consistently decried the recent

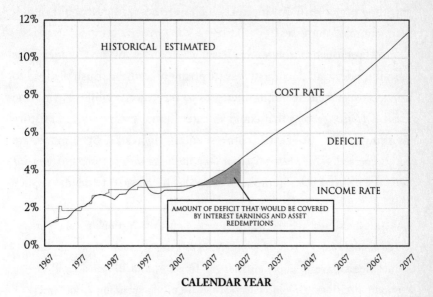

Figure 2. Social Security & Medicare

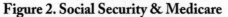

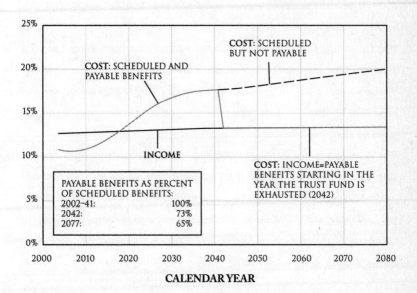

Figure 3. Social Security & Medicare

INTRODUCTION

"spending orgies" in Washington, which were hosted by Republican, not Democratic, Congresses.

However, Bush's strongest criticism was found in his first budget. This typically pedestrian document was surprisingly scathing. Bush pledged to "provide reasonable spending increases to meet needs while slowing the recent *explosive growth* that could threaten future prosperity . . . History has shown that—unlike tax cuts—spending increases, once made, are rarely reversed. *This pattern cannot long continue without jeopardizing our Nation's long-term goals"* (emphasis added). The president added,

> We must also reshape the way that we conduct the Nation's fiscal affairs. *The annual budget process increasingly has become a spectacle* of missed deadlines, legislative pileups, cliffhanger finishes, and ill-considered last minute decisions. *Gimmicks abound* for disguising spending as an "emergency" or advancing spending into the next year to avoid limits. Congressionally adopted *overall spending limits have become hurdles to be cleared, not ceilings to be honored.*
>
> In addition to higher spending, budget surpluses have led to a dramatic increase in congressional earmarks. The result is that the *Government is not only producing more spending, but more unjustified spending.* During this past year, the explosion in spending was accompanied by an unprecedented 6,000 plus earmarks in appropriations bills.
>
> A budget is not just about numbers. Far more it is about priorities—and integrity. *One great test is whether a budget legitimately supports the initiatives it purports to advance. A budget not only says a lot about how much we will spend, but it will inevitably reveal how we do the people's business. In other words, it is time to restore accountability and responsibility to Federal budget making.* (emphasis added)

President Bush's first budget encapsulated the frustrations of a handful of House conservatives who were, by 2001, the remnant of the

1994 revolution. Many career politicians in Washington, of course, cling to the illusion that spending is under control and that a day of reckoning will never arrive. For example, one of the official lines of the Republican conference is that government spending has been reduced as a percentage of the gross domestic product (GDP) under Republican control. This is correct, but disingenuous. The size of government shrunk as a percentage of GDP in recent years in spite of, not because of, the actions of Republicans in Congress. Now, government spending is actually increasing again as a percentage of GDP. Also, this comparison with GDP does not change the reality that the status quo is unsustainable. This argument is like a pilot saying everything is under control when his plane goes from a ninety-degree nosedive to an eighty-degree nosedive; the descent might be slightly less severe, but it is hardly enough to avoid a crash.

Careerism in Washington also is responsible for the premature surplus celebration that fueled public distrust of government, and, one could argue, created undue anxiety about the condition of our economy. Whenever a citizen hears long-term economic projections from Washington they should remember that career politicians in both parties spent much of the past few years competing with each other for credit for a surplus that "stretched as far as the eye could see." Both President Clinton and many leading Republicans perpetuated this farce. I was among a handful of members that included Mark Sanford (R-South Carolina)—the newly elected governor of that state—and John Shadegg (R-Arizona), who refused to talk about a surplus that did not exist and probably would never materialize because of Congress's inability to restrain spending. One of the few high-ranking Republicans who had the guts to call the surplus talk what it was—"bulls—t!"—was former Treasury Secretary Paul O'Neill. The capacity of an entire city of experienced, professional, and brilliant national leaders to be willingly and utterly deluded about an economic forecast as important as the surplus is chilling and should cause any person of common sense to be highly skeptical of projections from Washington that downplay bad economic news or promote good economic news.

Is it reasonable to hope that Republican control of the White House and both houses of Congress will restart the Republican revolution and help the federal government pull out of its nosedive? I find it difficult to be optimistic when some of the Republican leaders who could restart the revolution are busy undoing some of the revolution's accomplishments. For example, in January 2003, Republican leaders in the House dramatically relaxed the ban on gifts from lobbyists—a ban we had celebrated as an achievement in 1995. In 1999, Republican leaders replaced the total ban with a fifty-dollar gift limit, then allowed lobbyists to value ninety-dollar skyboxes at the MCI center at fifty dollars to fit under the limit. Now, Republican leaders have reopened a loophole we closed in 1995 that allowed corporations to buy members all-expense-paid vacations to "charity" events. One lobbyist told the *Washington Post,* "We plan to drive a Mack truck through this loophole," and predicted younger members would be particularly attracted to free vacations.

Republican leaders, former generals in the revolution, have also worked to undo other important items from the Contract era such as limits on committee spending and term limits for leadership offices. However, what has been particularly disturbing in Congress of late is its refusal to make tough spending choices after the September 11 attacks.

When President Bush spoke about "Operation Enduring Freedom," he wisely told the nation that success in this operation would come at a cost of blood and treasure. Our soldiers and ordinary Americans understood what this meant. Enduring freedom would require continued sacrifice. For our soldiers, this means being willing to pay the ultimate sacrifice in defense of freedom. Among ordinary Americans, this means enduring disruptions in their daily lives, such as extra security at airports and public places.

Yet some in Congress seemed to think they were exempt from

making sacrifices for the cause. Beneath a veneer of bipartisanship coop-
eration and good governance, Congress was up to its old tricks. In
October of 2001, Mitch Daniels, President Bush's director of the Office
of Management and Budget, chastised lawmakers for making "oppor-
tunistic spending sorties masquerading as 'emergency' needs." Daniels
was furious with lawmakers who were taking advantage of the chaos and
confusion of the moment to loot the public treasury for their own
personal political gain.

Just two days after planes slammed into the World Trade Center and
the Pentagon, Citizens Against Government Waste noted that the
Senate approved $6 million for the National Infrastructure Institute in
Portsmouth, New Hampshire, $2 million for the Oregon Groundfish
Outreach Program, and $850,000 for Chesapeake Bay Oyster Research.
Congress also increased spending for the corporate welfare-laden
Advanced Technology Program $191 million above the president's
request of $13 million. Every dollar spent on these pork projects was a
dollar that was *not available* for rebuilding and defending our nation.
The $213 million spent on these items was enough to buy 113 cruise
missiles and give 20,000 soldiers a $5,000 bonus. Congress's failure to
exercise self-restraint during our most dire hour since 1941 illustrates the
extent to which Republicans in particular have abandoned the spirit and
substance of the Contract with America.

It is my hope that educating the American people about how and
why career politicians in Washington refuse to take the political risks
necessary to produce real change will inspire the public to elect a new
generation of political leaders who will grab the tattered banner for
genuine reform in government. The stakes could not be higher. As we
face a menacing enemy abroad, we need to do everything possible at
home to streamline government so we can be in a strong position to
defend and preserve our freedoms.

The danger of inaction could be a sudden collapse of our economy or social safety net, but what is more likely is a steady decline of our relative power in the world. The nature of career politicians today is to make only those changes that are necessary to ward off imminent disaster while putting off the real problem for future generations. The long-term consequence of this cowardly and politically expedient approach will likely cause the United States to slip under the rising tide of another power, limiting our ability to defend our national security and our ability to pursue our ideals of freedom at home and around the world. Terrorists and tyrants would like nothing more than for our domestic complacency to weaken our posture abroad and embolden other nations to not only oppose but also block our efforts to preempt future threats.

My purpose in calling for bold change on the domestic front is not necessarily to see a restoration of the Republican revolution, but to see the revolutionary ideals of our founding fathers. Now, more than ever, we need men and women of principle in positions of leadership who understand that freedom will endure only in a system in which federal power is restrained. We need our leaders to negotiate on the basis of principle, not political expediency. Compromise is a reality of life in a representative democracy, but compromising one's principles is not.

Sadly, I am convinced the present Congress will not make the changes necessary to right our course. Because of the intransigence of careerists in Congress, we must look to new vehicles and methods to restore our founding principles. This book will describe the real workings of Congress—or lack thereof—and what must happen among us, the electorate, to restore our system of representative government.

"This country, with its institutions, belongs to the people who inhabit it," said Abraham Lincoln. "Whenever they shall grow weary of the existing government, they can exercise their constitutional right of amending it, or their revolutionary right to dismember or overthrow it."

Lincoln's comment is a timely reminder that concerned citizens still have the ability to overhaul the government if they so choose and reshape it in a fashion that better represents their interests. Our representative form of government is damaged, but it is not beyond repair. The ideas within the Contract with America may be lost among former Republican revolutionaries, but it is alive and well among the American people. If this great American experiment is to continue, the American people and principled leaders must rise up and take back a government that can still be of the people, by the people, and for the people.

1

STORMING THE CASTLE

When people are oppressed by their government,
it is a natural right they enjoy to relieve themselves of the oppression.

—U.S. GRANT

O NE SUMMER MORNING in June of 1994, I woke up with the
sudden realization I should run for Congress. This might not have
been a startling revelation for someone who ran in political circles. But for
me, a family physician in Muskogee, Oklahoma, it seemed ludicrous.

During the first half of 1994, I was like millions of Americans who
were growing increasingly frustrated with Washington. I was growing
weary of an elitist Congress that was out of touch with ordinary
Americans, and, as a doctor, I was horrified by President Clinton's
attempt to socialize medicine. I knew I would vote for change in the next
election, but running for Congress myself was the furthest thing from
my mind.

At that time my medical practice was thriving, and my wife, Carolyn,
and I were about to enter a new season in our lives. Sarah, the youngest
of my three daughters, was heading into her senior year in high school
and would soon be heading off to college. My middle daughter, Katie,
was already studying at Oklahoma State University. And my oldest
daughter, Callie, had recently moved back to Muskogee with her new

husband, Jeff, after graduating from the University of Oklahoma. If I harbored any secret ambition at the time, it was to be a grandfather.

My only political experience before 1994 was volunteering for Nixon's 1968 presidential campaign. One of my classmates who had also worked on that campaign happened to be Mike Synar who, in 1994, was an eight-term liberal Democrat congressman representing me in Washington.[2]

My true background was in business. After graduating from Oklahoma State University in 1970 with a degree in accounting, I went to work for my dad, O. W., as manager of Coburn Optical Products in Virginia. At the young age of twenty-two, I was responsible for thirteen employees in a company that was producing ophthalmic lenses. Even though I knew there were smarter people in the business who had more sophisticated marketing plans, I wasn't going to let anyone outwork me. My business plan, built on little more than tenacity, paid off. By 1978, we had 350 employees and had captured 35 percent of the U.S. market.

My experience in business played an important role in shaping my political views. Since I started working in 1970, I could feel the government gripping me a little tighter year after year with new regulations and higher taxes. As my freedom to run my operation on my terms began slipping away, I grew increasingly resentful of the federal government's intrusion into my business. I'll never forget an incident in 1976 when an FDA inspector walked into my company and said I couldn't be licensed to operate a new expansion of our business until I moved a bathroom wall eight inches to comply with federal regulations. I could tell the inspector wasn't simply doing his job but was also enjoying the power and leverage he had over me. You would imagine a reasonable person in this situation saying, "Gosh, I know this is a bit ridiculous, but I've got to ask you to move this wall." Instead, the inspector treated me like a criminal when I let him know how ludicrous, unnecessary, and costly this

---

[2] Congressman Synar passed away just two years later in 1996.

request was. "You don't understand," he insisted. "You can move this wall, or you can wait forever to get your permit."

Not long after this, my career took a radically different turn when I decided to move back to Oklahoma with my wife and three children and enroll in medical school. As a thirty-one-year-old first year student at the University of Oklahoma, I earned the nickname "Gramps" from my classmates. My decision to go to medical school was motivated by a desire to move on from my business experience and get back to Oklahoma, but it was also influenced by an event that occurred a few years earlier.

When I came home for Christmas in 1975, my mother, Joy, noticed that a birthmark behind my left ear had changed. She said what she wanted for Christmas that year was for me to have that checked. I wasn't worried, but, wanting to grant my mom her Christmas wish, I went to the doctor. The doctor took a small biopsy sample but wasn't particularly concerned. However, a couple of days later, he called me and said I needed to come back to his office. The doctor told me I had cancer, but he needed to do more tests to see how far it had spread.

Next I went to a specialist who, after running a series of tests, dropped a bomb on me that has forever altered my life. He said, "Tom, you have a malignant melanoma, a form of skin cancer. Unfortunately, the survival rate for this depth of invasion isn't very high. I'd say you have about a 20 percent chance of surviving beyond one year."

When I left the office, I drove around aimlessly. I wasn't scared because I've always had a deep faith and trust in God. I believe that we can influence some things in our lives to a degree, but I also believe there is an ultimate plan over which we have no control. Still, I was angry at the situation. I wondered if I would be able to see my young girls grow up, and I worried about how they would be taken care of without me. I also wanted to know if I could grow old with my wife and wondered whether I would be able to continue managing a thriving company.

By the time I pulled the car into the driveway, my perspective on life had changed. Facing death helped me put my priorities in perspective in a hurry. I had always known what was important in life before that, but I hadn't acted like it. My relationships became more important. My desire to help others grew. My drive to make my company flourish intensified.

I had one minor operation and then had to return to the hospital for major surgery after the doctors realized the tumor had invaded deeper than they had expected. The surgeon performed a procedure called a radical dissection on the left side of my neck, removing a large section of flesh and leaving a scar that is quite noticeable to this day. Although they believed they had removed all of the cancer, the operation couldn't be declared a success for another five years, which meant five years of waiting to know whether I would live through my early thirties.

The culmination of my battle with cancer came in 1992 at my daughter Callie's wedding. My sister, Mary, came up to me and said, "Well, you made it. You lived to see your daughter married." Every special event since then—the wedding of my daughter Katie and the births of my three grandchildren—has been even sweeter knowing what a privilege it is that I am still on this earth to enjoy those blessings.

Needless to say, my bout with cancer gave me an ability to empathize with people struggling with illness and disease. My career as a doctor is extremely fulfilling. As a family practice physician specializing in obstetrics, I am blessed to participate in one of the most joyous events in life— bringing a new person into the world.

Still, however much I enjoyed my new career, I could not escape the reach of big government. I had to hire extra assistants simply to comply with the torrent of paperwork generated by government agencies and insurance companies. Trying to keep bureaucrats from stepping between my patients and me became a constant battle, which, unfortunately, is even worse now than it was in 1994.

Also, while specializing in obstetrics allowed me to participate in life's great joys, it also opened my eyes to some of life's greatest tragedies, such as sexually transmitted diseases, unintended pregnancies, and the problems associated with abortion. Witnessing these tragedies inspired me to become active in my community by speaking to students—and anyone who would listen—about the risks of STDs and the benefits of abstinence outside of marriage. Still, the thought never occurred to me that I would be a more effective spokesman for these issues in Washington, D.C. than I was in Oklahoma.

My life took yet another drastic turn one day in June of 1994 when I read in the *Muskogee Phoenix* a comment from my congressman, sixteen-year incumbent Mike Synar, about nationalizing health care. Synar tended to take positions that were a 180-degree departure from the values of the people in the district. I said to myself, "Somebody has got to run against this guy." It was a few days after reading his comment that I woke up realizing I should be the person to challenge Synar.

Synar, a very intelligent young man, was a liberal in a district that was conservative on social issues even though it was overwhelmingly Democratic by voter registration. Synar's major problem, however, was not that he was perceived as too liberal but that people thought he had completely lost touch with the district. Synar and his liberal colleagues in Congress liked to characterize his departure from the values of his district as admirable independence, but ordinary folks back home were concerned it was growing indifference and a capitulation to the ruling elite in Washington.

I tried to explain my road-to-Damascus experience to Carolyn the morning I awoke with my new purpose. She was not impressed.

"Tommy, no. Absolutely not," Carolyn said. I could tell by the look she gave me that she wondered if I was sleep deprived from delivering a baby during the night. Carolyn reminded me of what I already knew about myself. "You wouldn't fit into that arena," she said. "You don't have the right personality for politics." Carolyn knew better than anyone that I don't have a coy bone in my body. I was too direct and too bullheaded to succeed in the "go along to get along" world of politics.

I took Carolyn's perspective very seriously. The greatest gift and blessing I have ever had in this life has been my good fortune to be married to, cared for, loved by, and held accountable by Carolyn. Through my many careers and through life-threatening illness, she has always been by my side. She has been the keynote of my life.

We discussed the topic several times, but running for Congress still did not seem to be something she looked forward to with any eagerness. "Besides, everyone knows," Carolyn reminded me, "Mike Synar can't be beaten."

The next month, I sent a letter to my daughter Katie at the camp where she was working that summer to tell her that I was heading to Washington to investigate the possibility of running for Congress. "I thought it was the dumbest thing I ever heard in my life," Katie later recalled. "You just don't imagine your dad who has been a doctor your whole life suddenly running for Congress when this has never even been discussed before."

A few nights later, I floated the idea to a group of friends we had over for dinner. I'll never forget the blank stares and the silence, which was broken by the question, "Are you nuts?"

Later, Carolyn asked pointedly, "Why would you do something like that? You have a great practice. You are doing what you love. Why would you do something so counter to what you are? You don't want to be in that arena, do you?"

When I ran the idea by Fred Reufer, an orthopedic surgeon at the hospital, I got yet another blank stare as he said, "No Republican could win. Not you or anybody."

They were right, of course. I had no political background, no political sense, and no knowledge of how to get actively involved. I cared deeply about issues and was a registered Republican, but only because I couldn't stand how big government interfered with my business. I was pro-life, but I wasn't active in pro-life causes other than doing medical pro bono work for women in crisis situations and providing financial support to a counseling clinic for unplanned pregnancies. Yet if there was one reason for not running it was Carolyn's observation: *Politics just wasn't my style.*

Still, I had an overwhelming feeling that if those of us on the outside didn't make an attempt to change things they would never change. I had a deep sense that things were not right in our country. I saw Washington as a city dominated by self-serving career politicians who were more concerned with protecting their positions than responding to the needs of the country. After being controlled by the Democratic party for forty years, the Congress was now, more than ever, an island unto itself—and to folks in northeast Oklahoma, Congress seemed like a resort island unto itself.

STILL, I HAD AN OVERWHELMING FEELING THAT IF THOSE OF US ON THE OUTSIDE DIDN'T MAKE AN ATTEMPT TO CHANGE THINGS THEY WOULD NEVER CHANGE.

In 1994, I was also watching our culture decline from the vantage point of my medical practice. I saw firsthand the devastating consequences of the trend in our society to avoid responsibility and eliminate the consequences of any questionable behavior. Every week, teenagers would come into my practice with a host of sexually transmitted diseases and, in some cases, pregnancies. I was also witnessing the development of a massive HIV/AIDS epidemic that the government was almost covering up for fear of offending the politically correct free-sex and homosexual communities. The disease was newly infecting more than forty thousand Americans every year primarily because no one in government had the courage to implement common sense prevention measures the homosexual community had incorrectly labeled "anti-gay." I believe history will condemn our government for its lack of courage. Despite a few positive steps, I still believe we have an ineffective HIV prevention policy.

I saw troubling trends on other fronts. I saw a welfare system that increased the number of fatherless children by rewarding women for having children out of wedlock. I saw an education system that graduated students based on how much time they spent in school, not on whether they had learned basic skills with which to survive. I saw a judicial system that was casting aside the wisdom of our founders to fit the political whims of judges. I saw a criminal justice system that no longer administered justice but used behind-the-scenes maneuvering to ensure that public humiliation was not part of the process necessary to change a person's criminal behavior.

But what bothered me most was cowardice in public servants and elected officials who placed their political careers ahead of the best interests of the next generation. I understood that it had been this way for years, but the questions I asked myself were: Does it have to continue? Why shouldn't I do something about it if I feel so strongly about these problems? And could a bullheaded doctor from Muskogee with no political sense, but with some business and common sense, make a difference in Washington? If the form of government our founders created was still intact, I believed I could.

Despite the counsel of those I loved and respected, I decided to run. I told my hometown paper, "I don't believe in career politics and think the evidence of the representation we have now shows that career politics is not good for the state or the district. I'm tired of telling people we need to do something without doing something myself."

When I announced my candidacy in front of eighty supporters, I said my candidacy "pits the conservative people of the second district against a liberal Washington-based political elite represented by Mike Synar." I said I was concerned about the "professional political elite" in Washington and the impact they were having on the country. I noted that Oklahomans had already voted to limit the terms of state legislators and supported term limits at the federal level.

"Unfortunately, career politicians like Mike Synar do not share this vision [of term limits]," I told the crowd. "Our founding fathers never envisioned a situation in which people would make a career of elective politics. They viewed public office as a temporary sacrifice.... More and more we are represented in Congress by politicians who do not live in our communities, who do not share our values, who do not understand our problems, and who do not respond to our needs and wishes. They are a privileged political elite who justify their existence by spending our money, raising our taxes, and regulating our lives. They vote themselves huge salaries, hire large staffs who spend much of their time engaged in activities designed to re-elect their employers, and send us thinly disguised campaign mail at our own expense to convince us of our need to retain them in office."

In response to my announcement, Synar said he was "adamantly opposed" to term limits because they would damage the political clout of small states like Oklahoma and increase voter apathy. "This is just another gimmick by the Republicans who cannot win at the ballot box," Synar told the *Muskogee Phoenix*.

I found a few basic campaign themes and repeated them at every stop. I reminded citizens that this is still our government and we can take it back whenever we muster the will, the courage, and the commitment to do so. I said I was running against the institution of Congress and how it operates. I believed the goal for the congressman was to represent the values and attitudes of his district, not the values of Washington.

I said many of our problems stem from a breakdown in the family and that the reason our budget is in such a mess is because we were trying to get government to do what families used to do for themselves. I opposed Clinton's health care plan and said it would "drive up costs and taxes, reduce the options enjoyed by the average American, and place a crushing burden on small business." My platform also had a strong pro-life plank. "Our goal as a society should be to protect and enhance life," I said, "not make it easier to snuff it out before it has a chance to grow on its own."

I had to travel the northern and western part of the district extensively because I was virtually unknown outside of Muskogee. At a stop at the Sirloin Stockade in Claremore, I said careerism in Washington "goes to the heart of what's wrong in America right now. In Washington today, there is what I call an 'arrogance of power.' Our decision makers are more and more part of a privileged political elite, represented by professional politicians like Mike Synar and Bill Clinton."

Everyone in the district knew it would take a miracle to beat Synar, an entrenched and savvy eight-term incumbent. Therefore, in the Republican primary, I decided not to run against my two Republican opponents but instead to run against Synar, the incumbent. I never even mentioned the other two Republican candidates by name. We raised about sixty thousand dollars very quickly, allowing us to produce TV ads addressing important issues in the second district on which the present congressman was highly vulnerable.

In the Republican primary I was the liberal candidate. The leading candidate, a gentleman named Jerry Hill, had the support of pro-life and conservative activists and had an extensive grassroots organization within the Republican party, small as it was in northeast Oklahoma. Hill almost defeated Synar in a close election in 1992 (54 to 46 percent) after Synar narrowly defeated Drew Edmondson in a tough Democratic primary by only one percentage point. Hill had already been running for almost two years. Unlike Hill, I hadn't marched or carried signs in pro-life rallies. I had simply worked behind the scenes on pro-life issues and other causes. Because I wasn't overtly political, my conservative credentials were in doubt. I was a wildcard and a threat to the conservative establishment's candidate.

When my closest supporters gathered at My Place Barbeque in Muskogee to watch the election returns, I saw that my strategy of running against Synar and ignoring my primary opponents had paid off. I beat Jerry Hill 63 to 31 percent. In the Democratic primary, Synar failed to receive a majority of the vote, which forced a run-off between Synar and Virgil Cooper, a seventy-one-year-old retired schoolteacher.

A few weeks later it became clear our primary strategy worked too well. In one of the bellwether elections in 1994, Synar lost in the Democratic primary runoff to Cooper, a political newcomer. Cooper was a real wildcard because he was, in fact, more conservative than me and had even less campaign experience. At the time, I would have preferred to run against Synar, and I even told Senator Don Nickles (R-Oklahoma) I thought Synar was taking so many political hits that he might lose in the primary. Prior to Cooper's victory, we led Synar by thirty points according to our internal polling.

Representative Bill Richardson (D-New Mexico), who is now the governor of New Mexico, said Synar's defeat was "a major blow to the [Democratic] caucus and a major wake-up call. . . . It sends a message that we had better redouble our efforts, including those of us in supposedly safe seats."

Virgil Cooper was one of the most unique and colorful figures to ever run in a general election in Oklahoma. He ran an unconventional but contagious grassroots campaign. He introduced himself by saying, "I'm running against Mike Synar." This fact alone was usually enough to win the support of the voters. Cooper drove an old pickup truck around the district with a campaign sign on the back and stopped in parking lots to tuck business cards under the windshield wipers of parked cars.

State Democratic leaders were dismissive of Cooper during the primary. "Virgil who?" was their response to questions about the challenger to their man, Mike Synar. Synar himself was nasty to Cooper during the primary. He ran television ads claiming Cooper wanted to cut Social Security and Medicare benefits even though Cooper himself received Social Security. This cheap fearmongering tactic that works too often in campaigns did not stick on the folksy, likable, and elderly Cooper.

Cooper was incensed by the ads. Word got around the district that when Cooper saw Synar a few days before the runoff he said, "You just keep lying about me and I'll keep telling the truth about you, and we'll see who gets elected."

The general election campaign was difficult because Virgil Cooper is one of the finest gentlemen I have ever met, and I didn't enjoy running against him. Cooper had deservedly become a folk hero for defeating a sixteen-year incumbent congressman in his party's primary. I also had an affinity for Cooper because his friends, like mine, thought he was a little bit loony for wanting to challenge Synar. "We thought he was crazy," Cooper's eighty-one-year-old friend Howard Huff told Gannet News Service. "We thought he was just going to look into it."

My campaign against Cooper made for some great debates about conservative values in the Oklahoma countryside. In one memorable debate, Cooper accused me of supporting tobacco and alcohol interests because my wife's stock portfolio owned mutual funds that included shares of RJR Nabisco. We thought his attempt to find dirt on me in my wife's stock portfolio was a stretch, and many people laughed off the attack. But some people listened and thought it was simply terrible.

One attack I couldn't laugh off was when Cooper ran Democratic National Committee ads falsely accusing me of not accepting payments from Medicare and favoring cuts in elderly benefits. In response, I said Cooper was duped by the DNC and would fall prey to Washington insiders if elected. The low point of the campaign for me was realizing Cooper was being handled by the very people he wanted to drive out of power. Nevertheless, I still admired Cooper even though I disagreed with his decision to delegate so much authority to political hacks who didn't understand him or care about him.

One of the odd sensations in a campaign is reading glowing compliments from your friends in ads. My dear friend Charles Pearson said, "If our next congressman is really going to do something to help Oklahoma families, he can start by making sure every able-bodied man and woman who wants one, has a job. A good job. Tom Coburn has built a business, so he understands what it will take to create an economic environment capable of facilitating growth and stimulating job creation. Bottom line, he's put people to work. Whether you're a Democrat or a Republican, that alone ought to be a good enough reason to vote for him."

As my supporters were touting my experience outside of government, I was saying my lack of experience in government was a reason people should vote for me. "I don't know that things can't be done. Everyone in Congress is convinced they can't do things. I have the freshness of being able to say, Why not? Why can't we balance the budget? Why can't we cut government spending?"

On election night, six hundred people attended my watch party at West Middle School. A group of kids I had delivered and other patients of mine were assembled. One of the people at my watch party was seven-year-old Jacob Dickman. I'll never forget his particular endorsement: "I think he's a neat guy. He delivered me. He's my doctor." The fact that I had delivered nearly three thousand babies in my district certainly was a tremendous advantage in my campaign.

When the returns came in, I had won 52 to 48 percent and became the first Republican to represent my district since 1920. In my victory speech I said, "I hope tonight starts a trend to make government responsive to us again."

In hindsight, however, my victory was the number two story in the campaign. The defining moment in the campaign would always be Mike Synar's loss to a political novice in a primary. His loss was the tremor warning of the coming political earthquake in 1994.

In an interview with Gannet News Service after his defeat, Synar said he disagreed with the growing sentiment among Americans that "there's nothing government can do right and in some ways the government is the enemy. That's very dangerous."

"I don't come from that school," Synar said. "I think government can be an active and successful partner both with local and state government and private industry to develop a strategy for the future for jobs, for health care, for personal safety, and other things."

Unfortunately for Democrats who lost in 1994, including Speaker of the House Tom Foley, the school of thought that says, "In some ways the government is the enemy," was established by our founding fathers. The founders were weary of strong centralized governments and expected the people to dismember the government if it grew too large. As one of seventy-three freshmen Republicans headed to Washington, I believed this was a moment when the people had indeed risen up against a government whose inefficiencies were great and unendurable.

However, even as Republicans took control of the House, I remained skeptical of our ability to act on our mandate. I told the *Muskogee Phoenix*, "I was so pessimistic about politicians, I'm going to maintain my skepticism until I see that we're going to do what we say we're going to do. The future will tell how much of a historic event it is. It's easy to set an agenda and say this is what you're going to do and vote that way because you've committed to it. The tough thing will be six months from now when you have to make the tough decisions based on what you did. Will you stand up and make the tough decisions? That's when we're going to see the people who want to be professional politicians versus the people that want to be representatives."

History would show that the career politicians in the Republican party did not stand up.

2

OUR SACRED OATH

So you see, Colonel, you have violated the Constitution in what
I consider a vital point. It is a precedent fraught with danger to
the country, for when Congress once begins to stretch its power
beyond the limits of the Constitution, there is no limit to it,
and no security for the people.

—HORATIO BUNCE,
a constituent of U.S. Representative Davy Crockett

THE HISTORIC ELECTIONS OF 1994 revealed an aspect of the
American electorate that gives me great hope for our country.
Regardless of how well either party spins the truth, the American people
know when their government is off-kilter. Only 21 percent of respondents
in a 1994 University of Michigan poll said they trusted the government
to "do the right things most of the time." A 1999 Center of Policy
Attitudes study showed that 75 percent of the public believe the government represents "a few big interests" while only 19 percent believe the
government is truly concerned with the "benefit of all the people."

Some say such polls reflect a troubling level of cynicism among the
electorate. Yet, these polls also show that the public knows when
Washington is not truly representing its interests. The public may not
know what needs to change, but they usually know when change is
necessary. The good news is that when principled leaders communicate
a clear plan for change to a frustrated electorate, significant improvements can happen quickly.

In 1994, public outrage over careerism and the arrogance of power in

15

Washington led to the election of dozens of members who pledged to challenge the status quo. Abuses of power like the infamous House Post Office scandal had left the public crying for change. In that debacle, several members, including Dan Rostenkowski (D-Illinois), then-chairman of the powerful House Ways and Means Committee, were accused of embezzling cash from the House Post Office. Republicans in Washington led by Newt Gingrich (R-Georgia) seized the moment and did a masterful job selling a plan for change called the "Contract with America."

> YET THE REAL CHALLENGE IN OUR REPUBLIC IS, AND ALWAYS HAS BEEN, HOW TO MANAGE THE VERY HUMAN DESIRE FOR POWER, WHICH IS OUT OF CONTROL IN OUR SYSTEM TODAY.

Today, Washington is still suffering from the basic dysfunction the "Contract" hoped to correct—a chronic abuse of power and the unsustainable growth of government that is its natural consequence. Politicians and pundits of various stripes have different explanations as to why Congress does not seem to be representing the people, but most observers talk about the symptoms rather than the disease itself. John McCain (R-Arizona) has the view that the "iron triangle of big money, lobbyists, and legislation that for too long has put special interests ahead of the national interest" is the great evil in Washington. Many of my former colleagues say runaway federal spending is the real problem. Yet the real challenge in our republic is, and has always been, how to manage the very human desire for power, which is out of control in our system today.

Any plan to address change at this level is enormously difficult to sell and even more difficult to implement. Yet I am convinced that the basic dysfunction of power in Washington can be substantially improved. However, this problem will never be effectively addressed until the public and elected officials renew their respect for the principles of truly limited government found in a document to which politicians swear allegiance but flagrantly disregard—the U.S. Constitution.

THE CONSTITUTION AND
THE HUMAN DRIVE FOR POWER

When our forefathers were drafting the Constitution, their central concern was to fashion a system that would contain the human drive for power and channel the best and worst of human impulses toward ends that would serve the people. Our founders were wise and learned men who understood people and politics. As Alexander Hamilton said, "A fondness for power is implanted in most men, and it is natural to abuse it."

In particular, our founders believed concentrating too much power in any one person or body would erode freedoms, so they created a brilliant system of checks and balances to confine the human drive for power as a fireplace confines a fire. "Government is not reason," George Washington said. "It is not eloquence; it is force! Like fire, it is a dangerous servant and a fearful master." When that containment works properly it benefits everyone. But if it fails, the entire house can burn to the ground. Or, to use another analogy, power is like nuclear fuel in a reactor. When used in its proper confines it creates tremendous energy, but when it escapes, it contaminates everything in its vicinity.

The problem with government today is that the fire, the drive for power, is burning outside the containment chamber our founders built in the Constitution. The fundamental reason we are witnessing out-of-control spending is that the federal government has been doing many things our founders never envisioned, and now it does not know how to put the proverbial genie back in the bottle. Career politicians know we are on an unsustainable course but prefer to talk about anything but the real problem—the virtual meltdown of our containment system.

Rather than acknowledging this problem, too many politicians point to the symptoms of the contamination, not its cause. The debate about campaign finance reform, the great red herring in today's discussion about government reform, is a good example. Few politicians acknowledge the fact that the reason businesses and special interest groups spend huge sums to get politicians in their corner is because decisions made in Washington now touch virtually every aspect of our lives. What business executive would not use all legal means at his or her disposal to ensure that an ever-intrusive federal government not hurt the company's bottom line? Politicians who trade access and influence for campaign contributions are a natural consequence of a system in which the federal government is running more of our lives than our founders ever intended. Truly addressing the role of money in campaigns requires reining in an out-of-control government by restoring the integrity of the containment chamber called the U.S. Constitution.

Our founders were so concerned about the risks of a meltdown in our system they instituted the practice of requiring elected officials to take an oath to defend the Constitution. The Congressional Oath has been amended several times but its essential purpose has not changed. When members of Congress are sworn into office they stand in the chamber of the House of Representatives or the Senate and take the following oath of office:

> I do solemnly swear that I will support and defend the Constitution of the United States against all enemies, foreign and domestic; that I will bear true faith and allegiance to the same; that I take this obligation freely, without any mental reservation or purpose of evasion; and that I will well and faithfully discharge the duties of the office on which I am about to enter. So help me, God.

Politicians make a lot of promises, but the promise they swear to keep above all others is to defend the Constitution of the United States.

Members of Congress can belong to different political parties and hold divergent political opinions, but their highest loyalty should be to the Constitution. Without this commitment to the foundational rules of the governance, our system is destined to drift according to the whims of political parties and individual members.

Today, the oath is still held in high regard, if only in word. During the 2000 presidential campaign, Al Gore often referred to the fact that he had taken the oath of office six times to prove that he would be a responsible chief executive. However, Gore's voting record and the voting records of virtually every member of Congress reveal that the oath of office is more a ceremonial gesture than a sacred commitment. Today, almost all members of Congress—including me—are traitors to the Constitution. All it takes to subvert the Constitution is a "yes" vote on almost any modern appropriations bill, all of which include programs and federal responsibilities never envisioned by our founders.

THE CONSTITUTION AND LIMITED GOVERNMENT

The Constitution, ratified in 1789, established a clear and limited role for Congress. Article I, section 8, clause I of the Constitution gives Congress the power to "provide for the common defense and general welfare of the United States." The Constitution also conferred several other specific responsibilities on Congress. The House was given the power to levy taxes and regulate interstate commerce, while the Senate was granted the power to ratify treaties and confirm executive appointments. In 1791, the framers clarified the Constitution's intent to limit the role of the federal government with the Tenth Amendment, which reads, "The powers not delegated to the United States by the Constitution, nor prohibited by it to the States, are reserved to the States respectively, or to the people." In other words, Congress's role is limited to providing for the common defense, regulating interstate commerce, providing for the general welfare, and levying taxes. All other powers are reserved for the states.

Politicians who wish to defend themselves against this charge of treason argue the phrase "general welfare" gives Congress the constitutional authority to appropriate money for virtually any purpose imaginable. However, James Madison, whom most constitutional scholars recognize as the father of our Constitution, said quite clearly, "With respect to the words general welfare, I have always regarded them as qualified by the detail of powers [enumerated in the Constitution] connected with them. *To take them in a literal and unlimited sense would be a metamorphosis of the Constitution into a character which there is a host of proofs was not contemplated by its creators*" (emphasis added). In other words, Madison had the foresight to discredit any elected official who hoped to use the words "general welfare" to justify an expansion of the Congress's constitutional role.

Other founders consistently warned against the dangers of a large and powerful centralized government. Thomas Jefferson said, "Government big enough to supply everything you need is big enough to take everything you have. . . . The course of history shows that as government grows, liberty decreases." Jean-Jacques Rousseau, a political philosopher who influenced our founders said, "The bigger a state becomes, the more liberty diminishes."

The public debate surrounding the ratification of the Constitution also leaves little doubt that the founders envisioned a federal government with very limited powers. In the late eighteenth century many Americans were concerned that the proposed Constitution would establish a federal government just as tyrannical as the British crown. Many early Americans wanted a very weak federal government, if any centralized government at all. The framers were eager to ease these fears and convince the public that their intent was for the states and private citizens to be responsible for virtually every civic responsibility aside from providing for the common defense. Two of the framers of the Constitution, Alexander Hamilton and James Madison, along with another founding father, John Jay, made this case in a series of essays intended to persuade the state of New York to ratify the Constitution. These *Federalist Papers* provide perhaps the most authoritative account of the intent of the founders.

In "Federalist No. 45," Madison writes the following:

The powers delegated by the proposed Constitution to the federal government, are few and defined. Those which are to remain in the State governments are numerous and indefinite. The former will be exercised principally on external objects, as war, peace, negotiation, and foreign commerce; with which last the power of taxation will, for the most part, be connected. The powers reserved to the several States will extend to all the objects which, in the ordinary course of affairs, concern the lives, liberties, and properties of the people, and the internal order, improvement, and prosperity of the State.

The operations of the federal government will be most extensive and important in times of war and danger; those of the State governments, in times of peace and security. As the former periods will probably bear a small proportion to the latter, the State governments will here enjoy another advantage over the federal government. (emphasis added)

In other words, Madison expected the federal government to preempt state governments only in times of war. In times of peace and security state governments would enjoy an "advantage over the federal government." Furthermore, he said that the states, not the federal government, would have primary power over the "ordinary course of affairs" in the everyday lives of Americans. The situation in which we find ourselves is the opposite of what Madison intended—the federal government, not the states, is regulating the daily affairs of Americans.

21

Other federalist papers insisted the essential function of the federal government would be to ensure that the Union would be just strong enough to guard against potential foreign enemies and to protect the Union against internal dissension. The framers were trying to improve upon the Articles of Confederation, which governed America in the period between the end of the Revolutionary War and the ratification of the Constitution. The framers feared the Articles left the Union too vulnerable to attack and disunion. They said history was full of examples in which weak confederacies disintegrated from within. During the debate over ratification the framers argued about how strong the federal government needed to be, but no framer suggested the federal government should perform roles that could be performed by the states. Their goal was to create a federal government that would hold the Union together, not micromanage the everyday lives of Americans.

Despite these clear warnings, Congress has been pushing the bounds of its constitutional role since the early days of the Republic. In 1792, James Madison, our fourth president, chastised Congress when it appropriated $15,000 to assist French refugees: "I cannot undertake to lay my finger on that article of the Constitution which granted a right to Congress of expending, on objects of benevolence, the money of their constituents."

One of the most colorful clashes about Congress's constitutional responsibilities occurred early in the nineteenth century when U.S. Representative Davy Crockett had the audacity to question whether Congress had the constitutional authority to perform the charitable—and politically popular—act of appropriating money for the widow of a distinguished naval officer:

Mr. Speaker, I have as much respect for the memory of the deceased, and as much sympathy for the suffering of the living, if suffering there be, as any man in this house, but we must not permit our respect for the dead or our sympathy for a part of the living to lead us into an act of injustice to the balance of the living. *I will not go into an argument to prove that Congress has no power to appropriate this money as an act of charity. Every member upon this floor knows it.* We have the right, as individuals, to give away as much of our own money as we please in charity; but as members of Congress we have no right to appropriate a dollar of the public money. Some eloquent appeals have been made to us upon the ground that it is a debt due the deceased. Mr. Speaker, the deceased lived long after the close of the war; he was in office to the day of his death, and I have never heard that the government was in arrears to him.

Every man in this House knows it is not a debt. We cannot, without the grossest corruption, appropriate money as the payment of a debt. *We have not the semblance of authority to appropriate it as a charity.* Mr. Speaker, I have said we have the right to give as much money of our own as we please. I am the poorest man on this floor. I cannot vote for this bill, but I will give one week's pay to the object, and, if every member of Congress will do the same, it will amount to more than the bill asks. (emphasis added)

When Crockett took his seat, no one rose to challenge him, and the bill failed. Crockett later explained that he took such a principled stand after being chastised by a constituent, Horatio Bunce, for voting for another bill that appropriated $20,000 to victims of a fire in nearby Georgetown.

Mr. Bunce explained to Crockett:

Well, Colonel, you gave a vote last winter which shows that either you have not capacity to understand the Constitution, or that you are wanting in the honesty and firmness to be guided by it. . . . In the first place, the government ought to have in the Treasury no more than enough for its legitimate purposes. . . . *The power of collecting and disbursing money at pleasure is the most dangerous power that can be entrusted to man.* . . . If you have the right to give to one, you have the right to give to all; and, as the Constitution neither defines charity nor stipulates the amount, you are at liberty to give to any thing and everything which you may believe, or profess to believe, is a charity, and to any amount you may think proper. *You will very easily perceive what a wide door this would open for fraud and corruption and favoritism, on the one hand, and for robbing the people on the other.* . . . There are plenty of men in and around Washington who could have given $20,000 without depriving themselves of even a luxury of life. The congressmen chose to keep their own money, which, if reports be true, some of them spend not very creditably; and *the people about Washington, no doubt, applauded you for relieving them from the necessity of giving by giving what was not yours to give.* The people have delegated to Congress, by the Constitution, the power to do certain things. To do these, it is authorized to collect and pay moneys, and for nothing else. Everything beyond this is usurpation, and a violation of the Constitution.

So you see, Colonel, you have violated the Constitution in what I consider a vital point. It is a precedent fraught with danger to the country, for *when Congress once begins to stretch its power beyond the limits of the Constitution, there is no limit to it, and no security for the people.* (emphasis added)

The honesty and firmness with which Mr. Bunce defended the integrity of the Constitution is sorely lacking among professional politicians today.

Crockett's argument in favor of Congress's limited and constitutional role was part of a larger ongoing debate. In the nineteenth century the most important debate in American politics, according to Forest McDonald, distinguished research professor of history at the University of Alabama, concerned "the nature of the Union and the line to be drawn between the authority of the general government and that of several states."

In *States' Rights and the Union: Imperium in Imperio, 1776–1876,*

McDonald argues that the War of 1812, in which the British burned Washington, D.C., strengthened the hand of those who wanted a strong federal government to provide for the common defense, but the real blow to the doctrine of states' rights was the Civil War, in which the Union was nearly torn apart. In the aftermath of the Civil War, the nation struggled to restore a healthy equilibrium between the federalists—those who wanted a strong federal government—and staunch defenders of states' rights. The trauma of that event and lingering bitterness over the South's attempt to secede from the union made it difficult for defenders of states' rights to assert the founders' vision of limited government.

The Civil War was the first of two great shifts in our history when the balance of power between the states and federal government dramatically tilted to the federal government. This first shift was less a result of an ideological campaign to undermine the Constitution than of the South's tragic and unwise attempt to secede from the Union. The Civil War and its aftermath consolidated much more power in a centralized federal government than existed prior to the war. The second shift, however, was an ideological campaign initiated by a group of thinkers and politicians called "the progressives" who unabashedly called for a dramatic expansion in the role of the federal government in the social and economic life of the nation. The progressives, who held a dim view of the Constitution and the old order of things, created the momentum for Woodrow Wilson's "New Freedom," which was the precursor to Franklin Delano Roosevelt's "New Deal."

The "New Deal" opened the floodgates of federal spending and is the second great fulcrum on which power shifted to the federal government. The "New Deal" either created or laid the foundation for today's entitlement programs, such as Social Security and Medicare, that consume nearly half of our almost $2 trillion annual federal budget. Spending on national defense, by contrast, consumes only 15 percent of our annual budget.

Franklin D. Roosevelt is revered as a decisive leader who led our nation through war abroad and economic crisis at home and is memorialized between Jefferson and Lincoln in our nation's capitol. While FDR's gifts as a leader and visionary are beyond question, his calculated and relentless campaign to expand the role and scope of the federal government flew in the face of everything our founders warned of concerning the dangers of an ever-expanding federal government. FDR's response to the trauma, confusion, and near choas of the Great Depression was not a list of temporary emergency measures but a reshaping of our system of government. His infamous attempt to pack the Supreme Court with justices who understood "these modern conditions" as he viewed them revealed his intent to fundamentally subvert the Constitution. FDR derided the "Nine Old Men" in the court and called for all federal judges to retire by the age of seventy. Those who did not retire would be paired up with another justice thereby increasing the size of the court from nine to fifteen, the new appointees being his and thus sure to back his agenda. FDR's power play backfired in the short-term, but he won the long-term battle through carefully chosen appointments.

In the twentieth century, the expansion of federal power compared to local power was astonishing. In 1900, prior to the "New Deal," as detailed in *Restoring the Dream,* edited by Stephen Moore, the percentage of total government spending by local government was 60 percent while the federal government spent 20 percent. By 1940, the situation was reversed with the federal government accounting for 52 percent of all government spending while local government spent 23 percent. In 1990, local government accounted for 19 percent of government spending while the federal government accounted for 67 percent.

Paul Carrese, an associate professor of political science at the U.S. Air Force Academy, describes the trend this way:

> For the past century most American political scientists, following Woodrow
> Wilson, have disdained the principles of our constitutionalism—separation

of powers and federalism—as undemocratic, backward looking, and ineffi-cient. We have learned, however, that Wilson's blend of populism and scien-tific administration yields bureaucrats, demagogues, pollsters, overreaching judges, and journalists who can practice versions of elitism and tyranny quite well.

Americans today have grown so accustomed to the welfare state that it is difficult to imagine any other scenario, even as the status quo falters. Politicians who aggressively work to push Congress back into the confines of the Constitution are derided as extremists who want draconian, slash-and-burn cuts to vital services. Both parties encourage sentimental and patriotic references to the Constitution, but any member of Congress who tries to force the body to respect the Constitution is dismissed as naïve. Arguments about the theoretical importance of respecting the Constitution are easily drowned out by demagoguery. It is easy for politicians who want to protect the status quo to suggest that efforts to reduce the size of government will harm chil-dren, the elderly, and the poor. For example, in 1995, when Republicans wanted to *increase* spending for federal school nutrition programs by 4.5 percent annually instead of 5.2 percent, they were accused of wanting to starve underprivileged children. History, in my opinion, will judge those who resorted to cheap scare tactics to hold back necessary reforms as extremist defenders of the status quo.

Still, most members of Congress are either ignorant of or indifferent to Congress's constitutional guidelines and the warnings in history that should caution us against consolidating too much power in a large central government. The courts themselves have overreached and under-mined the founders' design for limited government. I always found it ironic when my Republican colleagues would deliver passionate speeches criticizing the judicial branch for not respecting the Constitution when they were gladly joining their colleagues in the legislative branch in violating the very same document. The next time a member of Congress criticizes the Supreme Court for not respecting the Constitution they should be prepared to offer legislation rescinding about half of the federal budget that is used for purposes never envisioned by our founders.

The 1994 "Republican revolution" could have been the third great fulcrum on which federal power shifted in our history, and it would have been the first time power shifted *away* from the federal government. The past two shifts, the Civil War in the 1860s and the "New Deal" in the 1930s, occurred in about seventy-year intervals after the ratification of our constitution in 1789. We are due for another shift, and the combined problems of the impending entitlement bankruptcy, unsustainable spending, and war costs will soon force a shift in one direction or the other. I believe one of the key reasons why the Republican revolution failed to produce revolutionary changes was because fewer Republicans than we imagined really believed in our founders' vision of limited representative government as described in the Constitution. Today, there is but a remnant of the revolutionary spirit and vision of our founders in our government.

Congress, of course, will never look like the Congress of the late eighteenth century. But to dismiss the parameters of Congress's constitutional authority as outdated is arrogant and dangerous. While our founders designed a Constitution that would be flexible enough to stretch with the times, they also established clear and responsible boundaries they hoped future generations would not cross. The founders' definition of these constitutional boundaries is clear and straightforward. Congress should provide for the common defense and perform any functions the states cannot do for themselves.

The budget shortfalls many states are experiencing are, in large part, a consequence of federal power being exercised outside its original boundaries. Dollars that should be used for education and health care programs at the state level are instead being consumed by a ravenous federal government. The burning of our tax dollars in Washington on useless bureaucracy is literally sucking the oxygen from the states. So-called "matching fund" schemes in programs like Medicaid mask the fact that the federal government is doing things for the states that the states and private entities should be doing for themselves—and doing it poorly and inefficiently.

Today, Congress is like a ship that has been cut from its constitutional moorings. We go wherever the political winds take us, and we have sailed into the dangerous waters of massive government expansion that is threatening to bankrupt our nation and sacrifice our children's future.

No civilization in history that has indulged in a massive expansion of its central government has long survived. Unless members of Congress and the American people restore their allegiance to the constitutional principle of limited government, America will follow the path of other great civilizations that decayed because of their own excesses.

The American people should ask themselves whom they are willing to trust: modern politicians who will say anything and support any program that will help them win reelection or the founding fathers who drew from several thousand years of political and world history during the drafting of the Constitution. The choice for America is clear: We can govern according to the career politicians' vision of how to win the next election or Madison's vision of how to preserve our freedom for the next generation.

THERE'S A DOCTOR IN THE HOUSE

3

THE CULTURE OF WASHINGTON

Power tends to corrupt, and absolute power corrupts absolutely.

—Lord Acton

As the seventy-three freshmen prepared to enter Congress in 1994, we did not fully appreciate that the forces that had caused the federal government to spin out of control could not be solely attributed to Democratic rule, nor could those forces be easily reversed by a changing of the guard. While the Democrats certainly expanded the size of government to a ridiculous degree, we did not anticipate how difficult it would be for Republicans to put the genie of big government back in its bottle. We understood that liberty decreases when government increases, but we did not fully understand the power of the tide we hoped to turn.

THE SEDUCTION OF POWER

As I discussed in the previous chapter, our founders were concerned that if the human drive for power escaped its constitutional confines our form of representative government would, in a sense, melt down, polluting our political institutions and its members. The system of checks and balances and limits on federal power was designed to prevent such a calamity.

Politicians have been tempted by the allure of power since the dawn of time. It was Adam's desire to be like God, to have an extra measure of power, which led him to eat the fruit from the Tree of Knowledge in the Garden of Eden. Some of the greatest works of literature, such as J. R. R. Tolkien's *Lord of the Rings* trilogy, have focused on this theme. In Tolkien's classic story, the hero embarks on a quest to destroy a ring of power that corrupts its user and becomes harder to destroy the closer the hero gets to the source of the ring's power. The struggle in Tolkien's story parallels the very human tendency for most members of Congress to become more addicted to power and devoid of principle the longer they stay in Washington and the closer they get to the centers of power within leadership and committees.

As a physician, I see the world through the lens of the medical profession. When I came to Washington, D.C., I was troubled to observe so many similarities between the behaviors of drug-addicted patients and my political colleagues. In Washington, power is like morphine. It dulls the senses, impairs judgment, and leads politicians to make choices that damage their own character and the machinery of our democracy. It seems more power is needed each year to satisfy the addiction.

Just as drug addicts sometimes stop at nothing to obtain their drug, a politician will often stop at nothing to gain access to more power. Principles, commitments, and even family relationships can be casually discarded if they stand in the way of the object of their addiction. Reason, logic, and morality all go out the window in an all-consuming blind drive to get a power fix.

C. S. Lewis called chasing after power "the quest for the Inner Ring"—the place where decisions are made, the place where one is "in-the-know," and the place where, once inside, one can feel pleasure when those on the outside feel excluded.

The sensation of stepping inside the Inner Ring of Congress is exhilarating. A member of Congress, especially one with little exposure to

Washington, can't help feeling awed while walking through the rotunda and Statuary Hall. Realizing that you are part of such an exclusive club that counts John C. Calhoun, Henry Clay, and John F. Kennedy as its members is truly intoxicating.

In fact, wherever members of Congress go, it seems everyone is reminding us that we are at the center of the universe. The typical meeting with constituents or a business group begins with them showering praise at the feet of their representative. "Thanks for all of the hard work you've done." "You're doing a tremendous job." "We don't know what we'd do without you." These are comments I heard dozens of times from visitors even when I had almost nothing to do with delivering the results for which I was given credit. Visitors are often paying respect to the office rather than the individual member, but most members gladly lap up the praise for themselves. It is easy to see how after receiving this adoration for a term or two most members become convinced they are indispensable to their district.

When I was elected to Congress, reporters were suddenly fascinated by my opinion on every subject. Simply being elected to Congress somehow made me an expert on every subject from foreign policy to the economy even though the typical member is at most an expert in only one or two areas. Being treated like an expert leads some members to believe they do in fact possess great wisdom about every subject, and they therefore speak about every subject from the floor. Others become what some of my friends from the Class of 1994 call "camera moths"— members who run toward a television camera whenever they see its bright light. In fact, when one of us seemed to be getting a lot of "face time" on television we would needle each other with this accusation. Still other members, as newly christened experts, make exaggerated claims, as Al Gore did when he took credit for inventing the Internet.

However, soon the thrill of being in the Inner Ring of 435 in the House or 100 in the Senate loses its potency, and the goal becomes to make it into the Inner Ring of subcommittee chairmen, then committee chairmen, then leadership. Lewis said that of all passions the passion for the Inner Ring is most skillful in making a man who is not yet a very bad man do very bad things. "As long as you are governed by that desire you will never get what you want," Lewis said. "You are trying to peel an onion; if you succeed there will be nothing left. Until you conquer the fear of being an outsider, an outsider you will remain."

IN THE MODERN CONGRESS IT SEEMS THE ENTIRE SYSTEM IS GEARED TOWARD SPENDING INCREASINGLY HUGE SUMS OF MONEY.

Unfortunately, our leadership and a majority of career Republicans never overcame that fear of being an outsider. They had waited so long to be in the majority that almost everything they did was based on not losing the majority. As a result, we governed from a position of fear rather than courage and failed to bring about revolutionary changes. I saw, time and time again, members and leadership make politically expedient decisions because they could not bear the thought of being on the outside. During the Republicans' forty years in the desert of Democratic rule they took the long view. Once they gained power, however, they too often switched to a short-term approach.

Lord Acton's famous axiom, "Power tends to corrupt, and absolute power corrupts absolutely," is as true today as ever. The struggle between power and principle in the hearts of politicians is, and always will be, a central part of the story about why our government is not functioning as it should.

The Inertia toward Spending

If power is the great motivating principle in Washington, greed is its great organizing principle. In the modern Congress it seems the entire system is geared toward spending increasingly huge sums of money.

THE CULTURE OF WASHINGTON

The primary reason Congress has such a hard time controlling spending is that it is performing functions it was never intended to handle. The system our founders designed has been breached, allowing the corrupting force of power to seep out and eat away at the institution of Congress itself and its members. Members of Congress now control an appropriations process that touches nearly every aspect of our lives from health care to education to retirement. The surest way a member of Congress can stay in power is to preserve and expand those programs.

My dear friend John Shadegg (R-Arizona) has a quote sitting atop one of his bookcases in his office that is the key to understanding how power is distributed in Congress: "The greatest pleasure in the world is to spend someone else's money." Whoever has the ability to provide or withhold this pleasure—to direct where money is spent, or not spent—holds ultimate power in Washington. No one has more control over the purse strings in Washington than the "cardinals"—the chairman and subcommittee chairman of the Appropriations Committees in the House and Senate and their staff.

In Congress, as in most organizations, there is a formal and informal power structure. The formal structure that consists of titles and a chain of command often does not align with the informal structure of how power is actually distributed. In any organization, individuals with less authoritative titles but greater access to key resources or information often exercise more power than those officially in command. The same is true in Congress.

The official role of the Appropriations Committee is to set spending *priorities*. Overall spending *levels* are supposed to be determined by the Budget Committee, which drafts an annual budget resolution setting spending levels for the upcoming fiscal year. Once the House and Senate pass the budget resolution, the task of the Appropriations Committee is to make the difficult decisions about which programs to fund and at what level within the limits outlined in the budget resolution. However, these formalities are routinely ignored by the appropriators.

35

The real power the Appropriations Committee exercises far exceeds its official, formal mandate. The Appropriations Committee not only determines spending priorities but also has more control over total levels of spending than the president or any other committee or body in the House, including the elected leadership.

The Appropriations Committee controls Congress's most important process. Congress debates a wide array of important issues every year from taxes to abortion to health care reform, but the bread and butter of Congress's actual work are the thirteen appropriations bills it must pass every year. How much, and where, money is spent in the appropriations bills affects virtually every other issue the House considers.

An excess of power has been concentrated in the Appropriations Committee because it is Grand Central Station for the spending requests and campaign contributions that flow through Congress. The committee is so powerful precisely because of its ability to spend. Every appropriations bill affects numerous constituencies who rely on the funding within that bill and will make large campaign contributions to the members who will fight to increase or protect that funding. The committee is also the biggest pork-processing center in Congress. Orders for pork barrel projects are often processed according to a member's seniority, popularity among committee members, and vulnerability in their next election.[3]

---

[3] Chapter 6 will focus much more extensively on pork politics. As a point of clarity, pork barrel projects are unnecessary or lower priority projects that receive funding not because of their merit, but because of their political utility; usually they are political payoffs or bribes to powerful constituents. Pork spending is one of the common abuses of power in Congress.

THE CULTURE OF WASHINGTON

TEN THINGS CONGRESS DOES NOT WANT YOU TO KNOW ABOUT HOW IT DOES BUSINESS

The First Thing Congress Does Not Want You to Know about How It Does Business: The Appropriations Committee staff knows more about the content of spending bills than elected representatives serving on that committee.

The Appropriations Committee has a large staff that wields tremendous power in a process that is far too complex for any one elected member serving on the committee to track. Modern appropriations bills are so vast and expensive that they often exceed the gross domestic products of many developing countries. Staff members have enormous power in leveraging information and overall spending levels. Staff can withhold or provide information and adjust spending levels. On several occasions I confronted members of the Appropriations Committee with questionable spending items their staff had inserted into bills without their knowledge or consent. When Republicans took control of Congress we did not necessarily take control of the Appropriations Committee because our leaders chose to retain much of the existing staff. Our leaders believed they needed the previous majority's staff to govern. Had they taken a risk and brought in people with a different perspective about how government should function, our revolution would have been much more successful.

Nevertheless, requests for spending do not appear out of nowhere. Individual members who want to spend more money are as much to blame for the inertia toward spending as the appropriators. As Shadegg says, "The appropriators are only a symptom of the problem, not the problem. Appropriators may carry the fight, but they are only reflecting the [members of the Republican] conference."

Representative Lindsey Graham (R-South Carolina), now a member of the Senate and another member from the Class of 1994 who often joined Shadegg and me in budget fights, agreed:

A lot of appropriators like the power that comes from taking care of themselves and their buddies, and we like being on the receiving end of that as a body. So, when we criticize the appropriators it's almost like you are claiming to be a helpless victim. They don't do anything we don't want them to do. The appropriations process works based on the will of the body and the will of the body in each appropriations item is to make sure that the things important to you locally and personally are satisfied. The appropriators are inundated with requests. They're responding to their constituency [individual members]. That's never going to change.

Appropriators will always respond to member requests, and this process is not inherently evil, just out of control. The appropriations process is not corrupted when members want to do good things for the country and for their constituents. Rather, the process becomes corrupted when funds are dispersed according to political considerations rather than true spending priorities. What typically happens is the neediest politician, in the political sense, gets taken care of first. If a member is in political trouble back home, he can usually count on a pork project for his district. While his press release will say he is spending money for the district, it is more often an insurance policy for his own seat.

Of course, every dollar Congress spends should be prioritized according to its constitutional duties. Providing for a strong defense should be its first priority, then regulating interstate commerce, and so on. If a member requests something for his district, it should be measured against every other request and should not be affected in any way by his chances for reelection or his previous votes. Unfortunately, this is not how the system works. Members on the Appropriations Committee have an unwritten agreement to use the process as a tool to help members of their respective parties win reelection, which is why members of the Appropriations Committee work so well across party aisles. Yet rather than being an oasis for bipartisanship, the committee is the center of gravity for the real force that directs Congress: *careerism*.

One episode that best illustrated the Appropriations Committee's bipartisan commitment to spending and to pork occurred in October of 2000 when House Appropriations Committee Republicans refused to release a list of Democratic pork projects to leadership. Members of leadership were irritated because Democrats were attacking Republican pork projects and wanted to mute their criticism by releasing a list of Democratic pork projects. The appropriators would have none of that, however, insisting that projects remain confidential. The episode revealed the appropriators' preference for secrecy over transparency and exposed their readiness to defy the wishes of leadership to protect spending as usual.

Nevertheless, one has to remember that the fault does not rest solely with the appropriators. It is at the request of individual members that appropriators serve as the guardians of a political spoils system that transcends the official Republican and Democratic platforms. One of the more grand acts of bipartisan elitism that occurred during my time in Congress happened in 1999 when Senators Tom Harkin (D-Iowa) and Arlen Specter (R-Pennsylvania) tried to use an appropriations bill to have two federal institutions renamed after themselves. Harkin wanted to rename the Center for Disease Control and Prevention the "Thomas R. Harkin Center for Disease Control and Prevention," and Specter wanted to name the Department of Health and Human Services National Library of Medicine the "Arlen Specter National Library of Medicine." I issued a statement drawing attention to this embarrassing display of taxpayer-funded self-flattery, and the bid to rename the institutions was pulled from the bill.

Even though this system of excessive spending, pork projects, and self-flattery seems absurd to ordinary Americans, the pressure to conform to it in Washington is enormous. Appropriators will punish members and block them from pursuing legitimate projects for their district if a member challenges this system. One unwritten rule is that if the Appropriations Committee chairman or a subcommittee chairman does you a favor, you are expected to vote for his bill. If you don't vote for the bill, the implied threat is that you can never again ask for anything. For example, in 1995, Appropriations Committee Chairman Bob Livingston (R-Louisiana) eliminated funding for Indian education in my district. I told him there was a better way to do what he was trying to do by folding the program into another program. He took my suggestion and changed the bill. When I voted against the overall bill because it spent an obscene amount of money, Livingston was livid. He assumed, it seemed, that because he did something for me, I would give him a blank check to spend as much as he wanted.

In another instance, during my final term, Mark Souder (R-Indiana) and I urged Sonny Callahan (R-Alabama), Foreign Operations Subcommittee chairman, to direct more money in his bill to border security and other needs in the Republic of Macedonia, a volatile nation in the Balkans. My office had been in contact with the office of the president of Macedonia, Boris Trajkovski, to determine how to help prevent a Kosovo-like situation in his country, which we feared could lead to a humanitarian catastrophe and another costly intervention by the U.S. and NATO. We asked for Callahan to pay for the increase by redirecting funds within the bill rather than increasing the overall level of spending.

After my brief remarks, Callahan said, "The time will come when the gentleman will have the opportunity to vote on whether or not we are going to have an increased allocation. And if indeed that allocation comes, which I am sure the gentleman will then not object if we are going to fulfill his request, I will certainly consider that." After Souder supported my remarks, Callahan said, "I would also give the same message to the gentleman from Indiana that when the time comes for an increased allocation whereby we can facilitate these things, we would very much appreciate the support of the gentlemen."

Callahan's real message was in effect, "I'll look at this request when you promise to vote for my bill." Callahan knew I didn't play that game, but I hoped that as a statesman Callahan would look at the potential for conflict in that region and make a reasonable judgment based on competing priorities in his bill. For whatever reason, the request was not ultimately fulfilled, and the next year Macedonia nearly descended into civil war in part because rebels from Kosovo crossed the porous border we were working to secure.

THE PUBLIC'S AMBIVALENCE
TOWARD BIG GOVERNMENT

If the appropriators are carrying the fight for individual members, individual members are carrying the fight of their constituents. The American public has a curious love/hate relationship with government. The public despises big government generally but loves it specifically. Shadegg says, "There are all kinds of people who come in to see me and say they are card-carrying conservatives, but we need money for this one project."

I had the same experience during my service. My response to constituent requests for more money for any program from education to health care was usually something like this: "I'll look at freezing spending in this area so there won't be a cut, but if we increase spending here the money will come out of the Social Security and Medicare surpluses." I would then find the most polite way of asking if they wanted to spend their children's and grandchildren's Social Security and

Medicare money on their project. I would also ask, "What program do you want to cut to make funds available for your project?" When I explained that most additional spending would come from Social Security and Medicare if there wasn't a cut in another program, most constituents left happy I was fighting to protect those programs and their children's and grandchildren's future. I always believed that my constituents sent me to Washington to fight for smaller, not bigger, government. And if they did not want that kind of representation, they would not have elected me.

I also didn't have to worry about alienating powerful lobbies in my district because, having taken a term limits pledge, I knew I would not be in Washington long. Most members bend over backwards to pursue funding for constituent requests. Every time one New York Republican met with a constituent who asked for money, he wrote a letter to the Appropriations Committee asking for funds for that project. When one constituent who didn't believe HIV caused AIDS wanted to fund a study to support this scientifically baseless and reckless position, the member wrote a letter anyway requesting funds for this "important" project in his district.

Columnist Walter Williams sums up this aspect of the problem well: "Today's politicians can't be held fully responsible for our growing constitutional contempt. . . . The lion's share of the blame rests with 270 million Americans. Our elected officials simply mirror our contempt for constitutional principles and our desire to live at the expense of our fellow American."

LOBBYISTS: THE PROGENY AND PROTECTORS OF BIG GOVERNMENT

Another important aspect of the culture of Washington today is the proliferation of special interests groups and lobbyists. Outside interest groups have always been a part of government since the dawn of time, but only in the last few decades have lobbyists attained such a significant role.

The primary reason for the explosion of lobbyists is the size and scope of government itself. As our elected officials have expanded government to reach into more aspects of our lives, lobbyists have arisen to direct and influence the nature of that involvement. Yet even though the intrusiveness of government itself is a reason for the existence of lobbyists, the incentives in the lobbying community are to expand, not limit, the scope of government.

Reducing the size of government too much would put many lobbyists out of a job. In many instances, I observed that even when the mission of an organization was to limit the scope of government that group's lobbyists put their own desire to keep their jobs ahead of their organization's goals. This is not to say that there is no place for lobbyists, who can be an excellent source of information that would be very difficult to obtain from any other source. However, the lobbying culture in Washington is a microcosm of Congress in which ego, power, persona, money, and personal connection get rolled into an effort to achieve a specified objective. What is really happening in many cases is an effort to advance one's career through accomplishment. Too often the goal of lobbyists is not positive policy change for their client and the public but the perpetuation of a process that is beneficial to themselves and their firms.

One of the best examples of the disconnection between an organization's goals and the goals of its lobbyists was the American Medical Association (AMA) and their role in the patients' bill of rights debate. The AMA failed, in my opinion, to play a constructive role in that debate because their lobbyists were completely out of touch with the needs of doctors and patients. The battle was ironic because the lobbyists were—with rare exception—lawyers, not doctors, and the doctors that did have influence over the lobbyists rarely practiced medicine. So here I was, a congressman who was actively practicing medicine and a member of the AMA, arguing back and forth with lawyers from the AMA who had never had one experience with Health Maintenance Organizations or managed care firms that eliminate necessary and adequate care for patients. The AMA's chief goal was to get the deal done and look good to the board of the AMA. It seemed they could not have cared less if the bill actually helped or hurt doctors or patients. From my vantage point, internal politics, not the needs of patients or doctors, were driving their position. The AMA instructed its lobbyists to avoid any compromise that might alienate doctors in Texas or Georgia, states that had already passed a patients' bill of rights that protected the right to sue in state courts.

The lesson I learned from my experience from the AMA patients' bill of rights debacle is the same lesson I was taught by John Kasich (R-Ohio) shortly after I arrived in Congress: Don't trust what anyone says in Washington because more often than not a political calculation will undermine their commitment. One of the first things I did when I retired from Congress was to cancel my membership in the AMA. It was clear from working with the AMA in Washington that they do not represent most physicians but rather the ruling political elite in medicine, and, as a consequence, they harm the interests of patients.

Another important aspect of the lobbying community is their relationship with congressional staff. The same principle of pursuit of the Inner Ring applies to those who work in Congress as it does to those elected to the institution. The twenty thousand or so staff members on Capitol Hill are human too, and sometimes their desire for power overcomes their desire to do the proper and appropriate thing. Staff will often advocate the politically expedient position that will enhance either their position within a committee or their position within their office. Also, staff members often go on to work for organizations that are under the jurisdiction of the committee for which they work, or on which their bosses serve. For example, it is common for committee staff to take a higher paying job with a lobbying firm that has legislation before that committee so that the staffer can lobby his or her former colleagues, creating an incestuous revolving-door effect.

The nexus between staff and lobbyists is most evident in the Appropriations Committee where staff on the various subcommittees are the true power brokers with lobbyists. Many of the cardinals never knew the details or the ultimate consequences of the bills they so lavishly praised during floor debate. Daylight rarely shines on appropriations bills for a reason. Members and staff do not want the public to know the true extent of the political favoritism and influence that controls that committee. Rarely are appropriations bills written in plain language to explain the effects of expenditures. But you can bet there is at least one (and often only one) lobbyist and staff member who knows where the money is going and whose political friend or bank account might benefit.

CAREER POLITICIANS DO NOT HAVE THE COURAGE TO PRIORITIZE SPENDING AND SAY NO TO DEMANDING SPECIAL INTEREST GROUPS WHO DO NOT REFLECT THE BEST INTERESTS OF THE COUNTRY.

I even saw tendencies in my own staff to overreach their authority because they worked for a congressman on Capitol Hill. On a few occasions, my own staff sent letters or made agreements with other members without my knowledge. This was limited but is a natural aspect of human behavior. However, when not held in check by the member, this behavior can grow to unlimited heights. Staff also have the ability to control the agenda by not giving a member or committee member timely or complete information they might need to make a proper choice. Members of Congress need staff to be their eyes and ears, but staff are very capable of inserting their own philosophy in lieu of the district's desires or constitutional limits.

In 1994, the strength of the forces that formed the culture of Washington—the seduction of power, the powerful inertia toward increasing spending, and the nexus between lobbyists, members, and staff—made it much easier for members to join the system rather than fight it. It is very tempting for members to appropriate funds for new programs and enjoy the power that comes with that activity when Congress, by default, already increases spending every year.

If anything could combat these forces and turn the tide, I believed, and still believe, it was principled leadership. Too often, career politicians do not have the courage to prioritize spending and say no to demanding special interest groups and narrow segments of constituents who do not at all reflect the best interests of the country. Fighting the status quo requires not only guts but also hard work and determination, qualities that rapidly dissipate after three or four terms in office, as the years after 1994 would reveal.

4

A BRIEF REVOLUTION

Insurgents are like conquerors: they must go forward.
The moment they are stopped they are lost.

—DUKE OF WELLINGTON,
British general who helped Spain to resist Napoleon

IN JANUARY 1995, the freshmen Republicans from the Class of 1994 marched into Congress determined to overrun the old guard in Washington. Our leader, Newt Gingrich, who often compared himself to the Duke of Wellington, seemed to understand the need to push forward swiftly to maintain and build upon our momentum. We had stormed the castle. Now it was time to occupy the keep, the traditional last bastion of defense in medieval times.

Gingrich really did make us feel like soldiers in a revolutionary army. We were not merely the new party in the majority; we were on a mission to change the culture of Washington. After having been swept into Washington in a historic election, we believed we had a mandate from the American people to overturn the old regime. In our minds, this previous regime wasn't simply the Democratic party; it was a way of doing business that separated Congress from the American people. We took this zeal and determination to turn Congress upside down into the first hundred days of the 104th Congress, which was a march unlike any other in the history of Congress.

THE FIRST HUNDRED DAYS

On our very first day in session, the new Republican majority unleashed a barrage of bills designed to complete our conquest. The eight measures passed on that single day exceeded the output—in terms of real reforms—of any single Congress in decades.

We started by passing a bill requiring Congress to live under the laws it imposes on the rest of the country. For years, Congress had exempted itself from complying with laws such as the Civil Rights Act of 1964, the Equal Employment Opportunity Act, and the Freedom of Information Act. Congress's brazen attempts to hold itself above the law typified what voters perceived as the arrogance of power in Washington.

Next, we wanted to begin the process of making Congress leaner, more efficient and responsive. Many of us proudly wore buttons declaring, "Cut Spending First." We believed the best way to demonstrate our commitment to that goal was to scale back Congress itself. We passed a bill calling for an independent audit of the House that would scour its books for signs of waste, fraud, and abuse. By exposing any residual corruption in the institution we hoped to set the Republican Congress apart from past Congresses. We also wanted to prevent any hidden scandals from blowing up in our faces. The recent House Bank and Post Office scandals were the kind of fiascos we didn't want to repeat.

In the spring of 1992, the public learned that at least a dozen members of Congress were deliberately writing large checks for insufficient funds while the Office of the Sergeant of Arms covered overdrafts for free. One House member, Mary Rose Oakar (D-Ohio), was indicted for trying to funnel $16,000 through a fake donor. Even though members of both parties were guilty, the Democrats, who controlled Congress at that time, took a savage beating. The scandal, which fueled the perception that politicians treated tax dollars as play money, helped solidify the belief among the public that most members of Congress had been there way too long. The criminal stupidity of trying to write hot checks at the taxpayers' expense was a classic example of how long-term exposure to power corrupts and impairs judgment.

Next, we cut the number of House committees and committee staff by one-third. With 35,000 aides, Congress had nine times as many staff as any other legislative body in the world, including the old Soviet Parliament. We then proceeded to end proxy voting on congressional committees—when one member votes on behalf of absent members—and opened all committee hearings, except hearings that dealt with national security, to the public. The veil of secrecy surrounding committee hearings was a radical departure from the principle of transparency, which is a key part of any healthy democracy.

We also passed significant tax and spend reform measures, including legislations requiring that any bill that increased the income tax rate pass by a three-fifths margin. Had this measure been in effect in 1993 it would have blocked Clinton's tax increase. However, I was convinced the most important reform we made to Congress that day was limiting the terms of the Speaker to four two-year terms and committee chairs to three two-year terms. This act provided the strongest institutional check against career politicians who could use powerful positions for personal political gain. By increasing the chances that principled statesmen and citizen legislators would occupy these important posts, we believed we made it much more likely that in decades to come Congress would pass laws based more on principle and less on politics. Unfortunately, this reform would be severely eroded by future Republican Congresses.[4]

We also took steps to end the perks that made Congress look like a

---

[4] When committee chairmanships expired in 2000 many simply played musical chairs and became chairmen of other committees. In the 106th Congress, the House repealed term limits for the Speaker, but, on a positive note, conservatives led by Pat Toomey (R-Pennsylvania) defeated an attempt to repeal term limits for committee chairmen.

resort island unto itself. We started with stopping the daily delivery of ice to congressional offices. Ending this wasteful and indulgent practice was so popular that Speaker Gingrich started carrying an empty ice bucket to remind and inspire members that we were here to end business as usual in Washington.

In those initial days our leadership gave us every indication our "up with the people" enthusiasm, idealism, and determination was justified. Speaker Gingrich had our trust and confidence; in fact, many freshmen were enamored with the man. As promised, he was bringing the items of the Contract with America to the floor for votes. I was also impressed that the new chairman of the House Appropriations Committee, Bob Livingston (R-Louisiana), was drafting appropriations bills that would actually cut spending. He was doing what almost everyone else in this country already knew was possible: trimming waste in the bloated federal bureaucracy.

Gingrich seemed to be following Wellington's advice. We were pushing forward and had no intention of stopping until we truly occupied the power centers of Washington. "We were far into the enemy's territory before they knew what had hit them," recalled Gil Gutknenct, a member of the Class of 1994 from Minnesota.

The events of the first hundred days prompted *Washington Post* columnist David Broder to write, "It is healthy for our politics—and politicians of any affiliation—when the public sees elected officials doing what they promised."

THE TERM LIMITS VOTE: HALTING THE MARCH

Of all the reforms the freshmen wanted to bring to Washington, I believed setting term limits was by far the most important. It was the soul of the Contract with America. Nothing would change the culture, and policies, of Washington more than replacing career politicians with citizen legislators. Political careerism more than anything else had separated Washington from the people. Careerism perpetuated big government and was a constant corrupting force in the system.

Our founders never envisioned members of Congress turning public service into a career. Instead, they believed in the idea of rotation. A public official could serve a few terms, step down for a time, and then perhaps run again for another office.

"One thing our founding fathers could not foresee," Ronald Reagan said in 1973, "was a nation governed by professional politicians who had a vested interest in getting reelected. They probably envisioned a fellow serving a couple of hitches and then looking . . . forward to getting back to the farm."

Abraham Lincoln only served one term in the House from 1847-1849. He wanted to run for another term, but his supporters back home said it was someone else's turn. Had he stayed in the House he might have never run for president.

George Washington voluntarily stepped down as president after two terms. He created a precedent that was followed for 140 years until Franklin Delano Roosevelt was elected to four consecutive terms. Despite their love for FDR, the nation preferred Washington's example and passed the Twenty-second Amendment, limiting our president to two terms.

By 1994, the nation seemed poised to apply term limits to the legislative branch as well. Twenty-three states had already passed term limits laws, and polls showed that the public supported term limits by margins of more than two-to-one. Even though only a handful of us pledged to leave after three terms, the vast majority of freshmen at that time imagined they would make some positive changes in Washington before returning home to their real lives and jobs. Few of us seemed to be in love with the idea of serving in Congress and making Washington our home. Most of us left our families back in our districts and dreaded the weekly trips back and forth to Washington.

Even though term limits was one of the most popular items in the

Contract, we knew it would be difficult to enact. We knew we could not get the votes to pass a constitutional amendment, but we did think term limits legislation had a good chance of passing. We thought a fair number of Democrats would support the measure. For the Democrats, the 1994 election was a bloodbath, and many of them felt lucky to be alive politically. Even though most Democrats disagreed with term limits, many feared opposing a popular position that was a critical part of the effort to drive them from power. We also assumed we could count on the support of senior Republicans who made term limits part of the Contract with America and who owed a debt to the term limits movement for helping to give Republicans a majority in Congress.

WE BADLY UNDER-ESTIMATED WHAT CAREER REPUBLICANS WHO HAD NEVER BEEN IN THE MAJORITY WOULD DO TO REMAIN IN THE MAJORITY.

The first warning sign that the term limits measure was in trouble came before the 104th Congress convened when House Majority Leader Dick Armey (R-Texas) said, "Now that we have elected a Republican House, maybe there is no more need for term limits."

The debate over term limits legislation in the House was between those who supported a three-term limit, those who supported a six-term limit, and those who were honest enough to oppose term limits altogether. Leadership itself was not united on a position. In the end, leadership rigged the vote to make sure that every Republican could go on record voting for term limits of some kind while ensuring that no measure received a majority of votes. The freshmen were outraged by their deceptive tactics.

The term limits debate was the first setback in our nascent revolution. We naïvely assumed Republicans were now going to do all of the good things they had waited their entire careers to do but had been blocked from doing by the Democrats. We badly underestimated what career Republicans who had never been in the majority would do to remain in the majority. Many Republicans had spent ten to twelve years languishing in the minority, and they weren't about to do anything that would return them to their state of exile. We thought all Republicans thought like we did, but many of the Republicans who came before us really thought like careerists. We were confident Republicans would support term limits *because they were Republicans.* It was sad when we realized that our leaders were more interested in term limits as a campaign issue than as a real reform. This was the first of many battles in which Republicans weren't willing to risk their position to fight for the principles we had campaigned on in 1994.

THE GOVERNMENT SHUTDOWN: THE END OF THE REVOLUTION

In May of 1995, Congress passed a budget resolution that cut spending in real terms for the first time since 1981, the first year of the Reagan revolution. Unfortunately, this would be the last time a Republican-led House would bring such a bill to the floor.

Later, in 1995, the House passed a budget plan that would balance the budget in seven years—producing the first balanced budget since 1969. The plan would trim projected spending by $1 trillion over a seven-year period, which was roughly the equivalent of eliminating all new federal spending that was enacted after fiscal year 1992. The *Muskogee Phoenix* called it "the first serious attempt to reduce the role of federal spending and activities since the New Deal."

Republicans said the bill was a repudiation of decades of Democratic policies that expanded government. "We tried your way," said Bill Archer, chairman of the House Ways and Means Committee. "For 30 years we raised taxes and increased spending. We want to cut spending, and we want to balance the budget. That's what this bill does."

Before the shutdown, the Democrats had been blasting the GOP for being "extremists" because we wanted to cut fraud and waste out of Medicare. There had been considerable heated and dishonest rhetoric from both political parties on the subject that caused unneeded fear among many people. When I held a town hall meeting in Wagoner, Oklahoma, I assured a group of nervous seniors that the GOP had no intention of denying their Medicare services. I explained that under our plan there would be a 6 percent increase in spending each year for seven years. When I walked into the meeting, there were about fifty seniors who had serious concerns. After I explained the plan, I asked how they wanted me to vote. Not one person raised a hand in opposition. Almost everyone said yes, I should vote for the plan. I believed that if I explained the facts to people in a way they could understand, without any self-serving spin, they would almost always support me. I had been sent to Washington to make government smaller, not bigger.

Another early warning sign to me of a conflict between the insurgents and the career politicians in the Republican party occurred in early 1995 when two other newly elected doctors, Greg Ganske (R-Iowa) and Dave Weldon (R-Florida), and I met with Bill Thomas (R-California), then-chairman of the powerful House Ways and Means Health Subcommittee, to offer our perspectives as physicians on Medicare issues. We thought our combined forty-plus years of experience of dealing with patients and Medicare might be an asset to Thomas and his committee. Yet as we met Thomas early in an empty cloakroom off the House floor, he informed us, "There is nothing you can teach me about Medicare." Thus began and ended a fruitless meeting that typified the attitudes of many of Washington's elite.

In the fall of 1995, Newt Gingrich and Bill Clinton collided over the budget. The president was refusing to sign appropriations bills that reduced spending or even slowed the rate of increase in spending. To keep the government open, we passed continuing resolutions, which allowed spending to continue at the same level as the previous fiscal year, until President Clinton refused even to sign these resolutions. Although the responsibility for funding the government technically lies with the Congress, a president's refusal to sign a continuing resolution essentially stops all funding for the government. The result was a government shutdown.

Career Republicans were scared to death. They were terrified the public would accuse the party of not being able to govern, and we would lose our majority. Twice in the twentieth century Republicans held Congress for only two years, and they dreaded the thought that this could be the third time.

I thought the fear that the public would punish us for not being able to govern was nonsense. This fear was the product of a Washington mentality that had nothing to do with the desires of ordinary people across America. Career politicians assumed that keeping the government open was the measure of good governance. It was my opinion and, I believed, the opinion of most Americans that if we kept the government open just to avoid criticism, while the government was still spending too much money, then we were not doing our duty. We were brought into the majority to make the government more efficient. If anything, the public wanted us to not govern and not pass new laws or spending bills.

Even my political consultant, Tom Cole, who recently replaced J.C. Watts as the representative of Oklahoma's fourth district, said, "The last thing you want to do is shut down the government." That's a true statement if you intend to fold. But if you intend to keep the government closed until the president will agree to change the direction of the country, it's a fine strategy. It is only a bad strategy if you choose such a position and then back down, which is exactly what happened.

The freshmen were resolute during the shutdown. During a meeting of the Republican conference, Lindsey Graham said, "If we don't hold the line here he's [Clinton's] back in the ball game. This is critically important. Don't give in now. It's all about him not keeping his word. He never honored his word [about putting forward a plan that balanced the budget in seven years as scored by the nonpartisan Congressional Budget Office]. Keep it on the trust issue and we'll win over time."

The real failure of the shutdown was that our leadership did not prepare members that, in the event of a shutdown, there could be no backing down. Leadership did not educate members that they had to stick together through thick and thin until it was over. Walking into a shutdown situation unaware of the determination of our opponent was like landing on the beaches of Normandy and assuming the machine gun placements on the cliffs had been taken out. Our generals simply did not prepare us for the political barrage of attacks that would come our way.

During the heat of battle I said to Gingrich, "This is like negotiating with a union. If you show weakness once, you will never win again against Bill Clinton." I told him a story from my days at Coburn Optical when the Teamsters wanted to unionize my employees. The package they were demanding was so ludicrous and burdensome from a financial standpoint that I would have had to lay off employees to cover the costs. "You never give an indication of what you might do and you never, ever back down," I told Gingrich. In response, he offered one of his classic reactions to a freshman's proposal: "Hmmm."

Gingrich talked a lot about the importance of listening, but he was often not interested in discussing our ideas. He had a saying on his wall in the Speaker's office that he quoted often: "Listen, learn, help, and lead." The freshmen later developed our own quote about Gingrich: "Fire, Ready, Aim."

Gingrich would receive our input, but he rarely took it seriously. He usually made us feel as if we didn't have much value because we didn't know anything about the political game in Washington. We were from the outside and wet behind the ears in terms of politics, and we obviously didn't know as much about history as he did. It would not take long for us to become "the conservatives" to him.

As Gingrich floundered in negotiations with the president, he repeatedly blamed the freshmen for the impasse. We weren't sure how to take this. On one hand, blaming gridlock on an intractable party who is not in the room can be a useful negotiating tactic. You can say, "I'd really like to move in your direction, but these guys just won't let me." On the other hand, we were afraid he was using us as an excuse for his own inability to negotiate with Clinton. Without a doubt, Clinton was a master negotiator. With his charm, he could mesmerize and manipulate almost anyone in his presence. But Clinton was hardly infallible. He made his share of blunders during his first two years, and we believed we could beat him. We thought Gingrich believed this as well. Senator Bob Dole (R-Kansas), however, was a different story.

As the negotiations continued without much progress, Steve Largent (R-Oklahoma) and I went to visit Bob Dole. Over at the Senate, we found Dole sitting in the cloakroom behind the Senate chamber. We told Dole we wanted a resolution to the problem, but we didn't want a resolution that gave up our ability to change the direction of the government. Dole was wishy-washy, which made us nervous. He said he didn't want the government shutdown at all and was almost disdainful of what the House was doing. It was clear that if he had his way, we would have acceded to the president's demands long before shutting down the government. As we made the long walk back to the House, I felt as if we had just talked to someone who was not our ally but was, in fact, part of the problem.

A week later, our fears about Dole came true when he went to the Senate floor and said, "Enough is enough," and essentially reopened the government.

The freshmen were castigated in the media for believing we should keep the government shut down until the bitter end. Yet history shows that the shutdown fight was a fight we could have won. George Stephanopoulos writes of the shutdown in his memoir, *All Too Human*:

BREACH OF TRUST

Publicly, the President was resolute; privately, he was wavering. "I'm not comfortable being this hard-line," he said in a [Dick] Morris residence meeting. . . . But during the two government shutdowns that occurred in November and December, the Republican leaders themselves were our secret weapon. As much as I would love to think that we were the sole authors of our success, their self-inflicted wounds and tactical blunders made the crucial difference.

Despite these gaffes [Stephanopoulos here is referring to Gingrich throwing a fit over his seat assignment on Air Force One], the Republicans were still in a strong position. On Sunday, November 19, six days into the first shutdown . . . our coalition was cracking.

To ward off that disaster, our budget team drove to the Capitol with an offer to meet the Republicans' demand for a balanced budget in seven years "if and only if" they agreed to provide "adequate funding for" the president's priorities: Medicare, Medicaid, education, and the environment. In our minds, the two halves of the resolution canceled each other out; nothing would be agreed to until everything was agreed to. Certain that the Republicans would reject it, we returned to the White House and waited . . . until Betty cracked the door and handed Leon the Republican counterproposal, fresh from the fax machine.

Reading over Leon's shoulder, I saw that the only changes were cosmetic, replacing "if and only if" with "and," and adding language praising veterans and citing the need for a strong national defense. "This is it!" Panetta exclaimed. "Yes!" I screamed in his ear. The president high-fived the whole room. Our fellow Democrats back on the Hill immediately agreed to accept the amendments, and the government was back in business. We Democrats emerged from the shutdown more unified, while the Republicans fractured. Whether the cause was hubris, naïveté, or a failure of nerve, the Republicans had blown their best chance to splinter our party; from that point on, everything started breaking our way. . . .

By now, [Gingrich] lost control of his troops. They refused to reopen the government unless we agreed to their terms, and the second shutdown began. The freshmen had become Newt's Frankenstein monster—and my new best friends. The more they dug in, the better off we were. Even pragmatic veterans adopted their kamikaze spirit. "We will never, never, never give up," thundered Louisiana's Bob Livingston on the House floor. "We will stay here until doomsday."

Not Bob Dole, though. . . . "I've got to get to New Hampshire," he confided. "One way or the other, it's over on the thirty-first, because I'm out of here."

Message or mistake? Doesn't matter. All we have to do is hold on one more week. They'll break. "It's over on the thirty-first. . . ."

On New Year's Eve, the budget talks at the White House recessed for the holiday. The two sides were still far apart, and, true to his word, Bob Dole was about to bolt. In two days, he'd announce that Senate Republicans were abandoning their House colleagues and voting with Democrats to lift the government shutdown.

Our leadership's reversal on the shutdown stunned us. No more than three days before our leadership told us we had to reopen the government, Republicans gathered in HC-5 in the Capitol to reinforce and reaffirm our position.

Shadegg recalled, "One of the most amazing experiences of my life was going into this conference room and seeing 200 plus members of the U.S. Congress, adult leaders of the country saying in stone, 'By God we're doing the right thing. I'm being told back home I'm doing the right thing. We all agree, no matter what it takes, we ought to stand tight.' And then our leadership comes back and says we ought to open it up."

Just before the final vote to reopen the government after the second shutdown, Shadegg delivered a speech to the Republican conference explaining why we shouldn't reopen the government. Shadegg argued that we could put the monkey on Clinton's back by telling him that we will pass a law that funded the government when he sends us a budget that balanced in seven years. Gingrich followed with a speech explaining why we should reopen the government.

Shadegg recounted the events that day:

At the conference, one of Newt's staffers came over and grabbed me and said, "The Speaker wants to talk to you before you leave." . . . [Newt] sees me out of the corner of his eye and says, "John, I don't care how you vote on this issue, just don't work against me."

[Later that day] I came to the floor and voted no. After I voted no, I went into the cloakroom. Within a minute or two, one of Newt's lieutenants grabs me and says, "Newt needs to see you." I stepped back onto the floor behind the railing. Newt jumps me and says, "Shadegg, what are you doing? You can't vote no." I was stunned. I said, "What do you mean I can't vote no?" Newt said, "You just can't vote no. This has to be a unanimous vote of the conference."

"Well, Newt," I said, "you yourself this morning said to me nose to nose, eyeball to eyeball, not more than 8 hours ago, you didn't care how I voted. You just didn't want me to work against you. I've kept that commitment, Mr. Speaker. I haven't spent the day working against you. I haven't rabble roused. I haven't gone to other freshmen colleagues and said this is a bad idea and they should join me in voting no. But you gave me permission this morning to vote no. . . . I think opening the government back up and getting nothing for it will make us look terrible across America. It will be a disaster, and I don't understand why you're upset with now having said to me this morning point blank you didn't care how I voted, you just didn't want me working against you. . . . If we were right in not conceding to the president in spending demands which led to the shutdown, then we're wrong to open it back up without anything happening. And I think we were right in not conceding to him in his demands, and therefore, since he has not changed his position one iota—all that's happened is Bob Dole has lost his nerve—then this is a mistake."

We went back and forth like that for a few minutes. Finally, Newt looked at me in disgust and said, "Well, it doesn't matter." "Well why?" I asked. "Because," Newt answered, "somebody else has already voted with you." Newt was looking at the screen above us. He had become kind of dejected because he lost his goal of 100 percent of Republicans agreeing on this. That second Republican was Mark Souder.

My decision to vote in favor of ultimately reopening the government was one of my biggest failures in Congress. I had been so against reopening the government and had worked hard to help hold our position. I was determined that we could in fact shrink the size of the government and get President Clinton to cave, which he almost did. Yet by the time Bob Dole sold us out, I was so discouraged and disheartened I gave in and voted with the majority. It was one of the worst votes I made. I succumbed not so much to expediency, but to apathy. I had given up on us.

Here is Gutknecht's recollection of the ordeal:

From an emotional standpoint, the shutdown took the fight out of the troops. Probably the greatest disappointment I had since I came to Washington was when I heard Bob Dole go to the floor of the Senate and say, "Enough is enough." We were on the verge of one of the greatest budget victories probably in the history of the Republic. I believed that then, and now it has only been reinforced. Had we won, we would not have suffered the casualties we did in '96 and '98. We paid so dearly for every inch of ground, and victory was in sight. Then it was snatched away.

Largent recalled, "The shutdown revealed the weakness in our armor. Clinton never failed to exploit that weakness."

Unfortunately, our generals did not believe our survival depended on us marching like we did during the first hundred days. Rather than standing on our core principle of reshaping the federal government in an image closer to our founders' intent, we succumbed to the fear of losing control of Congress. Meanwhile, a presidential candidate folded for the politically expedient reason of improving his chances in November. Even though we maintained our majority—by the narrowest of margins—history has shown that losing the shutdown fight was the death knell for the Republican revolution of 1994. Once we collapsed and opened the government, our leverage in terms of spending was gone forever. In fact, in the years after the shutdown, government spending grew at a faster rate than in the years preceding the Republican takeover.

> NO VOTER ELECTS THEIR REPRESENTATIVE WITH THE EXPECTATION THAT THEY WILL ACT ONLY WHEN IT IS POLITICALLY SAFE FOR THEM TO ACT. CALILNG FOR CHANGE IS NEVER POLITICALLY SAFE.

The shutdown battle illustrates a chronic problem in a Congress dominated by careerists: Long-term vision and the long-term interests of the country are continually sacrificed at the altar of short-term political expediency. Members of Congress have a sacred trust to the American people to do everything in their current term to serve the public. No voter elects their representative with the expectation that they will act only when it is politically safe for them to act. Calling for change is never politically safe. It certainly wasn't safe for our founders to have risked their lives, fortune, and sacred honor in a campaign they knew could end in their deaths. Thank God they didn't wait for the perfect political moment before they acted. If our founders had listened to today's consultants, we may still be a British colony, because, as many historians believe, a majority of colonists in the 1770s did not favor a radical break with the British.

We ask our soldiers to risk their lives in defense of freedom, but do we expect politicians to risk their political lives? It is true, of course, that military and political generals have to assess the battlefield and the strength of the enemy before taking action. It is also true that in 1994 and 1995 our assessment of the enemy's strength and some of our tactics were flawed. Yet our retreat was not about regrouping so we could fight another day; it was the end of the revolution and the inauguration of a policy of appeasing and accommodating an enemy—tyrannical Big Government—that was not, and never will be, politically safe to fight. With the notable exception of welfare reform, our policy decisions after the shutdown would reverse, not advance, our cause. Our generals had ignored Wellington's warning. Once we were stopped, we were lost.

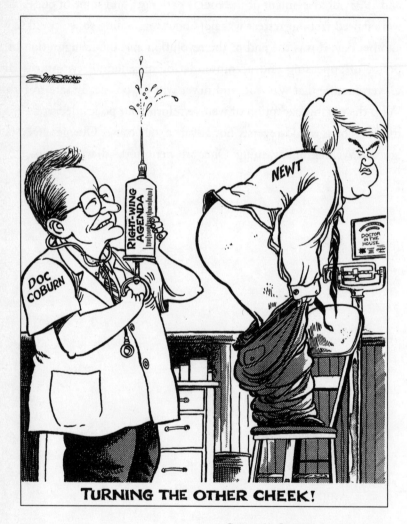

TURNING THE OTHER CHEEK!

5

LEARNING TO GOVERN

A reform is a correction of abuses,
a revolution is a transfer of power.

—E. G. BULWER LYTTON
(1803–1873), English novelist and member of Parliament

ONE OF THE SIGNS that long-term exposure to power can distort sound judgment is Congress's accepted definition of maturity in an elected official. Mature politicians who have "grown," according to career politicians, have generally abandoned their "up with the people" zeal and have learned to work within the system to get things done for their constituents. To the contrary, true maturity in a politician looks quite different; it is a persistent ability to stand on principle and pursue the long-term best interests of the country, not just their district or state, in the face of great political danger.

When Republicans took control of Congress in 1994, many of us believed what was taking place was more significant than merely one party switching places with another party in the majority. We believed we were ending one era in American politics and ushering in another. We were determined to end the long period of massive government expansion and start a new era in which a smaller, more efficient, and less intrusive government would allow states, local communities, and individual Americans to regain control of their own destinies. In 1994, it seemed that for most Republicans this was a genuine, heartfelt commitment and not merely election rhetoric. At least I knew this was true for me and many of my freshmen colleagues.

Most importantly, however, we wanted to change the culture of Washington and wrest power from the hands of the career politicians who were responsible for the reckless expansion of government that was threatening our future prosperity. Our majority would not just be a more conservative majority; it would be a majority that transferred power from the elite ruling class of career politicians in Washington back to the American people.

Yet after the betrayal over the term limits vote and the government shutdown debacle, it was becoming less likely this genuine transfer of power was going to happen. By the spring of 1996, our revolutionary majority had become a timid reform movement whose leaders were more interested in learning how to "govern" than in pursuing bold agendas. Perhaps fifty or sixty Republicans still wanted to continue the revolution, but we were outnumbered by career politicians in the Republican party who had more in common with the career politicians on the other side of the aisle than with us.

Columnist Bob Novak uses an apt illustration in his book, *Completing the Revolution,* to explain what was happening to Republicans at this time. Republicans, Novak explains, had to decide whether they would close down the executive washroom or merely change the locks. We may have entered Washington with the intent to end such perks, but we were opting to change the locks.

THE REVOLUTIONARIES BECOME THE REBELS

In the spring of 1996, our leadership was busy putting together a budget plan for fiscal year 1997—the first budget after the shutdown debacle—that was a return to business as usual in Washington. When the conference report for the budget came back to the House, we were troubled to learn that spending, and at that time the deficit, would go up $14 billion more than leadership had previously indicated for fiscal year 1997. To make matters worse, we wouldn't get around to reducing spending to bring down the deficit until 1999. To us, this appeared to be a classic career politicians' maneuver—avoid tough choices and kick the can down the road while creating the appearance of fiscal responsibility.

TRUE MATURITY IS A PERSISTENT ABILITY TO STAND ON PRINCIPLE AND PURSUE THE LONG-TERM BEST INTERESTS OF THE COUNTRY.

Many of my colleagues believed this budget was a sham. When an organization is facing a serious deficit, the last thing it is supposed to do is increase spending with the intention of cutting spending sometime in the future. What any responsible business owner does in that situation is to cut costs immediately so the business can recover. If we actually intended to reduce the size of government, I thought, we should do it now, not postpone the onset of cuts until a future year when they would be even more difficult to enact, not to mention possibly be blocked by a future Congress.

When the bill came to the floor, about two dozen freshmen, as well as a few other members disgusted with the direction of leadership, planned to vote against the conference report. From leadership's perspective, allowing a vote on a bill of this magnitude to fail would be catastrophic. They were terrified the party would appear to be inept and unable to "govern."

Leadership's whip (vote counting) operation was sophisticated enough to know they were in danger of losing the vote on the floor. What they were counting on in order to pass the bill was persuading enough members on the floor to vote with the team. With a narrow fifteen-seat majority, leadership could not allow many Republicans to vote "no" when, at best, only a handful of Democrats would vote for the Republican budget.

When the official time for the vote expired, the block of members that voted "no" was elated. The bill failed, or so we thought. We didn't want to embarrass our leaders, but they were asking us to violate our principles by voting for a dishonest and politically expedient budget. Though sending leadership and the appropriators back to the drawing board might be a short-term embarrassment for the party, we were convinced it would be good for the country in the long run.

Meanwhile, on the floor, the gavel had yet to come down to close the vote even though time had officially expired on the vote. Leadership ordered the vote to remain open until they could get enough votes to pass the bill. In a raucous scene on the floor, leadership frantically worked over freshmen to get them to change their vote. You could almost hear the bones cracking as leadership mercilessly twisted arms saying, "You can't do this to us," to members who had voted "no."

Leadership had plenty of ways to exercise carrot or stick leverage over rank-and-file members. They could threaten to pull them off of important committees, block special projects for their districts, refuse to campaign for them, and essentially chain them to the backbenches of the House. Leadership could conversely promise favors like pork projects, a campaign visit, or floor consideration of an issue important to the members. Leadership persuaded four members, Wayne Allard (R-Colorado), Barbara Cubin (R-Wyoming), Jack Metcalf (R-Washington) and Wes Cooley (R-Oregon), to change their votes from "nay" to "yea." The bill passed.

Sixteen of the Republicans who voted "no" were freshmen. After the vote, we tried to stick together and explain our reasons for voting against our party. I explained to reporters that it took a lot of political courage to oppose the leadership and vote against a plan we knew violated the principles the party ran on in 1994. I was discouraged that members who wanted to vote their conscience were being asked to ignore their principles. This ensured that the elitists and careerists in Washington could look good even as, in the long run, they damaged the country and the principles the Republican party stood for.

My colleague, Mark Souder, a member of the Class of 1994, who also voted against the budget, defended Steve Largent and me in a letter to the editor of the *Tulsa World:*

> The recent vote on the Fiscal Year 1997 Budget Resolution was one of the toughest this Congress has faced. The budget conference report would actually increase the deficit in FY 1997 before it would return on a path to a balanced budget. Several members of our freshman class, including Reps. Tom Coburn and Steve Largent, voted against the budget resolution despite the most intense arm-twisting from our own leadership to support the bill. The reason was simple: Washington always claims, with a wink and a nod, that all hikes in the deficit are temporary and will be fixed later. Despite all the pressure and all the threats, Tom Coburn and Steve Largent stood their ground and refused to accept the status quo. Tom and Steve held firm and voted the interests of the people who sent them to Congress. . . .
>
> *The reason there is a lack of confidence in Washington is because too many politicians are elected to office but never try to carry out their campaign promises.* The people of Oklahoma are lucky to have congressmen who bring their values to Washington and not the other way around. I greatly respect Tom and Steve's integrity and independence on this and other issues and am proud to serve with them in Congress. (Souder letter to *Tulsa World,* June 23, 1996, emphasis added)

After that vote, several moderates, many of whom signed—but didn't necessarily believe in—the Contract with America, urged the leadership to punish the freshmen who almost torpedoed the Republican budget. I explained to colleagues and reporters that those were votes of conscience, not votes of defiance. We were trying to be true to our constituents and ourselves, not undermine our leadership.

Newt Gingrich didn't attempt to exact any retribution, but he was irate, nonetheless. As *The Hill*, a local Capitol Hill newspaper, reported, during a meeting of Republicans shortly after the vote, Gingrich challenged any Republican who didn't like the direction leadership was taking "to have the courage to run for leadership yourself." He had no idea that some freshmen were taking that line as more than a rhetorical challenge. The more Gingrich tried to put us in our place, the less secure his place became.

After the vote, a group of freshman, myself included, were even more resolute in our determination to restart the revolution. We intended to seek cuts in other appropriations bills to hold Congress to its promise of working toward a truly balanced budget. The same week, I voted to eliminate tobacco subsidies and to stop production of the Seawolf submarine. "I'm not stopping," I told the *Muskogee Phoenix*. "The only way we stop spending in this country is live up to what we committed to do. . . . What I want to pursue is cutting the things that the military tells us we don't need. I want to spend slightly more money on defense, but I don't want us spending it on things that are paybacks for congressional seats."

After the debate on the fiscal year 1997 budget plan, the die was cast; from here on out the revolutionaries who would not "learn to govern" like the career politicians we were hired to replace would be known as "the rebels."

THE REVOLUTION'S FIRST REFERENDUM —THE 1996 ELECTIONS

As we approached the 1996 elections, the fear of losing control of Congress was becoming much stronger than the desire to fight for the principles that brought us into the majority. Therefore, it didn't surprise me that when Republicans faced voters in November, we lost eight seats in the House while gaining two seats in the Senate. The conventional wisdom, created largely by left-of-center pundits, was that our overreaching and extreme acts, such as shutting down the government, scared voters.

However, had we won the shutdown battle and continued our march of the first hundred days, I am convinced we would have increased our majority and Bob Dole would have had a much better chance of defeating Clinton. The shutdown battle was as much of a turning point for Clinton as it was for the Republican revolutionaries. We were demoralized while he and the entire Democratic party were reenergized.

After the election, Senate Majority Leader Lott formally and unilaterally declared that the revolution was over. "In '95, we were new, we were exuberant, we were excited, maybe a little out of control," Lott apologized to the *Washington Post*. "Now everything is different, the world is different. We're different, first of all, because we learned a lot. . . . We're not going to look for a reason to fight. We're going to look for a way to get things done." Besides, "I'm an 'order' kind of guy."

The *Post* reported that Lott was saying the following: "In the Lott era, there will be no 'first 100 days,' grand gestures or government shutdowns, as there were in the last Congress. Instead, as Lott describes his concept of 'regular order,' there will be a logical and expeditious sequence of events, decisions made by consensus."

The *Post* and many other papers were simply delighted by the results of the 1996 elections because it afforded them the opportunity to lay blame at the feet of the Republican insurgents. The press could tolerate career politicians like Bob Dole and Trent Lott who were not likely to dismember government, but they had little use for members of the Class of 1994 and welcomed every opportunity to discredit our philosophical underpinnings.

Many freshmen read Lott's statement as a capitulation and an endorsement of Dole's betrayal of the troops during the shutdown battle. It also signaled how, in the Republican Congress, a vague allegiance to process, or "regular order," would be more important than allegiance to principle.

From here on out the revolutionaries would be routinely criticized for not respecting the "order of things" in Congress. To us, this approach made our leaders seem like Pharisees. They would abandon the spirit of the law—the principles that built our majority—to follow an inside-the-Beltway understanding of the letter of the law.

THE REPUBLICAN TEAM VS. THE AMERICAN TEAM

This tension between process and principle once again surfaced in the spring of 1997. The last bill to be taken up before the two-week Easter recess was a bill that would have trashed one of the key items in the Contract with America. In 1995, we passed a bill that cut committee spending by a third. Now, only two years later, leadership had decided to increase committee spending by nearly 15 percent. Many of my colleagues were incensed that we were so casually going back on our word.

In order to keep the bill from coming to the floor, several members from the Class of 1994 threatened to vote against the rule. In Congress, the majority party dictates the rules of debate for bills that come to the floor. The procedural vote on the rule is typically a party line vote. Voting against your own party's rule is considered an act of treason. The thinking in Washington is that if the majority party can't count on all of its members to vote together on the rule, they might as well not be in the majority.

However, we knew that if this bill made it to the floor for an up or down vote, it would pass by a comfortable margin. I suspected a good number of Democrats would want to vote for the increase in committee spending to embarrass Republicans and portray them as retreating from a key item in the Contract—which we were. Even though I had no desire to undermine my fellow Republicans, I felt like I had been backed into a corner. I could either stand on principle and incur the wrath of my colleagues or betray the voters who trusted me to end "business as usual" in Washington. In that circumstance I had only one option.

Leadership knew it had a major problem. The whip's office believed there were twenty or so hard "no"s among Republicans, so throughout the day of the vote we had a series of "woodshed" discussions with leadership. We used that term because we were made to feel like misbehaving children who were being taken out to the woodshed for a whipping. "The funny thing was," Largent recalled, "*we* had to initiate (some of) those meetings." We were so determined to not let the party go back on its word that we were willing to put ourselves in an uncomfortable position with our leaders. In retrospect, the fact that leadership wasn't initiating much honest communication about the problem was a sign of dysfunction within leadership itself.

THEY WOULD ABANDON THE SPIRIT OF THE LAW— THE PRINCIPLES THAT BUILT OUR MAJORITY—TO FOLLOW AN INSIDE-THE-BELTWAY UNDER-STANDING OF THE LETTER OF THE LAW.

Leadership said the increase was necessary to give Dan Burton (R-Indiana), chairman of the Government Reform and Oversight Committee, the extra money he needed to continue his investigation into the White House's campaign abuses. They also talked about how important oversight is and how the little we spend on oversight saves the taxpayers billions. This argument wasn't terribly persuasive. First, oversight is a good investment only if the majority party has the political will to cut waste from the budget, which we weren't doing. Second, we knew the real need that triggered this spending binge had more to do with partisan politics than doing the hard work of scouring federal agencies for fraud and waste. Gingrich was convinced that he could make political hay out of someone else's miscues and became focused on Clinton rather than the job we promised the country we would do. Burton's investigation into White House campaign abuses was an appropriate, necessary, and essential function of his committee. Yet it was the right policy that was being pursued for the wrong reasons. Leadership was so obsessed with the political dimension of Burton's investigation they lacked the focus and discipline to make an exception to increase spending for Burton alone while slamming the vault door on other chairmen.

Just before the vote, a block of freshmen—Sanford, Graham, Souder, Steve Chabot (R-Ohio), Mark Neuman (R-Wisconsin), Joe Scarborough (R-Florida), Largent, and myself—as well as sophomore Pete Hoekstra (R-Michigan), were called into Dick Armey's office near the House floor. "I have never asked this of you guys, but I am asking now. Will you just give me the vote?" Armey asked. Armey then said something that struck us as odd. He said that if he could be perceived as having secured our vote, his position within leadership would be strengthened. That evening Largent wrote about that meeting in his diary: "It was revealing when he said that. There is obviously great insecurity, mistrust and lack of communication occurring within the leadership ranks. They are all competing with one another."

At one point Tom DeLay came in the room to do another whip check. We said we hadn't changed our mind about how we would vote, which surprised him. Because no one was saying anything to break the tension in the room, Mark Souder said diplomatically that while he couldn't speak for the group, he suspected if there was anyone we would give such a vote to it would be to a great conservative like Armey. "Just think about it," Armey said as he left the room, "we will hold the vote open for another ten minutes."

I was one of the first to follow Armey out the door. As I made the walk to the House floor in a long hallway lined with staff and reporters, I knew I was going to vote "no." I didn't know how the others would vote, and I was willing to be the only "no" vote if it came to that. After the meeting broke up, we each decided we would act individually and not in concert. As it turned out, I voted "no" and Matt Salmon and Bob Inglis (R-South Carolina)—who hadn't been in our meetings with leadership—voted "no." Nine others also voted "no." The rule failed 210 to 213 and was not resuscitated on the spot as in the previous year.

A few minutes later, the whip's office announced a mandatory meeting of the conference at 7:00 P.M. A few of us met in Graham's office before the meeting to prepare ourselves for what we expected to be the ultimate woodshed experience. After a short pep rally, we walked over together to HC-5, the room where Republicans and Democrats hold their caucuses.

When we filed in, it was immediately obvious Newt Gingrich was furious. The meeting began with a roll call, and Gingrich said every Republican would be meeting in HC-5 in the basement of the Capitol even if he had to send the sergeant at arms—the police—to track members down. Senior Republicans had never heard of a mandatory conference before. A few of us who voted against the rule stood along the south wall of a crowded HC-5 as we listened.

When Gingrich said, "The eleven geniuses who thought they knew more than the rest of the Congress are going to come up and explain their votes," someone leaned over to Mark Sanford and said, "I have never heard of anyone having to explain their vote." Gingrich continued, "Those of you who had planned to go to John Kasich's wedding on Saturday are not going. No one is going anywhere until we get the votes we need to pass this rule."

Steve Largent later wrote about the meeting:

His speech began by praising the moderates for voting with the team when they had every right to vote against the rule because of the partial birth amendment broken promise. He said he never wanted to hear from "you conservatives" about the moderates going south on the party. (Interesting to me to hear Newt refer to us as "you conservatives.") He went on to say that if every time someone didn't get their way and 10-12 of us parted, took our ball home and didn't play the whole conference and movement would be shattered. Then he wanted and looked forward to hearing from all eleven of us why we thought we were so much smarter than the rest of the conference. He also suggested if we didn't want to go along we should consider becoming independents and form our own party. By the time he finished I was ready to bolt to the microphone. I was sitting in the very back of the room next to Zach [Wamp]. I wasn't about to allow the Speaker to intimidate me or any of the eleven. By the time I got up front Boehner was introducing Armey to speak so I had to wait. Armey used analogies from war and soldiers fighting as a unit and also football and teammates all running the same play. I really resented the blatant inference that we were not team players and jeopardized everyone by what we did.

Largent, an NFL Hall of Famer, went straight to the podium after Armey was finished speaking. A surprised Boehner recognized him. "Mr. Speaker," Largent said calmly and directly to Gingrich who was no more than ten feet away, "I am not intimidated."

A hush fell over the room as all eyes darted back and forth between Largent and Gingrich. A sophomore was beginning to dress down the Speaker of the House:

I have been in rooms much smaller than this one when I was on the opposite side of teammates during a player's strike against the NFL. The guys in those rooms weighed 280, 320 pounds and not only *wanted* to kill me, if they had gotten a hold of me they probably *could* have. This isn't the case here tonight.

More seriously, I am not intimidated because I feel good about this vote and the principles behind it. The Speaker tonight talked about the eleven of us letting the team down. The more significant question and the question that never gets asked in Washington, D.C., is whose team are we on? When I was elected to represent the first district of Oklahoma, I wasn't elected to represent just the Republican or Democratic teams, but what I thought was in the best interest of the taxpayers back home. If you stop and think about it, the team that we're all on is the American Team. And, if, as a matter of conscience, I believe a vote is in the best interest of the American taxpayer I represent back home, well, then I just have to vote that way.

Second, in Washington people forget the significance of a person's word. Many of us were elected in 1994, and before that election we signed a document called the Contract with America. One of its pledges was to cut Washington committee funding by one third. We kept our word and did just that. Yet this proposal would reverse that cut. We owe it to those same folks to whom we pledged our word to either keep it, or go back to them and say, we're new to the business of running government. We cut too much and need to change our committee staffing numbers. Whatever we do, we shouldn't do what was proposed today, which typified the Washington way of doing business so many came here to change—take credit for cutting by a third and then below the radar screen quietly add back the spending.

By this point Largent had won over the crowd. I looked over at Jim Ramstad, a member from Minnesota in his fourth term, who was nodding his head in agreement. Several other members around him were doing the same.

Largent concluded by saying that for twenty years he has talked to kids all over the country about leadership and that leadership is about character and character is about leading by example. He said that if it doesn't work at home—or in Congress—don't export it. If we can't live with frozen spending levels, he asked, how can we ask others to do the same or even accept spending reductions with a straight face or any integrity?

Most of the conference applauded enthusiastically when Largent finished. Ramstad later told me, "That was one of the most inspiring speeches I've ever heard."

Lindsey Graham was the next to speak. "Well, unlike Steve Largent," Graham said, "I can be intimidated." Everyone broke out in laughter as Lindsey took the edge off the meeting.

Then I got up and said, "I'm just a doctor from Oklahoma. I admit I'm not much of a politician, but I know the difference between right and wrong. When you tell people we're going to lead by example then turn around and increase our own budgets, but ask them to make cuts, you lose all credibility. Maybe I don't belong in the Republican conference, Mr. Speaker."

Every one of the eleven members who voted against the rule said something and no one backed down or apologized for their vote. We believed we were doing the right thing, leaving no place for apologies. Gingrich's tactic backfired. He thought he could embarrass and intimidate us, but not one person was intimidated. He would never again use that approach.

THE REPUBLICAN "TEAM" WAS NO LONGER BEING HELD TOGETHER BY PRINCIPLES BUT BY CAREERISM AND THE DESIRE FOR POWER FOR ITS OWN SAKE.

Even though Gingrich had tried to shame us in front of our peers, the eleven of us who brought down the rule were more upset with the committee chairmen whose craving for more money was leading the entire conference to compromise our principles. It was ironic, and frustrating, that we were accused of not being team players when the cardinals and committee chairmen, not us, were leading the team away from the principles we all espoused. In our view, they were the real rebels and betrayers of our commitment to the American people.

This event exposed a more disturbing trend that we all understood but weren't quite ready to accept: the Republican "team" was no longer being held together by principles but by careerism and the desire for power for its own sake. The reason Newt Gingrich wanted us to explain why we were "so much smarter than the rest of the conference" is that we really were questioning what was holding the party together: the collective desire to create a Republican majority that would be in control for years to come. While we believed our actions defended the principles of the party, we were, in fact, undermining the party's ability to control the floor and temporarily derailing the effort to boost funding for Burton's investigation. Because our leaders believed breaking our promise in the Contract with America and increasing committee spending was a better way to keep us in power than keeping our word, we were accused of undermining the team. Gingrich's vitriolic response to us bringing down the rule for the bill confirmed to us that he was willing to trade our principles for a short term political advantage over the Democrats.

The increasingly partisan tone of Republicans had little to do with defining the differences between two competing Republican and Democratic visions for America and more to do with the desire to maintain the majority at all costs, even at the expense of our integrity and our word. In Washington, I learned that rigid partisanship usually signals a deeper faith in careerism than in conservatism or liberalism. Partisanship relies more on the power of intimidation than the power of ideas to persuade and unify the team. It's a truism in Washington that when a person is elected to Congress and wants to succeed all they have to do is become a rabidly partisan Republican or Democrat—someone has already made all of your decisions for you and will take care of your political needs as long as you serve the team.

What makes this mentality dangerous is that when the team is held together by careerism and mindless partisanship, individual members are punished for thinking for themselves. When members can't think for themselves their constituents are deprived of honest representation. For me to maintain partisan loyalty in the vote on the committee funding resolution, I would have had to first break a promise to my constituents and then mislead them about our work to undo the Contract to cover up

what my "teammates" had done. Voting against the rule was not a difficult decision because I always believed the people of Oklahoma would
much prefer that I be loyal to their needs and vote according to the long-
term interests of the country, not according to the political needs of other
careerists in Washington. As Largent said, I thought we should serve the
American team first, and the Republican team second.

At the end of the conference meeting everyone agreed to freeze
committee spending for thirty days except for Burton's committee.
Another vote on whether to increase committee funding would be held
in thirty days. This seemed reasonable enough at the time, but in retrospect we were being outmaneuvered by leadership. Gingrich knew that
with Burton out of the picture (no Democrat would support a bill that
increased funding to Burton's effort to investigate Clinton) they could
secure enough votes from the Democrats to significantly increase overall
committee funding from the Democrats even if a large number of
Republicans voted "no."

THE COUP

The showdown with Gingrich over the committee funding resolution
was the latest in a series of events that were causing some Republicans to
question whether it was in the best interests of the American, and
Republican, team for him to remain as Speaker. The key event that
started us thinking about whether Gingrich should be removed had been
the government shutdown. Gingrich's decision to join Bob Dole in
surrendering to Clinton in the shutdown battle had blind-sided much of
the conference. Those of us who wanted to keep fighting felt as if our
generals had abandoned us on the battlefield.

Before the government shutdown we thought Newt Gingrich was
invincible. After the shutdown, however, he was like a whipped dog who
still barked, yet cowered, in Clinton's presence. Our policies after the

shutdown were inconsistent, and Gingrich's leadership seemed erratic. He would often surprise and shock us with his midstream course corrections as he did with his attempt to increase committee funding. His inability to discipline himself in his public comments was also a serious liability. The best example occurred during the government shutdown when he complained about having to sit near the back of Air Force One. His untimely comments came across as petty and excessively partisan.

For me, the final straw was when leadership failed to keep their word about freezing overall spending on the legislative branch appropriations bill over which we had just clashed. Gingrich had assigned Bill Thomas to work on the problem of figuring out how to freeze every chairman's funding except for Burton. Thomas, however, set the stage for a spending increase, not a freeze. Thomas was, in essence, using a one-time increase to open the door for increasing every committee's budget. Republicans understood that what Thomas and leadership really wanted was an increase in overall committee funding, which they eventually received.

The Second Thing Congress Does Not Want You to Know about How It Does Business: Congress routinely uses "one-time" increases, often "emergency spending" measures, to permanently increase spending.

Congress can make spending increases look less severe by including the amount of any "emergency spending" from the previous year in the current year's baseline budget, the fixed point Congress starts with every year. For example, if Congress spent $600 billion last year and later added $20 billion in emergency spending, this year's baseline should be $600 billion, not $620 billion. Imagine this situation: Your teenager who receives a $50 allowance per month has an "emergency" and you give him or her an extra $10. If they came to you the next month and demanded a $60 allowance because that's what they had received in the previous month you would explain rationally that the extra $10 was a one-time "emergency" increase and should not be included in the amount they should expect the next month. Congress is like that teenager who wants to include one-time emergency expenditures in the total it gets to spend in the next year.

When I met with Gingrich, Thomas, Largent, and Sanford to discuss the problem, I told Thomas, "This isn't a freeze." Thomas replied defensively, "Oh, yes it is." We argued the point back and forth when I finally said to Gingrich pointedly, "You need to figure out who on your staff is lying to you." He said he would look into it. This was the night I decided Gingrich had to be replaced because he wouldn't intercede. He knew that his point man, Thomas, was the one who was guilty of distortions of the truth that enabled them to say they were keeping an agreement when, in fact, they were violating it.

Other Republicans at the time found that their loyalties to the American team and the Republican team were becoming harder to reconcile. Graham recalled, "People in the leadership were worried about where we were going, but they were also worried about political power. We were just worried about where we were going. Our motives were, this is not the team we signed up for."

After Gingrich confronted us in the meeting of the Republican conference Largent wrote in his diary:

Later that night a bunch of us met at Tortilla Coast for dinner. There was a lot of back slapping, bravado, and "we were with you in spirit" going on. Most people are beginning to feel this whole effort will have a positive effect on our leadership and the 105th agenda. . . . I don't know. I believe this could be the first shot in a long battle over who the leadership is in the 106th Congress.

Not long after this confrontation we learned that other members of leadership—Armey, Bill Paxon (R-New York), DeLay, and John Boehner (R-Ohio)—were meeting privately to discuss what to do about the "Newt problem." One meeting about the "Newt problem" in which I was a participant took place on July 9, 1997 with Armey and Sue Myrick of North Carolina, a meeting Armey would later suggest never happened.

When Sue and I entered Armey's office, his staff was excused. Armey sat behind his desk, something he would do only when the subject was extremely important, and lit a cigarette—the first of about ten he would smoke over the next forty-five minutes. Our entire conversation was about Gingrich, and Armey agreed Newt needed to go.

On Thursday, July 10, 1997, DeLay approached Lindsey Graham, the alleged ringleader of this effort, on the floor and said, "If you guys are going to do anything, you better do it now."

Graham asked, "What are you talking about?"

DeLay responded, "Well, there's going to be a story breaking. If you're going to act, you better act now."

Graham said, "Well, I'll get some guys together if you want to talk to us." Graham then went around the floor to tell the dozen or so of us that DeLay wants to talk with us about "the problem with Newt."

Graham recalled,

The lieutenants were no longer willing to follow the general so they came to the privates for help. We were the ones most concerned because we signed up for the Contract and came with all this zeal and you could see the conference slowly slipping away, spending more money, losing every confrontation with the president. . . . As Newt lost his focus, we became a rudderless ship. Newt deserved credit for getting us in the majority, but he became a voodoo doll they [the Democrats] would always bring out. Our intent was to not let this thing sink into the abyss.

Later that evening, twenty or so members of the Class of 1994 met in Graham's office with DeLay. We discussed our frustrations with Gingrich and all agreed that something needed to change. The key moment of the evening came when Graham asked, "Would you vote with us to vacate the chair?" (A parliamentary maneuver that would force Gingrich to step down.)

"Yes," DeLay answered. Graham repeated the question. DeLay again said he would vote with us.

While we discussed what would happen next, someone said Armey would become Speaker and Paxon would become majority leader. Then I jumped in and made a comment that would essentially unravel our effort to replace Gingrich. "But we want Paxon to be Speaker," I said, "not Armey."

Earlier that evening, before we gathered in Graham's office, Largent and I had spent an hour on the phone with Paxon, who agreed that Gingrich needed to go. Paxon assured us that everyone in leadership wanted Gingrich to go and were prepared to do what was necessary to oust him. Paxon also understood that we wanted him to be the next Speaker.

When I told DeLay it was Paxon, not Armey, who was our choice to succeed Gingrich, he seemed surprised. When DeLay brought this information back to the rest of leadership, Armey backed out and went to Gingrich, realizing it was Paxon, not him, who was our choice to serve as the next Speaker.

The next morning, July 11, the Associated Press ran an article reporting that a member of leadership had met with a group of lawmakers to quell a coup. Graham believes this "was somebody's effort over there to blame us for something they couldn't follow through with."

Soon thereafter Armey called the so-called "coup plotters" and Paxon into a meeting in a room to the right of his main office. (We found out early that morning that Armey and DeLay had gone to Gingrich, although Armey probably went to him the previous night.) We were stunned when Armey started to come after us. He wanted to know how in good conscience we could try to throw Gingrich overboard. I couldn't believe what I was hearing. Wasn't this the same Dick Armey who had agreed with all of us that Gingrich had to go? As Armey tried to take us to the woodshed, once again, I felt like I was listening to someone with two personalities. There was the Dick Armey who wanted Gingrich to be removed as Speaker, and then there was the Dick Armey whose political survival depended on not being perceived as trying to oust him. A few days later when Armey delivered a similar speech to the entire conference, Lindsey Graham exploded in anger. Lindsey threw back a chair and lunged toward Armey while calling him a liar. Lindsey was so irate he had to be physically restrained.

On July 22, 1997, Armey sent me and each member of the Republican conference the following personalized letter:

Dear Tom,

I know you are concerned about the events of the last two weeks. You have seen several versions of the story in press reports and I'm sure you've heard rumors and speculations from your colleagues. This has been a dispiriting two weeks for all of us. I would like to get this ugly episode behind us, but I feel I must respond to some of the things being written and said because my honesty has been called into question.

As Majority Leader, and in life, the thing I've prided myself on the most is my honesty and my integrity. Members know that I don't give my word easily and I don't make a lot of promises. I think you'll find Members across the spectrum agreeing that I have been an honest broker, a man of my word, and someone who has always looked out for the good of the Conference.

For me, I just want my good name back. I'm sure others, including many of the alleged dissidents, feel the same way. The reports of my involvement in this effort are all based on "we assumed he was involved," or "we were told he would go along with it." In addition, there are a lot of wild, inaccurate, and often contradictory stories being floated by unnamed sources that are doing damage to my and other Members' reputations. Let me be quite clear. My reputation is for telling it like it is. My friends constantly complain that I "don't do nuance well." I don't communicate with winks or nods. I just say it straight. Never have I said that I was in favor of any plan to remove the Speaker, and no Member can truthfully say they ever heard me say that, because I didn't.

At this point, I couldn't care less whether I'll be Speaker, Majority Leader, or dogcatcher, but I'll be damned if I'll let my name and honor be destroyed.

Knowing what I know now, I would have handled these past two weeks differently. No doubt I could have managed this mess better, but I believe in the end people will see my role as the following: 1) I assessed rumors about an action planned against the Speaker, 2) I warned the Speaker (which I did well before the infamous Thursday night meeting), 3) I rallied the top Leaders to stand with the Speaker, and 4) I explained to the dissidents why it would be wrong to carry out any action against the Speaker.

The Speaker is well aware of my actions over the past two weeks and he knows that I did not participate in any effort to dump him. In fact, *before the infamous Thursday night meeting, I relayed a message through my Chief of Staff to the Speaker that if there were an effort to throw Newt overboard they would have to throw me overboard also.* Alerting the Speaker in advance should be fairly strong evidence that I was not participating in some kind of coup. The Speaker has no doubt about my actions and my loyalty. His comments in *The Washington Post* make that quite clear.

I've made two mistakes in the past couple of weeks. One, I attended two meetings among Leaders where, based on reports of an uprising, we engaged in "what if" scenarios. At no time, however, did I advocate or prepare to remove the Speaker. In fact, from the time I heard from any Members outside of Leadership about the uprising, it took me less than half a day to move to stop the actions.

Two, when I went before the Conference about the article in *The Hill* last Wednesday, I spoke what I believed to be the truth. I believed that no Member of Leadership was involved. The reaction by Lindsey Graham frankly surprised me, and I began digging to find out why he and others began to call me a liar. I later learned that he and others had been given the impression that others and I were in favor of this action. I'll let others speak for themselves, but I never indicated any support for this type of action and certainly no one was authorized to speak on my behalf. I now understand why Lindsey was so upset, and don't blame him. I apologize for my initial belief that the dissidents were solely responsible for starting this mess.

How do we move beyond this episode? I think we have our best days ahead of us. We are very close to completing the budget and tax cut bills, and we'll move on to even bigger and better things. Anyone who reads the papers (with the exception of these last several days) can easily see that our side is winning on virtually every front. Sure, we have our share of problems, but we are cutting taxes, reducing spending, and improving the lives of American families, just as we said we would.

I'm sure you would not want your character and your honesty debated based on rumors or hearsay. Neither do I. I have no doubt that the real story of this episode will eventually be clear, and I have faith that my actions will be judged favorably. All I ask is that you listen to me and assess my actions based on what you know about my character.

If you have any doubt about my actions over the past two weeks, please call me and I'll be glad to discuss this with you at length.

Sincerely,

Dick Armey
Majority Leader

Regrettably, when Armey writes, "At no time, however, did I advocate or prepare to remove the Speaker," that recollection does not coincide with my recollection of our conversations. The day before we met in Lindsey's office for the Thursday night meeting, and long before Armey sent this letter, Armey repeatedly and unambiguously advocated the removal of Gingrich as Speaker and committed to help Sue Myrick and me change the leadership.

Armey also wrote in his letter, "From the time I heard from any Members outside of Leadership about the uprising, it took me less than half a day to move to stop the actions." Yet when Sue and I met with Armey more than twenty-four hours before the Thursday night meeting in Lindsey's office, we explicitly told him that Gingrich had to go. Armey concurred and never once discouraged us.

Also, based on our conversations with Paxon we knew that leadership, including Armey, was discussing how to dump Gingrich. The fact that Paxon, Boehner, Armey, and DeLay were meeting to talk about problems in leadership without inviting Gingrich doesn't exactly bolster Armey's argument that he was against removing Gingrich. Armey and the rest of leadership obviously wanted to keep Gingrich out of the loop regarding whatever it was they were planning.

The part of Armey's letter that is cause for even greater concern is his decision to describe the coup plotters as "the dissidents." His word choice explains the reasons we wanted to remove Gingrich in the first place. A dissident is, by definition, one who disagrees with and refuses to conform to established doctrines. In 1994, we all aspired to be dissidents. We were railing against the doctrines of elitism and careerism in Washington that were exerting a form of tyranny over the American people. By 1997, however, our formerly dissident leaders had taken control of a system they had vowed to dismantle. Rather than gutting the system of its careerist and elitist tendencies, our leaders left that system largely intact, regretted much of what they did dismantle, and were enjoying the political spoils for themselves.

For example, the next year Gingrich would secure $450 million for the construction of seven C-130J transport planes in his district, though the Pentagon ordered only one. As he secured one of the largest pork projects in history, Republicans lost seats. This was the type of thing we were raging against, and if this was a system our leaders wanted to defend, Armey was right—we were "the dissidents." The fact that our determination to be true to the principles we ran on in 1994 made us "dissidents" signaled how thoroughly the party had abandoned those principles.

The real story of the so-called coup has been and will be debated for years. No one will ever agree about how it all transpired. However, one part of the story that can be clarified is that Armey played a much more important role than he has admitted publicly. When Sue Myrick and I met with Armey before the Thursday night meeting, I remember him saying explicitly, "There has to be a change in leadership," and agreeing with us multiple times when we explained why Gingrich had to be removed. Why, then, would Armey write such a passionate letter in his defense?

Dick Armey is a decent and honorable man. However, he is also a human being who is capable of grossly distorting the truth when a position as powerful as Speaker appears to be within reach. As C. S. Lewis wrote, the pursuit of the Inner Ring makes "very good people do very bad things."

The coup was not a pleasant experience for anyone involved. I believe we were justified in our effort because the real power in our representative government should be at the bottom, not the top, of our society. Individual members work for the 600,000 or so constituents in their districts, and the leadership works for individual members. When the leadership stops working for the people and the people's elected representatives, individual members have a responsibility to intervene and remove those leaders. Referring to this as a "coup" is a bit overheated. Our goal was to change leadership, not topple our government. Speakers of the

House are not presidents or kings, and the Constitution provides avenues to remove them from power if they abrogate their responsibilities.

However, I do regret the unnecessary personal pain and anguish we caused Gingrich and several others involved by how we mishandled the process. In retrospect, we should have worked harder to replace him after the leadership elections following the 1996 elections. We were naïve to believe that our effort to appoint a new Speaker before the next round of leadership elections would work the way we imagined. John Shadegg had been warning me all along that leadership would tell us they'd go along but wouldn't betray Gingrich in the end, but I ignored his advice. He had been consulting with friends in the state legislature in Arizona who were telling him we'd never pull it off. He was right. As Graham recalls, "It probably wasn't artfully handled." Still, we would remember the lessons of the failed coup in 1997. They would serve us well in 1998.

6

GOING NATIVE

Revolutions never go backwards.

—WILLIAM HENRY SEWARD
*(1801–1872), American statesman, senator, and
secretary of state*

S OMETHING MY FRESHMEN REPUBLICAN COLLEAGUES and I
vowed never to do when we were elected in 1994 was to become like
the Washington insiders we were sent to Congress to replace—a process
we called "going native." In our second term, the trappings of
Washington were severely testing our new majority. "Nearly all men can
stand adversity," Abraham Lincoln said wisely, "but if you want to test a
man's character, give him power."

One of the defining characteristics of the culture of Washington we
wanted to change was the widely accepted practice of pork barrel
spending. We knew that since the dawn of time politicians had been
using their positions of power to fund pet projects that served narrow
parochial interests but undermined the best interests of the whole
community. In recent years, however, the problem has gone from a rash
to a cancer in our system.

At no time was this clash of cultures between the revolutionaries from
the Class of 1994 and the old guard in Congress more apparent than in the
debates surrounding the balanced budget agreement and the highway bill

in 1997 and 1998. Our determination to end business as usual in Congress collided with accounting gimmicks and old-fashioned pork barrel politics, as practiced by the grandmaster of pork in the House, Transportation Committee Chairman Bud Shuster of Pennsylvania. When the dust settled it was more obvious than ever that many Republican revolutionaries had already defected to the ranks of the careerists.

BALANCED BUDGET ACT OF 1997

In the summer of 1997, leadership was already thinking about achievements Republicans could run on in the upcoming November 1998 elections, more than a year away. They hoped one of those achievements would be an agreement with the White House on how to balance the federal budget by 2002 and end years of deficit spending. Members of the Class of 1994 and a few conservative Republicans who had already been fighting in the trenches for limited government hoped we would get it right this time.

However, when I caught wind of the actual budget numbers in the proposed agreement, I was anything but enthusiastic. If the numbers I was hearing were true, the plan would never work. Once again, all of the tough decisions about spending cuts would be put off to the so-called "out years." Congress would increase spending, then discover historic fiscal restraint in 2000, 2001, and 2002 when massive spending cuts would occur. If Congress saved its bad medicine for later, I knew it would never take it.

I remember spotting John Kasich, chairman of the House Budget Committee, during a hectic day in the Capitol. The restricted area behind the House chamber was crowded with clusters of members, lobbyists, and staff. When I saw Kasich head for Statuary Hall, I decided to chase him down. If anyone could talk sense into leadership it was Kasich, a conservative hero of mine who had waited his entire congressional career for this opportunity. No one wanted a balanced budget more than Kasich, and he was wise to the ways of Washington. I never forgot the time Kasich pulled me aside when I came to Washington to warn me, "You can trust what no one says in Washington in terms of commitments."

When I caught up with Kasich near the statue of Will Rogers, I could tell by the look of resignation on his face that he wasn't going to get what he wanted. There would be no plan to actually balance the budget based on controlling spending. He knew it. I knew it. Of course, no one at the time knew that tax revenues would end up growing as they would and temporarily absolve Congress of its fiscal irresponsibility in the eyes of the public.

"Tom, it's the best we could get," Kasich said in a slightly defensive tone as I pleaded with him to reject any plan that wouldn't do the job of balancing the budget. Our fifteen-minute conversation amidst statues of the great members who had served in the House was awkward. Kasich knew I admired him, and he knew this was less than what he had hoped for.

Kasich surely did not expect the appropriators and leadership to maintain the caps necessary to balance the budget. Yet even conservative stalwart Kasich would sell the plan as a crowning achievement in press releases and campaign stops. Had I not signed a term limits pledge that limited my time in Washington—and had I had presidential ambitions, like Kasich—I'm not sure I would have resisted the temptation to join the charade either.

Even as Congress was celebrating its historic budget deal, other members were plotting the deal's demise. Congress's true intentions about balancing the budget would be severely tested and revealed in a few short months as Republicans considered one of the most epic and notorious bills in its history.

THE PORK FEST OF 1998

The transportation bill was a key battleground because it was going to unravel, in symbol and substance, much of what we had achieved since

1994. At a cost of $217 billion, the bill was an astounding 42 percent more expensive than the last highway bill Congress passed six years earlier. More important, the bill was going to make the Balanced Budget Act of 1997 the Un-Balanced Budget Act of 1997. The bill spent $26 billion above the spending caps Republicans had recently passed with so much fanfare. A typically upbeat and positive Kasich called the bill an "abomination." Kasich knew better than any member that his historic budget deal was about to be bulldozed and paved over by Bud Shuster's highway extravaganza.

Aside from the excessive spending levels, the way in which the bill was put together mocked the very principles of responsibility and honesty in government that we ran on in 1994. The bill contained a record-shattering 1,467 pork projects—ten times the amount of pork in a highway bill President Reagan vetoed in 1987, which, bear in mind, came from a Democrat-controlled Congress. This following graph illustrates how the GOP Congress was taking pork to new heights:

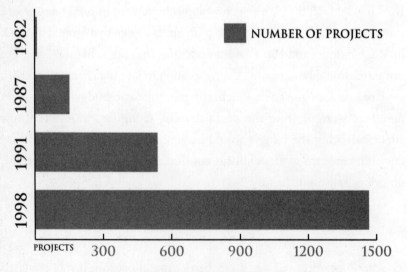

Figure 4. Pork Projects

The Third Thing Congress Does Not Want You to Know about How It Does Business: Members are routinely bribed for votes by being given total control over millions of dollars to be used for their pet projects—a process commonly referred to as pork barrel politics.

I have a simple definition of *pork:* If one member of Congress determines where the money is to be spent, it is pork. The merit, or lack thereof, of a project does not make it pork as much as the individual member's authority over how to spend the money. When politicians are given absolute control over these dollars they often make politics the priority, and scarce taxpayer dollars are squandered on lower-priority projects. Members who play this game, of course, always say one man's pork is another man's steak. While it's true that not all pork is as wasteful as Bud Shuster's highways to nowhere in Pennsylvania, a process in which one member can direct millions of dollars to projects of questionable merit is inherently wasteful, corrupt, and lacking in accountability.

Examples of Pork in the 1998 Highway Bill:

- $10 million to start "an advanced traffic monitoring and emergency response center" at Letterkenny Army Depot in Chambersburg, in Shuster's district.

- $640 million for 130 projects in Pennsylvania, home of Bud Shuster, including $7 million for a transportation museum in Allentown. (Shuster refused to disclose how much his district received.)

- $12 million for an Appalachian Transportation Institute at Marshall University (Nick Rahall, [D-West Virginia]) .

- $9 million for a Center for National Scenic Byways in Duluth to advise other communities regarding scenic byways. (James Oberstar [D-Minnesota] who earmarked $77 million for his district, $189 million total for state.)

- $12 million to fund an institute for "intelligent transportation systems" at the University of Minnesota.

- $3 million to produce a public television documentary on "infrastructure awareness."

- Senior Republican committee members Tom Petri and Sherwood Boehlert received $75 million. Howard Coble received $70 million. Don Young brought back $60 million to a congested Alaska, according to *Roll Call*.[5]

My colleagues and I believed the damage done by pork politics was not just to the federal budget but also to the public's trust in government. The public expects the government to fund projects according to real priorities, not politics. This brand of wasteful and self-serving politics was precisely the type of activity we came to Washington to end. In our view, the American people deserved to be represented by people who would spend their tax dollars on projects that mattered. Instead, many Republicans were leading the effort to squander the taxpayer's money on monuments to career politicians and advertisements for their reelection campaigns. The bill was a betrayal not only of our principles but also of the people who sent us to Washington to govern in a different way.

Another objection I had to pork politics was that it jeopardized public safety, something the purveyors of pork politics congratulate themselves for defending. For instance, allocating $7 million to a transportation

---

[5] For the latest examples of pork spending, go to the Citizens Against Government Waste website (www.CAGW.org).

museum in Allentown, Pennsylvania, means $7 million will not be spent improving dangerous two-lane highways and crumbling bridges.

Shuster and other defenders of pork politics said the process was clean because Congress had an official fourteen-point vetting process that judges projects according to merit. While it is true that this process can be used to help members weigh the value of projects, it is also a pork-laundering service. If a project goes through the fourteen-points, Shuster said, it is clean. However, when projects are offered in exchange for votes, no mention is made of the esteemed fourteen-point vetting process.

Shuster also tried to downplay this spending binge by reminding us that we were going to spend a mere $9 billion out of a $217 billion bill on "special demonstration projects." In other words, it was okay for career politicians to skim $9 billion from the taxpayers' transportation dollars to buy themselves political insurance—though any CEO would be thrown in prison for doing the same.

The previous year's debate on the Balanced Budget Act of 1997 set the stage for a confrontation over the highway bill. Shuster nearly succeeded in attaching an amendment to the budget bill that would have busted the spending caps before they went into effect. His amendment failed by only two votes, which called into question the House's willingness to do what it takes to truly balance the budget.

Shuster's tactics hardly surprised us. He had a reputation for being one of the most skilled dealmakers in Congress. What shocked us was the fact that Gingrich, who was supposed to be the torchbearer for fiscal responsibility, let this budget-busting amendment come to the floor for a vote when he had to know it had a chance of passing. This was yet another event that led us to contemplate his removal.

Gingrich wrote about this episode in his 1998 book, *Lessons Learned the Hard Way.* He called the highway bill "meritorious" because it would repair a highway system that was vital to the economy and had been neglected for too many years. However, as the balanced budget deal was being finalized in the summer of 1997, he knew he couldn't balance the budget *and* pay for Shuster's bill at the same time. Gingrich wrote, "We were in real danger of looking like a bunch of fools or hypocrites if we turned around and brought out a massive, multibillion-dollar, multi-year bill that destroyed the spending ceilings we had just written into law."

IF YOUR DECISIONS ARE BASED ON NOT LOSING A POSITION, YOU CANNOT EFFECTIVELY SERVE THE BEST LONG-TERM INTERESTS OF THE COUNTRY.

However, rather than force Shuster to streamline his bill to fit the caps, Gingrich avoided a confrontation with the wily chairman by convincing him it was best to postpone floor consideration of the bill until the spring of 1998. Gingrich had effectively decided, in my opinion, he would rather violate the caps than confront Shuster and the pork-caucus over spending. With a wink and a nod, Gingrich told Shuster to wait a few months, not because he wanted to keep the caps, but because he did not want to look foolish and hypocritical when we did break the caps. Gingrich either felt that he could not use his office to control spending or was not willing to lose his office to control spending. This goes to the heart of the matter: If your decisions are based on not losing a position, you cannot effectively serve the best long-term interests of the country.

The Fourth Thing Congress Does Not Want You to Know about How It Does Business: Powerful members of Congress in safe, noncompetitive seats often hold fund-raisers—thinly veiled shakedowns—outside of their districts to increase their leverage over other members.

In a bizarre prelude to the transportation battle, Shuster held a fund-raiser for himself with contractors in Oklahoma City, a city

---

that was hoping to secure federal funds for a major road improvement. What was odd was that Shuster had no opponent in his home state of Pennsylvania and had had none the previous two election cycles. Contractors eager to curry favor with the highway gods in Washington were quite eager to attend Shuster's event. Shuster didn't need the money for his own campaign, but he could use it to expand his kingdom and reach within Congress by giving excess funds from his campaign war chest to the party or other members.

Shuster wasn't the only career politician to play this game. Senior members often exploit their fund-raising potential not to protect their own seats but to maximize their leverage over other members. When a member can raise large sums of money, they can exchange that money for favors. They can essentially say, "If you vote for this bill I'll give you money for your campaign." J. C. Watts, the congressman representing Oklahoma City, wasn't invited to the event but his Political Action Committee contributed five hundred dollars. Watts sat on the Transportation Committee but wasn't exactly best friends with Shuster, having opposed Shuster on a key vote a few months earlier.

Was it conceivable Shuster wanted to intimidate other members? For a March 20, 1998 article, Jim Myers of the *Tulsa World* did what any good reporter would do and called the office of J. C. Watts, the lone Oklahoman on the Transportation Committee, and asked what Watts would get in the bill. Pam Pryor, Watts's press secretary, said she couldn't release the number because of a threat from the Transportation Committee.

"They gave us a number," Pryor told Myers. "They said we would lose every project in our district . . . if we released it."

When the two sides faced off in the spring of 1998, the first shot rang out at a press conference when Steve Largent accused the Transportation

Committee of trying to buy his vote. Largent said the Transportation Committee asked him where he wanted to spend $15 million in his district. A disgusted Largent said to the reporters, "I told them my vote was not for sale." Largent had exposed the pork game everyone understood in Washington but never discussed publicly: Members are routinely asked to sell "yes" votes on fiscally irresponsible bills in exchange for the authority to spend a certain amount of pork dollars in their districts.

Largent, like every member of Congress, had already forwarded transportation requests from his state's Department of Transportation to the House Transportation Committee. However, the official fourteen-point vetting process had no bearing on the question of whether Largent would sell his vote for a project of his choice. This was a one-point vetting process: vote "yes" and the money is yours to spend on anything you want.

Largent told Jim Myers of the *Tulsa World* that the bill "stinks" and "is everything I ran for Congress to be against. . . . Special projects should be based on need . . . not your relationship with the chairman of the committee."

Largent also explained that it was a well-known fact in Congress that members of the House Transportation Committee could receive up to five times as much for pork as non-committee members, and that the bill was being used to bolster vulnerable Republicans who wanted to show their constituents that they could bring home the bacon.

Soon, other members with the same experience with the committee as Largent echoed his assessment of the process. Soon thereafter, Matt Rader, my transportation legislative assistant, had received a voice mail message from Darrel Wilson, a staffer with the Transportation Committee. Wilson said, "We have a deal on the funding levels for that. I originally spoke to your boss, to your office, last September and we had notified you that there was $10 million in the bill for your boss. We're upping that by $5 million, so you have $15 million, and I'm just trying to figure out where you want to put the new money, the new $5 million."

Again, there was no mention of the venerable fourteen-point vetting process—just a pledge for $15 million to spend on whatever I wanted.

My staff wisely saved the voice mail message by bouncing it around to different phones in our office so our phone system wouldn't accidentally erase our smoking gun, which I cited extensively over the next few weeks. The message was played on ABC's "Evening News," referenced during floor debate, and cited in various press accounts. I knew certain members would not appreciate what I was doing, but I believed the public had the right to know how their tax dollars were being spent by their elected representatives in Washington. Plus, my limited-term status left me with nothing to fear from retribution.

After I was offered $15 million for pork, I told the *Tulsa World,* "This is just dirty power politics. . . . I don't want to be a part of that. It is exactly what's wrong with the U.S. Congress. Pet projects are going to be enacted into law so they can pay off political favors for people back home."

Lindsey Graham had also received a call from a Transportation Committee staffer. On March 19, 1998, Lindsey was told he was getting $15 million in the bill, more than twice as much as he had in last year's version, and he had until 5:00 P.M. to decide if he wanted the money. He also said no thanks. Lindsey told political journalist Bob Novak, "Of all the things I've been unhappy with that were done by the leadership this was the worst. It violates all our principles."

Sue Myrick had received a similar call and confirmed to ABC's "Evening News" that she was offered $15 million for her vote on March 23, 1998.

Our combined statements created an echo chamber effect in the media that produced various news stories about the vote-buying scheme in the House. The media loved the story because the public and the press assume that this sort of thing happens in Congress but is almost never confirmed by members.

Needless to say, Chairman Shuster was livid. On March 26, 1998, Shuster took to the floor of the House to raise a rare point of personal privilege that members can invoke when they believe they have been slighted by another member.

Ken Calvert, the acting chair, said that based on press accounts referring to Shuster, he could be recognized for a question of personal privilege. Shuster spoke:

Mr. Speaker, many years ago, Joseph McCarthy in Wheeling, West Virginia, stood up and waved papers and said he had the names of 57 Communists in government. Well, he got lots of headlines but, of course, he was eventually proved to be a liar. I am reminded of that event, although I certainly make no such charge here today.

Mr. Speaker, three of our colleagues have made numerous statements in the media that we have been, quote, "buying votes" to get them to support our BESTEA transportation legislation in exchange for projects which we have given them. Indeed, conversely, that we have been threatening Members that if they did not vote with us, they would not get the projects.

Let me make this very clear. I challenge these Members to name one person, one person whom I went to and said they will get a project in exchange for their vote. I challenge them to name one person who I threatened that they not get a project if they voted against us. [See Addendum 1 at the end of this chapter.]

Indeed, if we look back at the battle we had here last year on the budget resolution where we had our transportation amendment, I urge my colleagues to go look at Members who voted against us and then look at the projects they are receiving today. This is simply a blatant falsehood.

Now, no doubt many Members support our legislation because it is important to their district, because it is important to America, because they are getting projects that they have requested and which have been vetted through our 14-point requirement.

It seems that in life sometimes there are those who, when one takes a different view from their view, they must somehow ascribe some base motivation. They simply cannot believe that because someone disagrees with them, that another's motives can be as pure as theirs. Indeed, sometimes it seems as though the smaller the minority they represent, the more incensed they become, because they view themselves as more pure, more righteous, more sanctimonious than the larger majority of us who are mere mortals. But I do not ascribe any of these motives to our colleagues. I prefer to believe that they simply are misinformed.

Mr. Speaker, the supreme irony is that the three individuals who have been attacking us, attacking our motives, attacking our integrity have submitted projects to us for their own congressional districts.

Shuster completed his speech by introducing into the congressional record letters we had written and forwarded to his committee requesting projects in our districts. (My materials are contained in Addendum 2 at the end of this chapter.)

Shuster was misleading about the manner in which we forwarded requests from transportation officials in our state. Like every member of Congress, we asked the committee to fund, as funds were available, the projects transportation officials in our state believed were most important. We believed the Transportation Committee then had the difficult duty of deciding which project requests from all 435 were most crucial. However, when we were asked to trade our vote for absolute control over $15 million, we refused to participate in a process that had little integrity and was damaging to the country.

Later that day I went to the floor of the House to deliver a speech of my own:

Mr. Speaker, I rise today to discuss a matter of grave concern to me and many of my colleagues. I am in great hope that the American public is paying attention to what I am about to say.

Mr. Speaker, I am going to talk about transportation dollars and budget authority and busting the budget. The transportation dollars that are being handled in this country are being handled in a way that I believe does not support the best interests of the American public nor [does it] support the quality of this institution.

Next week the House will be asked to vote on a transportation bill that could cost the American taxpayers $216 billion, money they have already paid into a taxpayers' fund. This will make this bill one of the largest public works bills in our history. The chairman of the Committee on the Budget [Kasich] has called the bill an "abomination" because it will bust the budget by at least $26 billion. That is $26 billion that we are going to pass on to our next generation. We have the assurances that this will be paid for in conference. Anybody that has been here for any length of time knows that that is not much in terms of assurance.

This Congress has made important steps toward reversing the fiscal irresponsibility of its recent past, and we must stay that course. We must not lose our bearings when we are so close to making significant strides towards reducing our $5.5 trillion debt.

I want to explain to the American people how transportation dollars are divided up in this country and where that process is corrupt and needs to be reformed. Every time Americans fill their cars up with gas, a few cents goes towards a massive federal transportation fund. Congress has set up a committee to divide these funds. Each member of this committee exercises enormous influence over where these dollars are spent.

Every Member of Congress has the authority to request special projects, based on the needs of their district and the recommendations of their respective state's Department of Transportation. Money should be awarded to these projects based solely on their merit, but this is often not the case, as anyone who has observed this process recently will admit.

Instead of dividing transportation money according to the merit of projects, money is divided based on political favors and political expediency. Stories in today's Associated Press will help explain what I mean.

The AP [Associated Press] reports North Dakota and South Dakota are similar in size and population, but when it comes to the House's highway bill, they are nothing alike. The bill earmarks $60 million in special projects for South Dakota, six times as much as its neighbor to the north.

Mr. Speaker, let me ask my colleagues and the American public a question. Is it likely that the projects in South Dakota have six times more merit as the projects in North Dakota, or is there some political motivation involved?

In Minnesota, one district [represented by Oberstar] out of the eight congressional districts in that state received $80 million of the $140 million earmarked for projects in that state. Does that one district have such a disproportionate need for highway funds, or is there some other reason for this imbalance in funding? Is it a coincidence that an inordinately high proportion of transportation funds are targeted to districts represented by members of the Committee on Transportation and Infrastructure? Is it a coincidence that this bill sends outrageous sums of money to members in both parties who will face difficult reelections? [AP reported that in Alabama, more than half the state's $190 million in projects would be headed for two districts, one represented by Transportation Committee member Spencer Bachus and the other by Bob Riley, a freshmen who faced a tough reelection race.]

Also, if my colleagues examine this bill, they will find striking disparities in the amount of money one state receives over another, regardless of what they put into the trust fund.

Mr. Speaker, I invite the public and the press to examine this bill and decide for themselves whether this money is being divided according to merit or to politics. This bill includes over 1,400 special projects. In 1987, President Reagan vetoed a bill that had 150 such projects, which is just one-tenth the number in this bill.

We should ask ourselves what the typical American thinks of this process. I think we know. The public finds that it is sick, dirty, and corrupt, and a throwback to the system of "good ol' boys" that we came here in 1994 to end. We have $5.5 trillion worth of debt in this country. We cannot afford to play games with the public's money, and, more importantly, we cannot afford to play games with the public's trust.

That is why I and several of my colleagues turned down funds in this year's highway transportation bill. I made a statement to the press that the committee had approached me in hopes of buying my vote. I stand by that statement.

But this is not an issue of one Member against another Member or one Member against a committee. This issue is about whether Congress will continue to look the other way on a system that encourages Members to do the inappropriate and wrong things. This system not only wastes the public's money, it degrades the public's trust in this institution. It is difficult to put a dollar value on trust because it is invaluable. As legislators, the public's trust is our most precious and scarce resource. Once that trust is lost, we all know it is hard to earn it back.

If this Congress and the class of 1994 are known for one thing, I hope it is for our unwavering crusade to regain the public trust. Without that trust, we are governed by suspicion and cynicism, and our society cannot be sustained for long with that foundation.

The next day Kasich joined our side for a press conference to declare our intent to kill the bill. "They say pigs get fat and hogs get slaughtered. And frankly, this bill is a hog; it's way over the top. We came to Washington to change the culture of this town and frankly this bill . . . is a significant detour from where our party has been going," Kasich said.

Kasich's stand took real guts. He was contemplating a presidential run in 2000, and he was openly defying Newt Gingrich and the rest of leadership who, according to Dennis Hastert, then the chief deputy majority whip, were united in their support for the abomination. To me,

Kasich seemed to be motivated in part by lingering disgust over the fraudulent balanced budget negotiations that had wired the agreement to fail.

Going into the fight on the floor we had a small army and a courageous general in John Kasich. One of our plans was to return the pork dollars to the states. We knew we had virtually no chance of winning a vote on the issue, but we wanted to make a point. Largent told Myers of the *Tulsa World*, "I just think the more light we throw on this, the more we expose it, the better it will be. We will definitely be throwing excruciatingly painful light on it."

When Kasich appeared on "Fox News Sunday" a few days before the vote, he sounded like a revolutionary from the Class of 1994. "This bill is a throwback to the old ways," he said. "This is one where we fell down. . . . I just hope we don't get comfortable with governing in this way, because if we do, we wouldn't be any better than the way the Democrats ran the place."

However, Kasich admitted, "I think I'll get hit by a cement truck" when we attempted to cut spending and pork in the bill. He added that he thought and hoped President Clinton would veto the abomination. Matt Salmon from Arizona said, "It's a strange day when President Clinton is acting more fiscally responsible than the GOP Congress, but such is life in this strange city."

The bill was such an obvious monstrosity that we not only had Kasich publicly fight with us—the usual suspects—but also had moderates who saw the danger of the party walking away from the budget deal. The moderates didn't want to see a split in the foundation that held the party together, which they believed was a common commitment to balance the budget and restore fiscal discipline. At this point, I was convinced careerism above anything else was holding the party together. Chris Shays, a Republican moderate from Connecticut and a member of the Budget Committee, told the *Washington Post*, "This is the best indication that the Republican revolution is over. It's really obscene that we would get so close to putting our country's finances in order and then blow it with a $30 billion outrage. This is politics at its worst."

Shays later told a reporter with the Reuters news agency that if the bill passed it would bring the "Republican Revolution to a grinding halt" and lead to "war" between leadership and conservatives.

Outside groups were criticizing the bill as well. "The earmarking is reprehensible," Daniel Mitchell of the Heritage Foundation told the *Washington Post*. "It's the traditional logrolling—I'll scratch your back if you scratch mine—that created the welfare state and that voters probably didn't think would increase when the Republicans took over Congress."

We knew killing the bill was a long shot, but we had to try. At a minimum, we wanted to highlight the differences between the true fiscal conservatives and the careerists who were defending old pork-style politics.

The Democrats were already having a field day explaining how the bill busted the budget. They certainly weren't serious about a balanced budget and would have produced a bill with a similar amount of pork, but their criticism was on the mark. They were accusing GOP leaders of pursuing "spectacularly dangerous and reckless" changes to the budget process. Chet Edwards (D-Texas) put it well when he told the *Washington Times* that under this bill, "The five-year budget deal becomes a six-month budget."

The day of the vote, I supported an amendment that would return transportation dollars and decisions to the states. Under the current system, Oklahoma was only receiving eighty-two cents for every dollar it put into the federal transportation pot. Graham offered an amendment to cut the 1,467 demonstration projects from the bill, which totaled more than $9 billion. As expected, both amendments failed, and the bill passed with more than three hundred votes.

The exercise was worthwhile because it is okay to lose while standing on principle—especially if the debate educates the public. Even though we were crushed in the actual votes on the floor this was an instance when losing gave the public valuable insight into how Congress really works. If the public had a better understanding of what pork spending really is, they would demand that politicians in Washington reform the way they spend money.

Consider how the public would react if Shuster's brand of pork politics was applied to other areas of the federal budget, like health care. Shuster consistently argued that setting aside 5 percent, or $9 billion, from a $217 billion bill for demonstration projects was a very reasonable thing to do. "Angels in heaven don't decide where highways are going to be built," Shuster would say, "This is a political process. And it is not unreasonable for the members of Congress . . . to identify 5 percent of the pot for high-priority projects that are important in their districts."

However, imagine if the House gave individual members control over 5 percent of the total amount the federal government spends on a budget item such as cancer research. As a practicing physician, vice-chairman of the Commerce Committee's Health and Environment Subcommittee, and a cancer survivor, I would have no problem coming up with a list of worthy projects in my district. I could use my position of power on a key committee to direct even more funds to my district. However, were I to create a Tom Coburn Center for Cancer Research, it might do very good work, but it would be absurd, self-indulgent, and possibly damaging to cancer research as I directed scarce tax dollars to a lower-priority project.

Giving members this much power in such a sensitive area would create a firestorm of controversy. I would contend the transportation issue is not much different. Transportation can also be a life and death issue. Failing to allocate money to repair roads and bridges can and does endanger lives. Every $7 million transportation museum or $4 million bike path diverts funds from higher priority projects where safety might be a serious concern.

I did not doubt that Shuster cared very deeply and sincerely about the safety of people who travel on our nation's roads and bridges. However, I'm not sure that he, and others who defended this process, saw the trade-offs that inevitably occur when individual members of Congress are allowed to control 5 percent of the highway budget. In some cases, funds in that 5 percent pot are directed to projects that enhance the safety of roads and bridges, but in many other cases those funds are used to enhance a member's political career, at the expense of public safety.

The response back home was intense. People either loved or hated what we did, but most responses were positive. What Steve and I did was the opposite of what the public expects politicians in Washington to do. The public expects politicians to be for fiscal responsibility in every district but their own. It is shocking for a politician to turn down a chance to bring home the bacon in his or her own district. The voters supported our stand by a two to one margin, and both Steve and I were reelected by comfortable margins.

Our most vocal critics were highway contractors and a few editorial writers. For several years after this episode I received critical letters from contractors because of my vote—a price I gladly paid to combat the self-serving pork emanating from Washington.

Ken Neal, editorial page editor of the *Tulsa World,* wrote a column about our stand on the highway bill that was representative of the arguments of those who criticized our stand. Neal said the highway bill shows that "representative government—messy as it is—is functioning," and that, *"[t]o be a good member of Congress is to work within the system of representative government. To be a good member is to do as much for one's constituents as possible. That involves working with the other members of Congress"* (emphasis added).

Critics like Neal were implying that the way the current Congress does business is the way business has always been done, and always will be done, so it is naïve and politically suicidal to wage war against that system. The only way you can "do good" for the people is conform to the

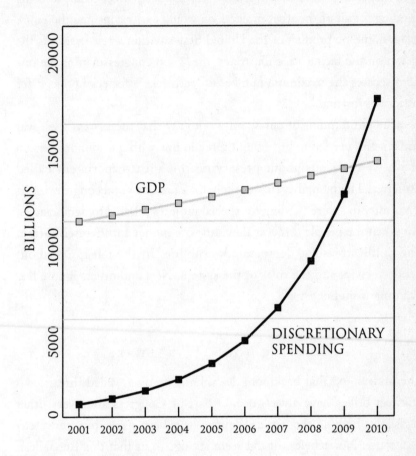

To illustrate the problem with the aforementioned definition of the "good congressman" consider the following thought experiment. If every member of Congress succeeded in being a "good congressman" during the fiscal year 2002 budget process, 18,898 earmarks would have been approved at a cost of $279 billion, a 43 percent increase in discretionary spending (*Washington Post*, July 8, 2001). If this "good congressman" standard was achieved in subsequent years and discretionary spending increased by 43 percent, federal spending would double by 2006 and consume our entire domestic product by 2010. In 2001, there were an estimated 6,400 earmarks, a threefold increase from 1995 (*Washington Post*, November 15, 2001).

Figure 5. The "Good Congressman"

system. Never mind the fact that if every member succeeded in securing funding for all of their pet projects we would easily consume the entire gross domestic product of the United States within a few years. As the graph on the facing page illustrates, the "good congressman" is the one who secures the maximum number of "earmarks" of special projects for his or her district.

The entire point of our stand was to say that the system itself was broken and needed to be brought more in line with our founders' vision if we were serious about preserving this great experiment called America. The mentality that the sole measure of a good congressman is his ability to secure funding for special projects is lethal to democracies, for when the people discover they can vote money for themselves from the public treasury, democracies crumble. In their lectures about modern civics and the rules of the system, Neal and others ignore this warning from history.

GETTING YOUR "FAIR" SHARE

We understood that backroom deals, horse-trading, veiled threats, and indirect bribes have always been a part of Congress and every other legislative body in the world. We may have been naïve, but we weren't *that* naïve. Nevertheless, it did seem strange to us that this Republican Congress was so intent on passing a bill that contained more pork than all of the highway bills Congress had passed in the previous twenty years. Yet we believed it was fatalistic to accept a corrupt system that pointlessly wasted billions of dollars on politically-driven, not need-driven, projects.

There was a day when Congress did not play pork politics nearly to the extent it does today. Davy Crocket, for instance, was more repulsed by pork politics than any member of the Class of 1994. Furthermore, a little known rule adopted by the House of Representatives in 1914 states: "It shall not be in order for any bill providing general legislation in relation to roads to contain any provision *for any specific road*" (emphasis added). Congress followed this rule for seventy years because congressional leaders understood that a breach in this dam would lead to a flood of requests for special transportation projects.

Business as it has "always been done," according to the civics lectures we were receiving in the media and from senior members, actually started in 1982 when the era of excessive highway pork spending began. That year, according to the General Accounting Office, Congress earmarked funds for ten demonstration projects at a cost of $386 million. In 1987, 152 projects were funded at a cost of $1.3 billion; in 1991, 539 projects for $6.2 billion; and in 1998, 1,467 projects for $9.5 billion.

Shuster, therefore, was not carrying on an ancient tradition. Instead, he was a pioneer of pork politics (see Addendum 1). Pork barrel politics is not an immutable law like gravity; it can be contained with statesmanlike leadership—which was absent during consideration of the highway bill.

During this debate, the *New Republic* published a thoughtful article that unabashedly defended the practice of loading major spending bills with pork. They said pork was the glue that held the bill together. Without promising members politically attractive projects for their district, they argued, leadership would have a much more difficult time cobbling together a majority of members to vote for the legislation. Even though some pork projects are wasteful they should be seen as "overhead" costs that keep the government running.

However, in the process I observed, pork acted more like acid than glue. Pork politics ate away funds for higher priority projects and further dissolved the public's trust in government. It is also worth noting that the largest highway construction project of all time—President Eisenhower's decision to build the interstate highway system—was accomplished *without* doling out pork projects.

The public, of course, wants roads and bridges, but I've never met a taxpayer who wants career politicians to use their tax dollars to reinforce their seats in office. Individual members have no right to take 5 percent of any bill and allocate it as they please. Setting aside 5 percent of a massive spending bill for members' personal use serves no other purpose but to maintain an elite ruling class of career politicians who are representing themselves and special interests, not the American public.

In our post-September 11 world, pork politics is especially shameful and harmful to our national interests. It is a style of politics that says, in effect, "Social Security and Medicare may be going bankrupt, our economy may be weak, and we may be struggling to pay the enormous costs of war, reconstruction, and development, but look what I've done for fishermen in Alaska (or whatever project in whatever state)." Fishermen in Alaska do have real and legitimate struggles, but so do our soldiers and the millions of working Americans whose retirement dollars are being squandered in today's Social Security Ponzi scheme.

Pork politics is the result of a public that has learned it can vote money for itself from the public treasury, and of a Congress that knows the inherent danger in this practice but does not want to give up the political hay that comes with handing out goodies back home. The best way for the people to get their money back is to vote for candidates who will cut taxes and reduce the size and scope of government. Receiving a pork project is a terrible return on the public's money. The best way to help the plight of oysters in the Chesapeake Bay (one of the post-9/11 pork projects) is to let people living in those regions keep more of their own money so they can support local researchers through local government initiatives. Sending that money to Washington to be processed by a bureaucracy that will send back less makes no sense. Pork politics in this sense is not unlike a congressional-run lottery that says, "Send us increasingly large sums of tax dollars and maybe your state will hit the jackpot," when the body being enriched by this scheme is the Congress, not the general public.

The public does have a right to its fair share, but its fair share is not the money pork barrel politicians want to send back home for their own political benefit. Rather, the public's fair share is the money they earn minus the money that is absolutely necessary to finance the federal government's essential functions, which does not include, according to our founders, pandering to parochial interests—especially during a time of war.

The real damage done by pork barrel politics, however, extends far beyond the dollars wasted on projects of questionable merit. Earmarks are a gateway drug on the road to a spending addiction. Each little project isn't that bad, but it leads to a habit of spending and a deep aversion to fiscal restraint. When a politician fights for special projects in his or her district, they typically compromise their ability to fight for fiscal restraint in other districts. The damage done by the earmarking process is greater than the sum of its parts.

Stephen Moore, then director of fiscal policy at the Cato Institute, summed up the impact of the highway bill: "Republicans and Democrats alike on Capitol Hill believe the highway bill is a political stroke of genius—rushing jobs and dollars back to their districts just in time for the elections. Even fiscal conservatives have calculated it's better politics to spend $30 billion of budget surplus funds on parochial transportation projects than to cut taxes on American workers. . . . It is to be hoped that come November voters will inform incumbents that they badly miscalculated."

Moore was right. Going native would cost us dearly in the next election.

As the following two addendums illustrate:

A postmortem analysis from *Roll Call*, a Capitol Hill newspaper, confirmed what everyone in Congress knew was happening. Its report supported Representative J. C. Watts's story when it found that some members would get a call and be told to not tell anyone how much they would receive. According to the *Roll Call* analysis, "Shuster's funding allocations were based less on pressing infrastructure needs than committee assignments, voting records, and demands from the GOP leadership."

Roll Call reported that the three Republican committee members who opposed Shuster's bill in 1997, when it was half the size it was in 1998, didn't fare so well. Freshman Chip Pickering only received $32 million, far less than other freshmen on Shuster's committee. Most freshmen on the committee received $40 million. According to *Roll Call:*

> Pickering was unavailable for comment, but several Members complained privately that the Mississippi freshman was penalized for opposing Shuster last May on his amendment to the budget bill that failed by two votes.
>
> "It's fair to say that we are convinced there's a system in place to punish Members (like Pickering)," said one high-ranking GOP Member, who like almost every Republican interviewed for this story, refused to talk candidly about Shuster unless his name was withheld.

Committee sources also told *Roll Call* that the bill was written to deliberately conceal how much money is earmarked for each member.

Roll Call reported that Shuster critics who didn't sit on the Transportation Committee were also punished. Rick Lazio was only offered $4 million, but he threw a fit and demanded to Gingrich and Shuster that he receive more. After a behind-the-scenes struggle he ended up with $27 million.

Jim McCrery, *Roll Call* said, was offered $10 million, two-thirds the minimum amount, and Rob Portman was told that his voting record would affect how much money he received. According to the *Roll Call* report:

As late as last week, National Republican Congressional Committee Chairman John Linder and other GOP leaders were complaining privately to Gingrich that Shuster was breaking his promise to not punish Members who opposed the chairman on key votes in the past.

"There's a lot of people who feel Newt is sending a bad signal by allowing Shuster to screw people who voted with leadership (against Shuster in 1997)," a senior leadership source said. "What message does that send for the next time we encourage Members to vote with leadership?" . . .

"Shuster made a deal with (Gingrich) that Members in vulnerable districts would be taken care of," said one leadership source. Rep. Robert Aderholt, one of the Democrats top targets in November, is the perfect example, this source said. Aderholt voted against Shuster in 1997, but was handed $25 million for projects in his district. . . .

Oberstar, who sources said controlled about 45 percent of the $10 billion pot, was the top Democratic recipient with $80 million . . . . Several Democratic sources said Oberstar, at the behest of House Minority Leader Richard Gephardt, paid special attention to Democratic Members whom Republicans are targeting for defeat this November. . . .

Democratic Reps. Leonard Boswell (Iowa) and Jay Johnson (Wisconsin), for instance, are top GOP targets and will head home to brag that they were able to steer $40 million each to their districts. And Neil Abercrombie (Hawaii) whom Democratic insiders consider one of their most vulnerable incumbents, pulled down $36.5 million.

Hon. Thomas E. Petri
U.S. House of Representatives
Chairman-Subcommittee on Surface Transportation
Rayburn House Office Building
Washington, DC

Dear Congressman Petri:

I encourage you to read the following testimony and letter. The enclosed detail very carefully the importance of Oklahoma's surface transportation.

I request that you give the State Highway 51 demonstration project proposal your full consideration.

In advance, I would like to thank you and your colleagues on the Transportation and Infrastructure Committee for your diligence and hard work on the upcoming ISTEA reauthorization.

Sincerely yours,

Tom A. Coburn, MD
Member of Congress.

STATE OF OKLAHOMA
Office of the Governor
Oklahoma, OK

February 21, 1997

Hon. Thomas E. Petri
U.S. House of Representatives
Chairman-Subcommittee on Surface Transportation
Rayburn House Office Building
Washington, DC

Dear Congressman Petri:

The significance of our surface transportation system should not be underestimated. Careful investment in our infrastructure increases productivity and economic prosperity at local and regional levels. Despite the importance of our transportation system to the nation's economic health, investment has fallen well short of what is truly needed. Dealing with these needs will require numerous approaches, including special project funding.

As you begin the monumental task of reauthorizing the Intermodal Surface Transportation Efficiency Act of 1991 (ISETA), we, the undersigned, wish to lend our support to the following special funding request, which is in addition to our existing obligation limit and is critical to the transportation needs of the State of Oklahoma.

SH 51 extending from Coweta east approximately 14.6 miles to Wagoner, Oklahoma. We commend your committee for its role in enacting ISTEA and for the subsequent improvements made with the passage of the National Highway System Bill last year. A sound national transportation policy is critical to our state's economy and our nation's ability to compete globally. To that end we urge you to evaluate our request and take the appropriate action.

Sincerely,

Frank Keating,
Governor

Neal A. McCaleb,
Secretary of Transportation

Herschal Crow,
Chairman, Oklahoma Transportation Commission

Demonstration Project Testimony
State Highway 51
Wagoner, Oklahoma

SUBMITTED BY: THE HONORABLE TOM A. COBURN, U.S. HOUSE OF REPRESENTATIVES AND NEAL A. MCCALEB, SECRETARY OF TRANSPORTATION, STATE OF OKLAHOMA

State Highway 51 (SH 51): SH-51 extending east from Coweta to the Arkansas border, has been identified as a Transportation Improvement Corridor. Eastern Oklahoma has an ever increasing population. Tourism has also increased in the Fort Gibson Lake and Tahlequah areas. These two factors form the basis of why reconstruction of SH-51 is of foremost concern.

The route has a high accident rate and contains bridges that are structurally deficient or functionally obsolete. For projected traffic, this two lane route with no shoulders is unacceptable, and could ultimately curb any future economic growth in the northeastern region of Oklahoma.

In addition to tourism dollars, the highway also serves as a major travel corridor and commuter route extending from the Tulsa Metropolitan area east to Broken Arrow, Muskogee, and the Arkansas state line.

SH-51 is crucial to the region's business, industry, and labor because it provides access to the Tulsa metropolitan area, McClellan Kerr Navigational System, and several recreational areas in eastern Oklahoma.

Nationally significant, SH-51 connects with I-44, I-244, the Muskogee Turnpike, US-412, and other major routes in eastern Oklahoma.

It is essential that SH-51 be expanded to four lanes to increase capacity, promote tourism, boost economic growth, and to improve safety and congestion. This project is estimated to cost $63 million, and although the state has expended nearly $34 million to improve this corridor, it is simply not enough in view of the overall critical needs of the entire highway system.

7

THE PERFECT STORM

*If the voters really understood what we were up to
they'd vote us out of office.*

—Senator Robert Byrd
(D-West Virginia)

Heading into the 1998 midterm elections, most of my
colleagues were extremely confident we would significantly
increase our bare majority. Many Republicans expected that President
Clinton's colossally foolish act of having an affair with a twenty-one-
year-old intern, and then lying to cover it up, would cause the public to
vote for Republicans in large numbers. Our consultants and leaders reinforced this expectation. In fact, in one meeting of the Republican conference, Gingrich told restless conservatives that we did not need to
mobilize our base with a bold agenda because Clinton had already motivated our base for us. In essence, all we had to do was not take any risks,
or make any mistakes, and we would be rewarded in November.

Meanwhile, our lackadaisical attitude was spilling over into the
appropriations process. We already knew that come October the costs of
the highway bill and other priorities were bound to collide with the cold
reality of the spending caps. Our take-no-risks strategy meant it was
even less likely we would do what was necessary to rein in spending.

Ironically, a political environment in which we thought we would harvest huge political gains was instead creating the conditions for a perfect storm. The Republican mishandling of the impeachment process was poised to collide with an appropriations process that was getting out of control. The consequences would be disastrous for us in November.

The appropriations season got off to a bad start in March when leadership could not decide whether to pay for a supplemental appropriations bill by borrowing from the Social Security surplus or by finding offsetting cuts. Almost every spring, Congress passes a supplemental spending bill that is intended to take care of unexpected needs or emergencies that were not addressed in the previous year's appropriations process—even though such bills are rarely necessary. Leadership and the appropriators liked passing supplemental bills because the additional spending did not count against the spending caps. A provision in the 1997 Balanced Budget Act waived the spending caps for emergency spending. Therefore, leadership and the appropriators felt no need to find offsetting cuts to pay for the supplemental.

The problem was that most of the so-called "emergencies" were not true emergencies. For example, Congress declared spending on the 2000 census as an emergency as if it were an unexpected crisis. This fiscally irresponsible approach was compounded by the fact that the total Congress spends on both nonemergency and emergency items becomes the baseline for the next year's budget.

In attempt to keep these abuses in check, a group of about a dozen conservatives in the House had formed an unofficial appropriations watchdog group to monitor the appropriations process. We asked to meet with Bob Livingston (R-Louisiana) and Gingrich to discuss spending levels in every bill. We did not necessarily expect to win many battles, but we were sick and tired of our leadership not trying. And we were not afraid to lose if losing framed the issue in terms that would help our cause in the long-term.

When we urged leadership to offset any additional spending,

everyone agreed that could be done except for Gingrich and Livingston. I thought their position was absurd. To claim outright that cuts could not be found was to assume that the federal government was running at peak efficiency and could not be cut back in any area. This was a difficult case to make in a body that had just designated $9 billion for special transportation pork projects, many to the districts of politically vulnerable members. Besides, common-sense people routinely cut back on expenses in their household or business budgets during tough times. Congress was hardly a model of the frugality families followed. Would it be painful to make cuts? For some, yes, it would. Would it be impossible? Hardly. When, in March, *The Hill* asked what I would think if leadership couldn't find the cuts, I replied, "Then we have a failed leadership."

Another warning sign of the looming confrontation over spending came in May when John Kasich was criticized for a plan to reduce spending during a meeting of the Republican conference. Bob Novak recounted the meeting well in his May 11, 1998 column "Rudderless Republicans": "Since Republicans retreated from their across-the-board tax reduction, their shrunken agenda now consists mainly of attacks on 'criminal' activities by the president. The GOP has tacitly bought into Clinton's clever campaign to expand government's role through incremental proposals. The sole hope of reversing this course is Kasich."

Kasich was hoping to cut spending by $154 billion—even though he admitted only $100 billion in cuts was doable—and pass along the savings in the form of a tax cut. When he approached me and other conservatives about an alternative budget, we were eager to help. Our five-year budget would reduce spending by $280 billion, cut taxes by at least $150 billion, and set aside 50 percent of any future surpluses for tax cuts. He wanted us to help pressure Republicans to support his plan because he was not finding much support from Newt Gingrich and committee chairmen.

When Kasich presented his plan to the entire Republican conference,

I was appalled, but not surprised, by the negative response he received. Livingston rose to blast Kasich's plan, reminding Republicans that he had no choice but to appropriate money for programs authorized by Congress. Once again we had to sit through this fallacious argument that we constantly heard from the appropriators. No two people in the room understood the hollowness of this argument more than Kasich and Livingston.

> *The Fifth Thing Congress Does Not Want You to Know about How It Does Business: Congress spends more than $100 billion every year on well over two hundred programs that are not authorized by law.*
>
> The rules of the House forbid Congress from funding programs that have not been explicitly authorized. One program, the Legal Services Corporation, which costs taxpayers more than $300 million each year, has not been authorized by Congress since 1979.

"Mr. Livingston can't have it both ways," I said to the conference. "He says we have to spend money for all programs that are authorized, but we also spend on programs that aren't authorized."

Livingston could have made cuts if he wanted to. Unfortunately, he did not want to. Gingrich's response was even more disturbing. He first defended Livingston's assertion that we had to pour money into unauthorized programs. Then he failed to mention that, of the federal programs that had been authorized, many could be streamlined or eliminated. Gingrich also demanded "less rhetoric" from Steve Largent and me. He said condescendingly that it was useless to embark on crusades, such as eliminating cabinet agencies, that had no chance of succeeding—even though in 1995 many Republicans supported consolidating and streamlining federal agencies. Gingrich's criticisms were probably partly triggered by his aggravation over our recent attacks against the highway bill.

We weren't entirely surprised by Gingrich and Livingston's tirades, but we were disappointed that Dick Armey and Tom DeLay, the two members of leadership who usually at least verbally advocated conservative policies, were silent.

Novak wrote:

Kasich, a career politician who is testing presidential waters for 2000, does not burn bridges and still has hopes of cutting government and reducing taxes this year. He will not criticize colleagues in the GOP leadership and stressed he has strong support from DeLay (despite his silence at the conference) and John Boehner (silent because he was presiding as conference chairman). By implication, Kasich was suggesting nonsupport from Armey and his own longtime mentor, Gingrich. The speaker's renewed partisanship is channeled into assailing the president's conduct, not the core Republican goal of cutting back government and its oppressive taxes.

As the appropriations process developed it became more and more clear that Republicans were simply hoping Clinton's misconduct would expand our majority. The House's July vote (July 21, 1998) to continue funding the National Endowment for the Arts (NEA) signaled the party's unwillingness to make serious cuts. The NEA, now funded at about $125 million annually, is a classic example of a program that is far outside the boundaries of the Constitution. Although Congress has reformed the NEA to some extent by limiting its ability to fund objectionable art and has more evenly distributed funds among all fifty states, not just New York and California, it still makes no sense to send state and local arts dollars to the federal government for bureaucratic management and redistribution. If states and local communities want to publicly fund the arts, fine. The federal government has no compelling interest or need to be involved other than to make career politicians look arts-sensitive.

The best way to support the arts is through private donations and by being an arts patron. An individual artist's success is not, and should not be, dependent on the federally managed NEA. In 1995, the NEA was contributing only 1 percent of the money that is spent on the arts in this country, and private giving to the arts was skyrocketing. Between 1965 and 1995, private donations to the arts quadrupled from $2.3 billion to $9.9 billion. By continuing to fund the NEA, and many other non-essential but politically popular programs, the House showed that it was not interested in explaining the need for limited government to the rest of America.

In September, another debate about supplemental spending flared. Once again conservatives wanted to find offsets for spending on the Y2K computer problem, agriculture aid, and peacekeeping, but leadership and the appropriators decided that would be too painful. Livingston told *CongressDaily*, "Short of changing the authorization process, we've cut appropriations about as much as we can do it and still get 218 votes." He was right, but that was because leadership lacked the guts to make it difficult for Republicans to vote for larger appropriations bills. I found it ironic that our leaders would enforce party discipline to compel members to vote for bills that busted the caps but would not enforce that same discipline to pressure members to vote for bills that were within the caps.

The unwillingness of leadership and the appropriators to find offsets was deeply frustrating to the revolutionaries from 1994. The previous year the president and Congress proclaimed an end to decades of budget deficits when the balanced budget agreement was signed into law. Yet the president, and some in Congress, were preparing to again break that agreement with bogus emergency spending that would steal about $20 billion from social security beneficiaries while asking our children and grandchildren to foot the bill.

While emergency spending would not count toward the spending limits imposed by the balanced budget agreement, it would reduce our $70 billion potential surplus, which was not a genuine surplus. Much of that money came from surplus in the Social Security Trust Fund, not the general revenue fund.

> **The Sixth Thing Congress Does Not Want You to Know about How It Does Business:** *Congress routinely raids the Social Security Trust Fund—taxpayer retirement dollars—to cover general revenue shortfalls.*
>
> In any business or company, an executive who "borrowed" money from his or her employee's retirement funds to cover an operating loss would be prosecuted. But this is precisely what Congress does with the Social Security Trust Fund and more than a hundred other trust funds that are intended to set aside money for a future need. Congress first started this practice in 1969.

I was one of a handful of members trying to remind colleagues that the purpose of the emergency spending provision was to ensure that the federal government can respond to war, natural disasters, and economic depressions—bona fide emergencies, not political padding for spending bills.

One member of the Senate, Judd Gregg of New Hampshire, did respond to the request for emergency spending in a statesmen-like manner. No request that year could have been more worthy of the designation "emergency spending" than the request to rebuild the American embassies in Kenya and Tanzania, and to increase security for all American embassies. Yet Gregg, the chairman of the Subcommittee of Jurisdiction, stated from the Senate floor that he was willing to find offsets for this spending. In an age of government largess, the best way to address this, and other emergency requests, was for Congress to fund urgent needs by reducing funding for other, less vital, programs. Unfortunately, Gregg's conduct was the exception rather than the standard in 1998.

Another way we tried to contain the damage of the supplemental spending excesses was to team up with moderates in the House, the group known as the "Lunch Bunch" after their regular weekly lunch. Several members from both camps were united in our commitment to enforce budget rules and work toward a truly balanced budget. In fact, a few months earlier we had joined forces on the highway bill but were unsuccessful in an effort to cut the pork from the bill. As members of the Class of 1994 were being dismissed by some in Congress and the media as neophytes who didn't know how to play the game, we were quietly building a powerful coalition with the Lunch Bunch. "If we are truly together," I told *CongressDaily*, "I don't think there's a larger [GOP conference] group. It's both ends of our conference, so you can assume that the people between us are with us."

We eventually persuaded leadership to offset the domestic spending portions of the emergency supplemental bill with cuts in other programs, while defense spending would not be offset with cuts. We presented leadership with $27 billion in cuts that could pay for the additional supplemental spending. I knew these would not be enacted at the end of the process, but I was convinced we had to try.

Then, at the end of September, the best fiscal news to come out of Washington in years was, paradoxically, the worst news as well. As expected, President Clinton announced that the federal government would end the year with a surplus of about $70 billion. "Tonight at midnight, America puts an end to three decades of deficits and launches a new era of balanced budgets and surpluses," Clinton said. Now that Washington was celebrating a mythical surplus, there would be even less incentive to restrain spending.

The GOP had long since decided to join Clinton's spin game with the surplus rather than expose the deception in his argument. The $70 billion surplus both parties were falling over each other to claim credit for was entirely from excess Social Security payments, which would need to be paid once baby boomers retired. Calling this money a surplus was like a business borrowing from their employee's retirement fund so they could call a loss a profit.

The superheated rhetoric celebrating the surplus indeed was making it even more difficult to restrain spending. As the session was drawing to a close, I told the *New York Times* that the only consensus was "to spend money and get out of town."

The Republicans were lulled into an even greater state of complacency as our Campaign Committee chairman, John Linder (R-Georgia), and other pollsters were predicting we would pick up at least a dozen seats in the November elections. Gingrich thought we would gain ten to forty seats. Prominent Republican pollster Ed Goeas was predicting we would gain fifteen to twenty seats, while even Democratic pollsters like Peter Hart were admitting we would gain seats. Hart, however, told *CongressDaily* in October that we had "not used our time in September well" and that we had irritated voters just as Congress was "riding a crest of feeling."

Our take-no-risks strategy caught up with us when leadership brought a forty-pound, four-thousand-page omnibus bill to the floor we were expected to pass even though no one had read it.[6] In defense of this monstrosity, Gingrich delivered what would be the final speech of his career from the floor of the House:

> I would say for just a minute, if I might, to my friends who were asking for a "no" vote, the perfectionist caucus, "And then what would you do under our Constitution?" It is easy to get up and say vote "no," but then what would they do?

---

[6] In Congress, an omnibus bill combines several different bills into one bill. Omnibus appropriations bills merge several appropriations bills into one massive spending bill. Spending levels of specific bills within an omnibus bill are often increased and obscured. Omnibus bills are often called "vehicles" (for moving special projects) or "Christmas trees" (because members load them up with extraneous items).

The fact is, under our Constitution, 435 Members of the House, each elected by a constituency based on population, work with 100 Members of the Senate, two from each State, then we work with the President of the United States. And surely those of us who have grown up and matured in this process understand after the last 4 years that we have to work together on big issues. And if we do not work together on big issues, nothing gets done. . . .

Now, my fine friends who are perfectionists, each in their own world where they are petty dictators, could write a perfect bill. And it would not be 4,000 pages, it would be about 2,200 of their particular projects and their particular interests and their particular goodies taking care of their particular States. But that is not the way life works in a free society. In a free society we have to have give and take. . . .

So I would say to each and every Member of this House, unless they have a plan that they think can get 218 votes over here, can pass through without a filibuster in the Senate and get signed, there is no responsible vote except "yes."

This was vintage Newt Gingrich. He justified his refusal to confront Clinton on spending with a civics lecture. However, one point Gingrich made that was fair was that too many so-called fiscal conservatives who were troubled by the size of the bill did in fact ask for projects for their districts. Yet what he and others in leadership refused to acknowledge was the power of their individual choices. They liked to believe they were constrained by historic inevitabilities. We had a hard time buying this argument when this was the same Speaker who, in this same bill, had earmarked $450 million for seven C-130 transport planes to be built in his district when the Pentagon itself had requested only one plane. A liberal Democrat in the White House hardly forced Gingrich to make this decision. We also knew that he could have exercised more leverage over Clinton if he had wanted to. The Balanced Budget Act of 1997 that

Gingrich supported and Clinton signed was one lever he could have used to fight for a more fiscally responsible bill.

Conservatives were calling the bill the "omni-terrible" bill. Nobody knew what was in the bill except for the Appropriations Committee staff and the president's staff.

The Seventh Thing Congress Does Not Want You to Know about How It Does Business: Members of Congress frequently do not have an opportunity to read the bills they are voting on.

Congress routinely ignores its own rule stating that members will have at least forty-eight hours to read bills prior to debate. This rule is frequently waived by the House Rules Committee, which sets the rules of debate, assuring that members will not know what specifically is in bills before they cast their vote. The reason this is done is that the leadership knows that all sorts of shenanigans take place in the final days and hours before spending bills come to the floor for a vote. If brought into the light, many more members would think twice before casting a "yea" vote. In one instance, my staff obtained a bill that had spending changes and adjustments literally written in the margins minutes before it came to the floor for a vote. This practice of withholding information from the people's elected representatives subverts our most basic standards of openness and transparency in government.

I released a statement that the omnibus bill violated almost every principle this Congress said it stood for in 1994. I called the bill "unconscionable, un-American, and untruthful." I said that four years ago I joined a Congress that was committed to reducing the size of government. Now we were passing a "Great Society" reauthorization bill.

I added that Congress had failed to distinguish desires from emergencies.

Giving the federal government emergency spending powers is like giving a teenager an emergency credit card; it's going to be used for nonemergencies.

I was also disgusted with how easily the president misled the American people about his commitment to reserve the surplus for Social Security. We were going to spend money we didn't need to spend and, as I later told *Reader's Digest*, we were going to lie to the American public. Clinton's own plan was to use the Social Security surplus to pay for his particular pet programs. The problem was, many Republicans also wanted to spend more, even if it came from Social Security. Congress could have opposed Clinton much more fiercely and was wrong to have conceded without much of a fight.

Members on both sides of the aisle agreed the bill was a monstrosity. Even Robert Byrd (D-West Virginia), a senator with legendary ability to deliver pork to his state, took to the floor to blast the measure calling it "virtually incomprehensible."

"Do I know what's in the bill? Are you kidding?" Byrd asked. "Only God knows! If the voters really understood what we were up to they'd vote us out of office."

Still, Byrd's outrage did not stop him from being an active participant in the process he was blasting. Byrd delivered $100 million for a new prison in his state and $2 million for the National Center for Cool and Cold Water Aquaculture in Leetown, West Virginia. Perhaps not wanting to be outdone by Byrd, *Reader's Digest* reported that Senate Appropriations Committee Chairman Ted Stevens (R-Alaska) directed $15 million to the tiny airstrip in the remote fishing village of King Cove (population 700). Local government administrator Robert S. Juettner told *Reader's Digest* he was "flabbergasted." He said he was not sure how $15 million would help the airstrip that receives so few planes because of high winds.

Meanwhile, David Obey (D-Wisconsin), ranking minority member on the House Appropriations Committee, was blaming members of the Conservative Action Team, a group of House conservatives that worked together to formulate and advance policy, for the omnibus disaster. He said we had pushed the party so far to the right we couldn't bring bills to the floor. Of course, Obey said anything that was not put forward by a Democrat was "pushing the Republican party too far to the right."

I disagreed. "The discipline to put the bills on the floor should have been there," I told *CongressDaily*. "That's what leadership is all about. . . . There's going to be an accounting for the process."

Gingrich had issued orders that the disaster be treated as a victory, but some members of the GOP had the guts to vote against the omnibus. Senate Majority Whip Don Nickles (R-Oklahoma) said, "I cannot vote for this bill because it busts the budget and spends the surplus that should be used to provide tax relief for working families and strengthen Social Security. I intend to work next year to improve the appropriations process so we don't suffer through this scenario again."

The Eighth Thing Congress Does Not Want You to Know about How It Does Business: One of the more secretive and anti-democratic ways in which Congress spends is directing money in report language that only members of the committee can vote on or amend.

Before a bill is passed, the Appropriations Committee staff writes report language that can direct millions of dollars to projects that were never directly voted on by the public's elected representatives. The report language is written literally at the whim of members of the Appropriations Committee and their staff. In one instance, several million dollars were made available in a defense appropriations bill that was to be directed to specific priorities and projects by individual members of the Defense Subcommittee. Yet, even this process was not secretive enough for some. During my final term I learned that committee chairs were attempting to secretly direct funds in letters to agency heads to avoid detection from watchdog

> groups who were reviewing report language for pork. When I raised this with leadership, they didn't believe this was happening but would check. I never heard back.

Meanwhile, at the same time that we were alienating our key supporters with a massive omnibus spending bill, Republicans were aggravating the public with the increasingly partisan handling of the Clinton investigation. The turning point came when our leadership decided to release the video of Clinton's embarrassing grand jury testimony. They were convinced it would be a political coup, but I was so convinced it would backfire that I sent out a statement on September 17 urging Republicans to not get too carried away:

> I have grave concerns that the release of the president's videotaped testimony will only heighten partisan conflict at a time when Congress cannot fulfill its duty without a high level of bipartisan cooperation. As we move toward the possibility of impeachment, Congress will face extraordinary temptations to exploit the situation for political gain. I fear that, in this particular case, this temptation will prove irresistible, and we will fail an important test.
>
> Members of Congress have a solemn obligation to the Constitution and to the American people to resolve this matter as quickly, fairly, and judiciously as possible. Escalating the public relations arms race in Washington will not move us toward a proper resolution of this matter.
>
> The release of this tape serves no purpose. The public will have the opportunity to read the entire transcript of the president's testimony, and Members of Congress—the people who may vote on impeachment—will have the opportunity to view the tape. Releasing the tape to the public will poison, not encourage, healthy debate. The American people are already making their views known on the information they have, which they consider to be sufficient. My office, like most offices, has been overwhelmed with calls and letters, mostly calling for resignation or impeachment

If the American people lose confidence in this Congress's ability to conduct fair impeachment proceedings we will jeopardize the prospects of a just resolution to this matter. We have nothing to lose by erring on the side of patience and restraint, but we have a great deal to lose by being rash. Releasing this tape is unfair and unwise.

I was criticized for my statement in conservative circles, but history proved me to be correct. The tape-release incident became a critical turning point in the impeachment saga. Several commentators said the incident "lanced the boil" and relieved pressure on Clinton. The White House, of course, did a masterful job of spinning this story to its favor. Before the tape was aired, it warned the media that Clinton storms out at one point. Clinton, however, did no such thing. When Clinton came across as more composed than expected, Republicans looked even worse. The release of the tape is a classic example of how a political calculation that looks good in the short-term can create serious long-term problems. The other part of the impeachment story, of course, is that few senators, Republican or Democrat, wanted to deal with the fact that Clinton had, in fact, committed impeachable offenses. Nevertheless, our fumbling of the process gave the Senate political cover for not taking the process seriously.

REPUBLICAN PARTY CANNIBALS?

In November, these two storms—a conservative base disgusted by Congress's spending orgies and a public confused and turned off by the GOP's handling of the impeachment process—converged, forming a perfect storm that nearly obliterated the GOP majority. Rather than gain seats, our majority was reduced to a mere five seats. Several conservatives decided to give Gingrich an ultimatum: resign, or be vacated from the Speaker's chair. The Speaker has to be elected by a majority of members of the House, both Republican and Democrat. We knew that if six Republicans refused to vote for Gingrich under any circumstance, the chair would be vacated because he would surely step down rather than see Minority Leader Richard Gephardt (D-Missouri) elected Speaker. Unlike our botched attempt to remove Gingrich in 1997, this leadership election was the time and place for his departure. We also wanted to act as discreetly as possible, not so much to avoid the threat of retaliation, but to minimize the pain for Gingrich and the party and to avoid the appearance of grandstanding about his removal. One member of our group, Matt Salmon of Arizona, talked to the press on our behalf.

The day Newt Gingrich resigned, he hosted a conference call in which he bitterly blasted the "cannibals" in the Republican party for his demise. The call was somber and very sad. The vast majority of Republicans by this point, not just the conservative "cannibals," had come to see Gingrich as a tragic figure who, through his own missteps and errors in judgment, had become more of a liability than an asset, in spite of his enormous gifts. Many liberal Democrats were sad to see him go because he had become a powerful fund-raising tool for their cause. The Democrat's attacks against Gingrich were unfair and ironic because he was moving toward their position, not away from it. From the perspective of many members of the Class of 1994, it was Gingrich who had drained the lifeblood from the Republican revolution with some of his political decisions.

The same day Gingrich resigned, Steve Largent challenged Dick Armey for the post of majority leader. J. C. Watts soon followed suit, challenging John Boehner of Ohio for the post of conference chairman, the top communications position in leadership. When Steve came back to Washington after the elections, he briefly considered running for Speaker before talking to Bob Livingston, who clearly would have more support for the position. Largent mounted a spirited challenge against Armey but fell short in a three-ballot vote, 127 to 95. Before the vote Largent said, "I feel like I did the day before a big game when I was very confident in my abilities but knew we were up against a really good team." The whole race felt like a third-and-long play. Largent came in ahead of Jennifer Dunn and Denny Hastert, whom several members attempted to draft as a write-in candidate. While we were disappointed with Largent's defeat, we were delighted about Watt's victory in the race for conference chairman.

The weeks after the 1998 elections became even more bizarre when, on the day of President Clinton's impeachment, Livingston, our presumed next Speaker, resigned on the floor of the House. After Livingston resigned some of us gathered in the members' dining room to decide whether Largent should run for Speaker. But, as we sat brainstorming, we started receiving scraps of information that DeLay's whip machine had already crowned Hastert as Speaker. We knew it was a done deal at that point. Largent would not be running for Speaker. Nevertheless, when the party woke up after the perfect storm of 1998, we found renewed hope that clearing away some of the old order in leadership would re-ignite the enthusiasm of 1994. As I headed into my third and final term I, for one, was going to do everything possible to get that fire started again.

The lesson for today from the pivotal and tumultuous 1998 elections is that bad policy really is bad politics. Political calculations that appear sound in the short-term, like our take-it-safe approach in the context of Clinton's scandal, can lead to long-term political disaster. The public does not want politicians to sit on a lead, and they will punish those who try. Conversely, I believe, the public rewards true political courage.

In retrospect, one could argue that the decision to remove Gingrich and the subsequent leadership shakeup was the best thing that could have happened to the Republican party. Still, gathering six members to remove Gingrich was not something we did flippantly or with malice. It is interesting to note, nonetheless, that the real instigators of the leadership shakeup were a small group of members who were mostly self-term-limited. Of course, some other group of members may have challenged Gingrich, but the people that had the guts to put their loyalty to the Constitution ahead of their loyalty to their political party were citizen legislators.

8

THE LAST STAND

To dare: that is the whole secret of revolutions.

—ANTOINE SAINT JUST

IN JANUARY OF 1999, I began my third and final term in office. I
had seriously considered leaving Congress one term early in 1998 but
decided to stick it out another two years when I thought there was still
time to re-ignite the revolutionary spirit that swept us into Congress. I
hoped our new Speaker, Denny Hastert, would rein in Congress's out-
of-control spending. I, for one, was committed to doing everything in
my power to help the Republican party do what it vowed to do in 1994.
I considered the fiscal year 2000 appropriations bills our last, and best,
chance to re-ignite the revolution. The 1997 balanced budget agreement
was in tatters—the caps had been blown away every year—but I was
hopeful Hastert would force the appropriators and rank-and-file
members to obey the budget law we had passed.

The fiscal year 2000 appropriations season, like every appropriations
season, started with the president submitting his budget to Congress.
Most presidential budgets are considered dead on arrival by congressional appropriators—even if Congress and the president are of the same

party. However, the president's budget reflects his priorities and is a starting point for negotiations. Clinton's budget for fiscal year 2000 reflected his confidence that he would once again extract a huge sum of money from the Republican Congress.

Something that always struck me as odd about our budget process is that the president's budget rarely comes to the floor of the House for a "yea" or "nay" vote—even though his staff spends millions of taxpayer dollars putting the plan together. I thought the sheer cost of the exercise was alone reason enough for me personally to bring Clinton's budget to the floor for a vote. Presidential budgets should mean something. Another reason I wanted the House to vote on Clinton's budget was to demonstrate how the president's rhetoric and his true intentions did not match up. Clinton had declared that the "era of big government was over" and said he was committed to protecting "every penny of Social Security" from the greedy hands in Congress. Yet the nonpartisan Congressional Budget Office reported that Clinton's budget would steal $146 billion from the Social Security Trust Fund to pay for his new spending over the next five years, while increasing taxes by $52 billion. Clinton's budget would also bust the budget caps Clinton himself signed into law by $30 billion for fiscal year 2000.

When Clinton's budget came to a vote on March 25, 1999, only two members had the courage to publicly support his plan. The Senate rejected Clinton's budget by a similarly lopsided 97-2 margin. In other words, less than 1 percent of Congress publicly supported Clinton's bid to use Social Security for additional spending.

I thought the ludicrous spending levels in Clinton's budget gave our leadership a great deal of leverage. His indulgence gave us the chance to seize the high ground by producing a budget that truly stayed within the budget caps. If Clinton wanted an end-of-the-year showdown over spending, we would give it to him. By being truly consistent with our rhetoric we could give the American people a choice between an honest, fiscally responsible budget and a budget that raided Social Security to pay for bigger government. If every Republican in the House and Senate repeated that message over the next several months, I didn't see any way we could lose.

A politically shrewd Clinton, however, did not expect us to take such an intellectually honest and confrontational approach. He was confident Republican appropriators wanted to spend nearly as much as he did and would agree to a final spending total not too far short of what he wanted. After all, this is what happened during the end game (the final stages of budget negotiations) the past three years. The fact that the Republican budget resolution that eventually passed *did* respect the budget caps meant nothing to Clinton. He knew the resolution was not worth the paper it was printed on. Clinton fully expected the flimsy budget resolution to be blown apart by both parties' lust for more spending.

> *The Ninth Thing Congress Does Not Want You to Know about How It Does Business: Each year, Congress spends countless hours preparing and debating a budget resolution it has no intention of keeping.*
>
> Every year Congress passes a budget resolution that is supposed to set in stone a maximum ceiling for spending. However, Congress routinely disregards this limit. Why? The passage of the budget resolution is an opportunity for members to send press releases to their districts, congratulating themselves for their commitment to fiscal discipline. Once the actual appropriations bills move through Congress, the budget resolution is cast aside to make room for new spending and pork projects.

The budget mechanism that is a much better indication of what Congress truly intends to spend is called the 302(b) allocation process. The 302(b) process (named after a section in a budget law) is hardly a topic of dinner table conversation among American families, yet it has an enormous influence on the total amount of tax dollars government spends every year. The public's lack of understanding about this process leaves congressional appropriators largely unaccountable—a situation they readily exploit.

The Tenth Thing Congress Does Not Want You to Know about How It Does Business: Congress circumvents its own budget limits, and avoids public scrutiny, by exploiting its own arcane budget procedures.

One way Congress conceals its true spending intentions is through the 302(b) allocation process. The 302(b) process divides the total amount allotted in the budget resolution among the thirteen appropriations bills Congress must pass every year. The 302(b) process is the budget within the budget; it essentially decides how much each bill receives of the total discretionary budget—dollars Congress has the power to spend—every year. Discretionary spending covers approximately one-third of the $2 trillion annual federal budget.

Congress can use the 302(b) process to call for fictitious cuts in later bills while increasing spending in earlier bills, creating an appearance of fiscal restraint that does not exist in reality. Congress can also use this process to choose which bills might be included in an end-of-the-year omnibus bill.

Imagine you're at Thanksgiving dinner with thirteen relatives and it's time to enjoy Grandma's pumpkin pie. Some slices (appropriations bills) will be larger than others, and it's up to the pie cutter (the Appropriations Committee) to decide how big to make each piece. If the first two people in line get a large slice, it's natural for those at the end of the line to be worried about the size of their slice.

The problem in Congress is that the total size of the pie is not truly fixed—it magically expands so those at the end of the line can get a large slice as well. While pledging allegiance to the spending limit in the budget resolution, members often work behind the scenes to expand the pie. In 1999, the 302(b) allocations made it clear that Congress had no intention of respecting the budget resolution, the budget caps, or Social Security.

Under the 302(b) allocations for fiscal year 2000, appropriators planned to increase spending in the first few appropriations bills while pretending to pay for those increases with dramatic cuts in the final bills. About $10 billion was to be cut from two of the last bills: those funding health, education, and veterans programs—politically-charged areas of the budget Congress was not about to axe. This would be like telling the two hungriest relatives at the end of the line at Thanksgiving dinner that they wouldn't get their share of the pie. However, by claiming they had a plan to cut spending in those bills, appropriators could spend more on bills that would come up earlier in the process. Throughout the process they would express their intent to respect the caps, while fully expecting that the pie would expand enough, with the help of Clinton, to restore their fictitious cuts in the final bills.

As a parent, you can imagine the 302(b) process as sending your son or daughter to college for the first time with his or her own bank account. You say, "I'm going to set up an account and trust you to divide it appropriately among your budget items." He or she says, "Okay, you can trust me."

In November, you get the call you were hoping you would not get, yet expected: "Mom and Dad, I have an emergency. Send me more money. I really want to fly home for Christmas, but I'm almost broke, and my meal card doesn't have much money left on it either." You ask a few probing questions. You then deliver the standard lecture about the importance of budgeting within one's means and discover your child spent $500 on concerts, CDs, and eating out, without making adequate provisions for important end-of-semester needs. But what, as a parent, do you do? Leave your starving child stranded in their dorm room during the holidays, or bail him or her out at the last minute by expanding the total size of the budget?

Congress is sometimes like that college freshman but, unlike newly independent eighteen-year-olds, this group of forty, fifty, and sixty-year-old lawyers, business executives, and professionals knows better. Appropriators don't make unreasonable cuts in vital programs without expecting to be bailed out later. That isn't just irresponsible—it's irresponsible *and* deceptive.

Several members of the Class of 1994 were incensed by these budget tricks. Our goal was simply to do what we said we would do, obey the laws we passed, and do our best to make sure future generations were not saddled with debt and higher taxes. However, our efforts to encourage the party to do what it said it would do made us "rebels" and "trouble-makers." Our disgust with similar shenanigans in the previous year's omnibus appropriations bill prompted Newt Gingrich to go to the floor of the House and lambaste the "perfectionist caucus." What he didn't understand in 1998, and what the appropriators—and to a certain degree, leadership—didn't understand in 1999, was that we didn't expect perfection. We simply expected our team to make an honest effort to bring bills to the floor that were consistent with our principles, our promises, and existing law. In doing so, we believed we could make Clinton pay a political price for his budget dishonesty and lust for bigger government. Integrity and honesty in government were, in our view, a win-win proposition. Yet by this point both Congress and Clinton were intoxicated with surplus fever, even though no real surplus existed—nor, I believed, would it ever exist.

Our moment of truth approached as leadership and the appropriators prepared to bring up the first appropriations bill in a 302(b) process we knew was designed to sabotage the 1997 balanced budget law. Everyone who tracked the budget process knew this plan to stay within the caps was a complete farce. There was zero chance the Labor Health and Human Services (Labor HHS) bill and Veteran Affairs-Housing and Urban Development (VA-HUD) bills, which fund critical health care, education, and veteran programs, would pass with such massive cuts. If the appropriators actually wanted to maintain the caps, rather than to merely create the *appearance* of keeping the caps, they would have spread the cuts among several bills, not eviscerated two of the most popular and politically-charged bills. The 302(b) scheme virtually guaranteed another end-of-the-year budget train wreck followed by a spending free-for-all.

The first bill out of the chute was the Agriculture Appropriations Bill, which included a $250 million increase over the previous year. The appropriators knew that we knew what they were up to, but they thought they were safe in starting with the agriculture bill. They assumed that no member in their right mind would oppose the agriculture bill and dare be perceived as working against farmers. As the representative of rural northeast Oklahoma, I was certainly for farmers, but I was convinced that perpetuating this budget charade and stealing from their Social Security was not in their best interest.

The only way I knew to halt a process that was obviously going to result in another spending binge was to resort to drastic measures. Congress as a whole seemed to be in denial about the direction we were heading. So I decided that rather than letting the appropriations process end in a train wreck, I could blow up the tracks before the train ever left the station. This would, at least, give our party another chance to develop spending allotments that would honor the caps.

On May 25, 1999, I sent an email to the Appropriations Committee announcing my intention to oppose the rule for the Agriculture Appropriations Bill and, should the rule be adopted, to filibuster the bill with 115 amendments. Although it was the rules of the Senate, not the House, that permitted filibusters, I could mount a de facto filibuster by offering an unlimited number of cutting amendments. Each amendment would consume at least five minutes of debate. I estimated that I could tie up the House for at least ten hours, or two legislative days. I thought this would provide ample time to spotlight the House's budget games and encourage members to obey the law and maintain the caps. I was not aware of any time a member of the House had effectively filibustered a bill by offering amendment after amendment, but I figured it was worth a try. If we did not protect the caps here, they would never be respected later.

I planned to press my case in two ways. First, I intended to point out that any dollar Congress spent above a $10 billion cut from last year's spending levels would bust the caps. The agriculture bill spent $253 million more than last year's bill. A spending binge in the first appropriations bill was a terrible way to start the difficult process of cutting spending—highlighting the fact that the 302(b) process was wired to fail. Second, I planned to remind members that any dollar Congress spent above a $10 billion cut would not only bust the caps, it would also automatically raid the Social Security surplus.

The so-called surplus that year was the result of excess Social Security revenues, not excess general fund, or operational budget, revenues. In reality, the federal government ran an operational deficit that they covered up by borrowing excess Social Security money, funds expected to be consumed when the baby boomers retire. This was the same trick the Democrats had used since 1969 when they wanted to use Social Security money to pay for "Great Society"programs. Thirty years later Congress was stealing Social Security money to buy a phony surplus and hide their betrayal of the balanced budget agreement. Because Social Security has been one of the few sacred areas of the budget, no career politician wanted to be caught stealing from it. My goal was to shine the brightest spotlight possible on their thievery.

In a statement I released in advance of the filibuster I said, "Every dollar Congress steals from Social Security betrays the public's trust and undermines public confidence in this body. . . . I understand the plight of our farmers, but I also know that our farmers don't want career politicians to steal their Social Security money so they will have an easier time winning the next election. Congress just provided $6 billion in emergency farm relief, and we do not need additional spending now."

I explained that my amendments would target only those lower priority parts of the bill such as $5 million for wood utilization research, $1 million for global climate change research, increases for marketing subsidies, and other increases for buildings and facilities.

I also reminded my colleagues that all but two members of Congress—those who voted for Clinton's budget—voted for budget resolutions that protected 100 percent of Social Security, and that going along with this budget farce was sure to violate the commitment they had made to their constituents through those votes. Unfortunately, very few members were up to keeping their commitments—except to get reelected.

AN HONEST DEBATE

During consideration of the rules for debate on the agriculture spending bill, I began by explaining my purpose for the filibuster I was about to mount:

> Mr. Speaker, I come to the floor today to talk about where we are going in this country. This rule is symptomatic of the problem that we face. There are two Members of the House who honestly agreed that we would not be able to live within the 1997 budget agreement with the President. Those two Members voted for a budget that would actually spend Social Security money. Everybody else that is a Member of this House voted for one budget or another that would preserve 100 percent of the Social

Security surplus this year. This bill is the first among many bills that will do exactly the opposite of that. The Appropriations Subcommittee on Agriculture, Rural Development, Food and Drug Administration, and Related Agencies states that this bill is a cut. That is an untruthful statement. This bill actually increases spending around $250 million. That money will come from the Social Security surplus.

There will be those today in the debate on this bill that will deny that. They will say there is no way you can know that this money will be coming from Social Security because we have not considered the other bills. To me that is intellectually dishonest, because we realize that this is the first bill of 13 appropriations bills . . . we will consider over the next several months. We have said with the budget that passed this House that we would preserve 100 percent of the Social Security surplus. My question to my colleagues is if we really do not intend to do that, it is time for us to be very, very honest with the American people. I put my colleagues on notice that I will vote for no appropriations bill and no rule that is intended to spend the first penny of Social Security surplus. The issue really is not Social Security. The issue really is are we going to regenerate faith of the American people in this body? We cannot in good conscience for our country, for our children, and for our grandchildren do anything but be fully honest about what our intentions are. . . . For America to thrive, America to turn around . . . the same principles have to be held in this body, and that is a principle of truth.

If in fact this body intends to protect Social Security, if it intends to do that, if we are true with our votes about what we meant on the various budgets, then there is no way if this rule passes that this bill should pass.

I come from an agricultural district. My district is farmers. It is rural. Everything in my district has lots to do with the appropriations coming from the Agricultural Department. But we can do better. We must do better. Because it is not about spending Social Security money. It is not about being true to our word. It is about the foundational structure of our country and whether or not we are going to operate on the principles that we want our children to have, that we are going to reinforce the positive aspects of honor, of commitment to your word. Are we going to set an example for our children in high school that we are going to do what we said we were going to do? Are we going to be true to the founding principles of this country?

I am in my last term, and I must say that I am very much discouraged as a Member of this body [about] whether or not we have a great future when in fact we say one thing and mean another. I hope that you will check your heart, not just your mind, especially not your political mind, but that you will check your heart. Do we really mean it when we say we are going to protect Social Security, or do we not? I believe we do not mean it.

Only ten members voted against the rule including three Republicans besides me—fellow usual suspects John Hostettler of Indiana, David McIntosh of Indiana, and Mark Sanford of South Carolina.

When the actual bill came to the floor I again tried to bring the debate around to the fact that we were poised to raid the Social Security surplus to pay for new spending:

If we expect to protect Social Security money, which on both sides of the aisle, save two Members of this body, voted for budgets that said they would protect 100 percent of Social Security, then we have to bring this bill back to the level of spending last year. What that requires is about $260 million worth of trimming amendments to be able to do that. I propose to offer offsetting amendments that will bring us down to last year's level. When we are at that level, then I will stop offering amendments. Until we get to that level, I plan on continuing to offer amendments. This is not done in any precocious fashion. My intention is to help us all do what we all voted, save two Members, to do, and that is to preserve Social Security. The best way I know of doing that is the first appropriation bill, to make a first start on that.

Joe Skeen, a Republican from New Mexico and the chairman of the Agricultural Appropriations Subcommittee, had a difficult task before him. He explained that the bill was a modest increase over last year's level but was much less than the president's request. Skeen also referred to the conundrum faced by every Appropriations Subcommittee chairman. "I have heard several hundred requests for more spending by my colleagues," Skeen said on the floor, "both Republicans and Democrats. Frankly this bill does not come near to paying for all those requests. But we did the best we could, and I certainly hope that no one who wrote us asking for spending will support this amendment."

Skeen added, "It is always possible to find fault with individual items in the bill, but this bill is a cooperative effort. *I believe it reflects the kind of legislation that a majority of our Members want to see for their constituents*" (emphasis added).

Skeen and other appropriators were, by and large, good people who were caught in a cycle of ever-expanding government. The fact that Skeen and other appropriators had said "no" to spending requests more often than "yes" illustrates the extent of the bipartisan longing for spending in Congress. Skeen was correct, but he should have added that a majority of members also would not tell their constituents they were breaking their word on previous commitments when they voted for such a bill.

Marcy Kaptur (D-Ohio), the ranking minority member on the Agricultural Appropriations Subcommittee was irate that I was stalling the agriculture bill. She seemed unconcerned that the bill was putting Congress on a path to raid Social Security. If Kaptur had had her way, we would have spent significantly more in the bill. She believed the Department of Agriculture agency was already "hemorrhaging." Kaptur thought it was catastrophic that the agency had 129,500 employees in 1993 while the bill on the floor would provide funds for 107,700 positions. Her argument that 21,800 positions had been cut, however, was misleading. Kaptur knew better than anyone that the Department of

Agriculture also had more than 80,000 contract employees. Most of those so-called cuts were converted to contract employees so, in essence, there were no cuts whatsoever—a fact of which Kaptur was well aware as she spoke.

Because I believed that one agriculture employee for every 1,500 Americans was too much, and that agriculture dollars should go to farmers, not a massive federal bureaucracy, the first amendment I offered would freeze the budget for the Office of Budget and Program Analysis at the previous year's level. The bill increased funding for the office by 7 percent, or $463,000.

I doubted that any one of my amendments would pass. However, if any had a chance of passing I thought this one might; it's hard to argue that a bureaucratic office can't live without a freeze. I said from the floor, "It is my feeling that the people in my district are best represented when the money that is spent for agriculture goes to our farmers, not to the bureaucratic administration of that aid to our farmers."

Sue Myrick from North Carolina then rose to support my amendment. I was relieved that a few members from the Class of 1994 were willing to stand with me and endure the ridicule I was by this point receiving from other members. At one point, Tom Latham (R-Iowa) walked up to me on the floor of the House and said without any pretense of parliamentary diplomacy, "You're a jerk." In a lighter moment, when my dear friend Jo Ann Emerson (R-Missouri) got huffy and scowled at me while we were sitting on the floor, I looked her in the eye and stuck out my tongue. She cracked up. Myrick spoke:

> Mr. Chairman, I rise in support of the Coburn amendment because I just believe it is time to keep our promise, and this is one place we have to start. We have told the American people that we balanced the budget, and I really believe that now we need to stick to our word, because otherwise we are not being true to them. . . .

It is time to put the good of the country ahead of personal ambition and tighten our belts. Without cuts now, and this is a relatively non-controversial bill, if we cannot do it here, how in the world are we going to reduce spending in the other twelve appropriations bills?

Mr. Chairman, for years, Congress has raided Social Security and funded pork barrel spending, and I believe it needs to stop; and today is a good time to stop it. I support the Coburn amendment, and I support fiscal responsibility.

Myrick put it very well. If we couldn't make cuts here, we were never going to make cuts in later bills.

My first amendment failed by a vote of 133 to 285, but I did manage to win the support of Chairman Bill Archer (R-Texas) of the powerful Ways and Means Committee, leading moderate Mike Castle (R-Delaware), Majority Whip Tom DeLay (R-Texas), and liberal stalwart Barney Frank (D-Maine).

My second amendment attempted to reduce the increase in funding for the Office of Budget and Program Analysis in half, lowering an 8 percent increase to a 4 percent increase of $231,000.

The scene on the floor was bordering on chaos, which is what most of the real work off the floor of the House is like. I thought it was healthy that reality was displacing the false and choreographed decorum of the typical floor debate. Many of my colleagues were obviously not as pleased by this disruption. For instance, I had difficulty fulfilling Kaptur's routine request for copies of my amendment. My appropriations legislative assistant, Neil Bradley, was literally writing amendments while I was on the floor, so we had very little time to make advanced copies, which was customary.

By this point, I had taken an incredible amount of heat from members of the Republican party who were furious that I was holding up business. I brought this up during floor debate:

I recently had a Member come up and say that I was a good reason to vote against term limits because I was offering amendments to decrease the spending in Washington and that I felt we should not spend any money that comes from Social Security. Well, I would [contend] just the opposite of that. I think that is a good reason to vote for people with term limits.

The fact is that we are spending $260 million more in this appropriation bill than we did last year. The purpose of this amendment is to trim some of that. . . . It is not anything but incumbent on Members of this body to try to spend the taxpayers' money in the way that they believe is in the best interest of the country and in the best interest of the long-term security for this Nation. I want to be measured by how I left our country. I want to be measured when my grandchildren, who are now three and one, look at their income tax statements and look at their payroll slips and know that we were not responsible for raising the FICA payments from 12 percent to 25 percent. . . .

We can change what happens in Washington. We do not have to spend more money.

My second amendment failed 146 to 267, but I was just getting started. On this amendment I managed to pick up the vote of Majority Leader Dick Armey. Archer, Castle, DeLay, and Frank also voted for the amendment.

After I offered my third amendment, which was designed to eliminate an excessive 9 percent increase to the Office of the Chief Information Officer, Earl Pomeroy, a Democrat from North Dakota, rose to challenge my claim that the bill would essentially raid Social Security. Pomeroy said, "I am informed that the Subcommittee on Agriculture, Rural Development, Food and Drug Administration, and related agencies has brought this bill to the floor within their 302(b) allocation and therefore am of the opinion that it is funded by general fund revenues and has nothing to do with the Social Security funds the gentleman is speaking to."

Pomeroy was the first to rise and deliver the spin from the careerists in the House. I was eager to refute his claim. Many careerist Republicans were embarrassed by what was happening. But I thought it was positive for the public to get a glimpse into the inner working of the Congress:

> Mr. Chairman . . . that is a literal statement that in fact at the end of the day will not be true. Because by saying that this is within the 302(b) means that you also would agree that Labor HHS could be cut $4.9 billion which is also in the 302(b) for Labor HHS. I assure you that neither you nor I would vote for an appropriation bill at that level. So what I would tell the gentleman is that the 302(b)s really are not applicable to the process that we are seeing going on right now because the end game is we are going to spend Social Security money and we are not going to be below the $10 billion. I understand how that works, you understand how that works, and although technically this committee is within the 302(b) allocation, the 302(b) allocations are designed so that in the long run we will spend Social Security money.

Having already bought into the budget charade, Pomeroy could not relent and went into an even more intense mode of spin. Pomeroy said, "If the gentleman will yield further, this House passed a budget. These are the early appropriation bills coming to the floor under that budget. Much was made by the majority in consideration of the budget that it was protecting Social Security. Here we have the chairman of the Subcommittee on Agriculture bringing his bill up within the allocation he had."

I responded,

> If the gentleman would agree to vote for this bill under its 302(b) and agree to vote for the Labor HHS bill under its 302(b), I will be happy to buy his discussion of this argument. But I would portray that I will not

vote for a Labor HHS bill that is cut by $4.9 billion and I would surmise that he probably would not do that under the same argument. The fact is that the 302(b)s are not an accurate reflection of where we are going with the budget process this year. They are in terms of total dollars, and I would agree with the gentleman in terms of total dollars, but what they are is front-end-loaded and at the tail end is the very things that most people are going to need besides our farmers, those that are most dependent on us, the veterans, those that do not have housing, those that are needy in terms of Medicaid, Medicare and the supplemental things that we do to help those people, those dollars are not going to be available. So what we are going to do is we are either going to pass a bill that cuts those severely, which neither of us I would surmise would vote for, or we are going to go into a negotiation again with the President and bust the budget caps and in fact spend Social Security money. So I will stick with my argument that this bill, because it is above last year and is not below last year, will in the end ultimately spend seniors' money.

Matt Salmon, a Republican from Arizona and another "true believer" from the Class of 1994 then rose to speak in favor of my amendment:

The fact is, the gentleman from Oklahoma has recognized, I think, as many of us do, that within this total budgetary process, he sees that train wreck coming. The fact is, at the end of the day, after it is all done, if we fund government, if we fund the bureaucracies at the level that all of these proposals are coming in at, we will end up having to rob Social Security to cover up the difference. Frankly, I am not going to be a party to that.

I know the gentleman has risked a lot to put forth, what, close to 100 amendments today because he believes so strongly in the sanctity, the sacredness of making that promise to the seniors in our country, the seniors in this land. Every amendment that he offers, you are going to hear arguments why the bureaucracy that they are defending is more important than the promise and the commitment, the sacred commitment, that we made to our senior citizens. Frankly, I am going to side with the gentleman from Oklahoma on this one.

The most revealing and climactic part of the debate occurred when Bill Young of Florida, the chairman of the Appropriations Committee came to the floor:

> Mr. Chairman, I take the time first to compliment my friend and colleague from Oklahoma for speaking out so strongly for those who rely on Social Security, because I have the great privilege of representing more Social Security recipients than almost every Member of this House of Representatives, and so I really appreciate the strong work and the strong message, and I am glad that Congress recognizes that it is important to keep our commitment to those on Social Security. And to do that we did adopt a budget resolution that provided the appropriators with a certain amount of money for discretionary spending. . . .
>
> So again, Mr. Chairman, to my colleagues I would say this bill is within the section 302(b) suballocations, which are within the budget resolution number, which are within the 1997 budget caps that all of the leaders of both political parties in the House, both political parties in the Senate and the President in the White House have all said we are going to live within. This bill lives within those budget caps and within its section 302(b) suballocation, and I would hope that we could resist these amendments and get on to passing this bill, and get to conference with the other body and get the funding to the agriculture community where it is really needed.

I appreciated Young's tone but I could not agree with the substance of what he said. My response:

> Mr. Chairman, I have the utmost respect for the gentleman. I believe his heart is right. As my colleagues know, when 1997 was agreed to, we did

not have a war in Bosnia, we did not have $13 billion that we are going to spend on an action over there. Where are we going to get the money to pay for that? Where did that money come from? That money comes from Social Security.

So the debate really is, is the climate in Washington going to change? Are we going to talk to the President? Are we going to bring things down and say: We are spending this $13 billion because we got to fight a war, and there is probably going to be more where that comes from. We want to plus up defense. I agree with that, but are we going to live within those budget caps as we do that?

Young responded by saying that he did the best job he could under the budget resolution. I did not doubt his sincerity. In his honesty, Young also made a tacit admission that the outcome of budget negotiations was out of his hands. Young said, "Mr. Chairman, I would respond to the gentleman that that is a decision [whether to maintain the caps] that neither he nor I will make. That is a decision that will be made by the leadership of the House and the leadership of the Senate. Then the Congress will work its will and decide if they want to agree or disagree with the decision made by the leadership."

Young was mostly right. Leadership and, unfortunately, money-hungry rank-and-file members would decide the fate of the caps. The problem was that leadership could not control the appropriators, the appropriators could not control rank-and-file members, and members couldn't say no to special interest groups and constituents who had grown comfortable with big government. There was no way we would keep the caps unless the American people curbed their appetite for big government or unless leadership summoned the courage to explain to the public why indulging its appetite was self-destructive.

Regarding the first problem of the public's demands for spending, Barney Frank offered one of the more insightful, though sarcastic, comments of the day:

Mr. Chairman, I would just say I think the issue is in fact, and I am not as sure as the gentleman as to what the American people think, but I think the American people may be conflicted. I think they may have a preference, on the one hand, for a low level of overall spending, and on the other hand, for particular spending programs that add up to more than the overall level. That is, I think the American people may be in a position where they favor a whole that is smaller than the sum of the parts they favor, and that is what we have to grapple with.

The phenomenon Frank referred to was what historians said would be the downfall of democracies: they collapse when the people learn they can vote themselves money from the public treasury.

Regarding the second problem—a lack of strong political leadership—Steve Largent offered one of the best speeches of the day:

I will tell my colleagues that, as one Republican, I am not ashamed of what we did in the 1997 balanced budget agreement. It is the best thing we have done since I have been here, and I am proud of that and will gladly defend it to my dying day. But are we all willing to do that?

What we have really is a logjam of ideals that are coming together in this first appropriation bill. The ideals are saving Social Security and the surplus, balancing the budget, and spending more money.

I would have bet my last dollar that several years ago, had my colleagues asked me a question, if we had a logjam of those three ideals, which one would win, I would have bet my last dollar that Social Security would trump all the others. But what we are finding evident in this process is that is not true. Spending trumps everything else in this body. Big spending trumps everything, including Social Security. . . .

So what the gentleman from Oklahoma is doing, he is not railing against agriculture, he is railing against this process. Sure, my colleagues are right, this is a problem within the Republican conference; and leadership is what is needed.

We need to talk about what is the end game, not agriculture. What is the end game? Where are we going? Are we going to end up with the same disaster that we had last year, where we end up spending billions of dollars above the budget caps . . . that is the point that the gentleman from Oklahoma is trying to make.

I was always taught, say what you mean and mean what you say. . . . Mean what you say is an integrity issue. That is what this issue is about. It is an integrity issue of this party. Because if my colleagues are going to ask me to go around the country and hail the Republican party and say we are the party that is to save Social Security first, then my colleagues better mean what they say, because I want to mean what I say. If we do not mean what we say, then I am going to quit saying it. . . .

Again, the gentleman from Oklahoma has had the foresight and the courage to take the high ground and look ahead and say, if we continue down this path, we have a disaster coming in the form of VA-HUD and Labor-HHS that none of my colleagues will vote for under the 302(b) allocations. Not one of my colleagues will vote for a $4 billion cut in VA-HUD and $5 billion cut in Labor-HHS. Not one of my colleagues will vote for it, not one.

The floor debate on this day became a major national news story featured on "CNN Headline News" and the major network shows. The *Los Angeles Times* said of the filibuster:

Bold is certainly the term that applies to the efforts by Oklahoma Republican Tom A. Coburn to block the appropriations bill for the operations of the Department of Agriculture. Attacking from the conservative side of the party, Coburn has used some deft parliamentary maneuvering in his effort to cut $250 million from the legislation. It is a direct challenge to the leadership of Hastert and, worse, an embarrassment to him because Coburn has even managed to get the votes of DeLay and Majority Leader Dick Armey of Texas for some of his amendments.

On June 8, 1999, after the Memorial Day recess, Hastert gathered Republican House members and assured us he intended to respect the caps but warned us that we risked losing our majority because of obstructionist tactics. Hastert said, "Some days you have to give your leadership the benefit of the doubt and just follow. That is the difference between a majority mentality and a minority mentality."

Before the meeting I had a different view of the situation, as I explained to the *Washington Post*: "My inclination is to try to get the Republicans to do what they told the American people they will do and not spend any money above the caps and not spend one dollar of Social Security money. The strategy we're doing now will only assure there won't be a Republican majority."

Nevertheless, I agreed to end to my de facto filibuster after Hastert offered two guarantees: a $102 million cut from the agriculture spending bill (we wanted $250 million in cuts) and cuts in every other appropriations bill. As appropriations bills came to the floor, Chairman Young did, in fact, offer cutting amendments that reduced spending by more than $500 million. This was a tremendous achievement and proved that Congress could cut spending with a little hard work and political will. Still, I doubted Congress, as a whole, would keep its commitment to stay within the caps. Mark Sanford summed up the feeling of conservatives well when he told the *Washington Post* after the meeting, "I'm very sympathetic to what they're trying to do . . . but you can't help but remain skeptical. I want to be a team member, but I don't want to close my eyes to the math."

It is important to note that leadership's true antagonists were not budget hawks but members of the Appropriations Committee who loved the power that came from spending. *Roll Call* exposed this tension when it reported on June 21, 1999,

Majority Whip DeLay has directed three of his advisers to comb through every spending bill to determine if the cardinals are misleading leadership about the dearth of noncontroversial programs to slash.... "The cardinals know if they can wait the leadership and membership out, their ability to spend more increases accordingly," said a senior leadership source. "The leadership, spurred on by Coburn, is pushing these guys as hard as they can move."

Nevertheless, after all of the drama, fighting, and promises of what DeLay called a "long, hot summer," Congress was not ultimately willing to keep its commitment to the American people as it busted the budget caps by $39 billion.

I was disappointed that during this debate the press tended to focus on the story of Republican infighting instead of the real policies that mattered to the American people. The story should have been that Republicans and Democrats alike were abandoning the commitments they made to the American people in 1997. Members of both parties, it seemed, would rather show their constituents they were good representatives by sending dollars to their districts instead of keeping their promises. I would suggest that the press would have far better served our Republic by outlining the deception and demagoguery used by career politicians in both parties to enhance and secure their positions in elected office. The fact is, the press decided that the best story was not about the manipulations of Congress but the gossip of the dirty details of Republican infighting. This shows the failure of the modern-day media to serve their intended purpose.

THE STORY SHOULD HAVE BEEN THAT REPUBLICANS AND DEMOCRATS ALIKE WERE ABANDONING THE COMMITMENTS THEY MADE TO THE AMERICAN PEOPLE IN 1997.

However, this last stand, more than anything, was about reminding members and the public of our founders' vision for America.

During the debate I said,

> I would love to have been in a room with our founding fathers, because while we talk about majority-minority parties, I am sure they did not talk about majority-minority parties. They talked about doing what was best for this country regardless of what an individual's party says. . . . It should be what is best for our [country], not what is good for our party. The founding fathers never once rationalized getting in power and having control so they could stay in power. What they said was, we are going to put this Union together and we are going to make it work because the people are going to have the integrity to do what is best for their constituents and they are going to have the vision to make sure that they do not make a short-run choice that sacrifices the long-run choice.

In 1994, I thought the Republican revolution was on course to remind the public of this vision and to reinvigorate the Congress with the basic principles of limited government. Regrettably, by my final term in office, I realized a majority of Republicans would rather play politics-as-usual than restore this vision. Our failure to stay this course was a missed opportunity for the Republican party and, more important, for the entire nation.

9

THE RETURN OF
BIG GOVERNMENT

There is nothing more difficult to take in hand, more perilous to
conduct, or more uncertain in its success, than to take the lead in the
introduction of a new order of things.

—MACHIAVELLI

THE OPEN WARFARE in the Republican party that marked the fiscal
year 2000 budget process prompted leadership to make a greater
effort to restrain spending in the fiscal year 2001 appropriations bills, at
least initially. The process started on a more honest, if not altogether
fiscally responsible track, when the budget resolution made no pretense
about the party's desire to stay within the caps.

On March 24, 2000, I reluctantly voted for the fiscal year 2001
budget resolution after House leaders adopted several enforcement
mechanisms designed to discourage what had become an annual end-of-
the-year spending binge. In previous years, spending limits in House
budget resolutions were blown away during negotiations with the Senate
and the White House. The final tally for appropriations bills exceeded
the budget resolutions by an average of about $25 billion over the
previous three years.

Even as I voted for the budget resolution I released a statement criticizing the overall spending level in the budget: "The excessive spending
levels in this budget imperil the projected surpluses and the future of

Medicare. I'm afraid that our robust economy has lulled Congress into a state of complacency that will threaten our future prosperity."

What salvaged the budget resolution was a clever "Save Our Surplus" (S.O.S.) provision sponsored by freshman Representative Pat Toomey (R-Pennsylvania) prohibiting the House from spending any unanticipated surplus dollars. Toomey was a bright and creative new member who quickly learned how powerful the inertia is toward spending in Congress.

In my statement I added, "Once government is allowed to grow, it is extraordinarily difficult to shrink. The enforcement mechanisms in this budget will constrain the growth of government and will help this budget be more than just another wink and nod from Washington."

During this final appropriations cycle before my retirement I worked very hard to avoid publicly embarrassing Speaker Hastert and the rest of leadership. John Shadegg and I met with Speaker Hastert early in the appropriations cycle to try to reach a private agreement on spending. We knew that the casualness with which the caps were discarded in the previous year made it certain the House would blow the caps away again this year. Shadegg and I wanted to limit the damage as best we could. Hastert personally agreed to guarantee that at the end of the process the total cost of the appropriations bills would not exceed the caps by more than 2 percent. Hastert shook our hands as we agreed to not block appropriations bills as I had done with the Agriculture Appropriation Bill the previous year.

Later that year when *National Journal* awarded me the "black ink" award for the second year in a row for my effective role in the appropriations process, they noted that some observers believed I had taken a less public, and therefore less effective, role in the appropriations process. The reason I was not more public in my approach was because the Speaker of the House gave me his word spending would not get out of control, and I trusted him to keep his word. Unfortunately, the Speaker couldn't keep his commitment. I once again recalled my encounter with John Kasich during my first term when he took me aside to warn me to trust no one in Washington in terms of a commitment.

It wasn't due to a dishonest nature that Hastert failed to keep his word. He truly is one of the more honorable people in Congress. He just couldn't follow through with his commitment because he lacked the resolve to contain the Republican conference's uncontrollable lust for spending. Hastert shouldn't have made the promise he made to John Shadegg and me unless he was willing to wage war against the appropriators and a majority of Republican members who wanted to spend more than 2 percent above the caps. He wanted to keep his word, but, in reality, he feared he couldn't keep his position as Speaker and his word at the same time. The political costs for him would have been too high.

In hindsight, my nonconfrontational strategy was a mistake. I had no desire to publicly embarrass anyone, but I forgot that the only language career politicians understand is power and leverage. Trying to keep the behind-the-scenes battles out of the press caused me to sacrifice leverage I could have used to more aggressively rein in spending. If I could do that year over again I would have used the filibuster strategy the entire year.

During my final year in office the Cato Institute published an insightful study entitled "The Return of the Living Dead" that described how the Republican party had abandoned its zeal for smaller government. The report stated:

> The 106th Congress is well on its way to becoming the largest-spending Congress on domestic social programs since the late 1970s when Jimmy Carter sat in the Oval Office and Thomas "Tip" O'Neill was Speaker of the House.
>
> A major reason for all the new spending is the inability or unwillingness of Republicans to eliminate virtually any government program.

Many of the more than 200 programs that the Republicans pledged to eliminate in 1995 in their "Contract with America" fiscal blueprint now have fatter budgets than they had before the changing of the guard.

Overall federal expenditures for 95 of the largest "living-dead" programs have risen a total of 13 percent since 1994. Many of President Clinton's favorite programs have received substantial increases, often in excess of what the president has proposed.

Congress has violated its own "spending caps" virtually every year as well. Comparison of actual spending from 1996 to 2000 with the original expenditure targets set in 1995 reveals that excess spending over the baseline totals $187 billion. Even after the budget caps were renegotiated upward in 1997, Congress still managed to exceed the revised budget cap for the following years by a total of more than $40 billion.

From FY 1998 to 2000, nondefense domestic spending increased by more than 14 percent, after adjusting for inflation.

Our first budget adopted in 1995 called for the elimination of more than two hundred wasteful and unconstitutional government programs, including three entire cabinet agencies: the Departments of Education, Energy, and Commerce. President Reagan had targeted many of these programs for elimination, as did former U.S. Representative and White House Chief of Staff Leon Panetta (D-California)—hardly a hard-right reactionary radical—when he was the chairman of the House Budget Committee. Yet from 1995 to 2000, no agency was eliminated, and the budget for the Department of Commerce alone grew by 45 percent.

Leadership's favorite argument in defense of excessive spending was "Clinton made us do it," and the dissidents in the alleged "perfectionist caucus" made the situation worse because they refused to accept the realities of compromise in representative government. While Clinton certainly made it difficult for us to reduce the size of government, he was hardly forcing us to fund some of his favorite programs at higher levels than he had requested. Between 1998 and 2000, the Cato Institute reported that our discretionary budgets exceeded Clinton's requests by more than $30 billion.

Still, leadership and many career politicians were insinuating that the Class of 1994 was in dire need of a Civics 101 lesson because we did not understand that compromise and helping our districts was how politics worked. The tension in both camps was not due to our lack of understanding of governing and compromise but a clash of paradigms. We wanted to restore the vision of our founders while it seemed to us that career politicians had cast aside the Constitution. We also believed it was possible to keep your promises and win, and that helping our districts should not be measured by how much pork we brought home. In fact, we were confident that reducing spending and eliminating federal debt would benefit every congressional district.

We couldn't cut programs because we had long since ceded the moral high ground. In today's Congress, the political costs of cutting or eliminating virtually any government program are extremely high. Most government programs are defended by an array of lobbyists and special interest groups whose purpose in life is to make it as painful as possible for any politician to limit their funds. The Republican leadership lived under the continual fear that those groups would mobilize the Democrats to start the chants about "right-wing extremism" and "draconian cuts." The only defense against that type of spin is to speak the truth and stand on principle. When Republicans broke the caps we lost all moral authority to cut spending.

In 1995, we pledged to reduce the size of government but failed. Cato said, "Having lost that battle to Clinton during the government shutdown, the gun-shy GOP has concluded that it mustn't shoot at *anything* at all." By the end of my time in Congress, careerism had trumped fiscal conservatism. Our party had grown so afraid of losing the majority that we no longer took the bold steps the American people wanted us take. Had we taken those steps, we probably would have increased our majority.

As the Cato study said:

In October 1999 Alison Mitchell of the *New York Times* gave a realistic assessment of the budget debate in Washington: "As President Clinton and the Republican-controlled Congress begin final budget negotiations this week, the combative debate and expected vetoes obscure a fundamental reality: the two sides have only modest disagreement about how much to spend." It seems clear that there is now a bipartisan consensus in the Clinton White House and the Republican Congress that the era of big government is here to stay.

One of the mantras from the Republican conference was "What a Difference the Republican Conference Makes," a claim that, for a time, was supported by good news in the economy that had very little to do with anything the Republican Congress did. The unfortunate reality almost ten years after the Republican revolution is that, when measured by the size of government, a Republican Congress has not made a significant difference. We made very little progress in achieving the goal of shrinking the size of government.

As I prepared to leave Congress in October of 2000, I summed up my feelings for my constituents in northeast Oklahoma:

Six years after the citizens of the second district sent me to Washington to fight for a smaller and more fair and efficient government, I'm ready to come home. I'm humbled and honored to have had the opportunity to represent my constituents, but I'm disappointed that the Congress has done little to preserve and protect future opportunities for the next generation and restore to them liberties that have been lost in recent decades.

I came to Congress as one of 73 freshman Republicans determined to transform an institution that had become complacent and detached from the concerns of ordinary Americans. As I look back, the Republican majority did some good by enacting welfare reform and slowing the spending of the Clinton-Gore administration, but we failed to change Washington. Instead, Washington changed the new majority.

Congress continues to be an elite ruling class that represents not the people but itself and special interests. The fault, however, does not rest solely with the Republican leadership. I have never shied away from criticizing my own party when I thought we were abandoning our core principles for a temporary political gain, but what happened in Washington the past six years reveals more about human nature and the addictive quality of power than the failings of either party.

The real hope for the long-term viability of the American experiment, therefore, does not rest with the Republican party—or any political party for that matter. Instead, it rests with the American people who decided to turn the political world upside down in 1994. If the American people can reacquaint themselves with our founders' vision and elect representatives with true political courage—which would exclude almost all career politicians—our course can be righted.

10

REVOLUTION FROM THE BOTTOM UP

The Revolution was effected before the war commenced.
The Revolution was in the minds and hearts of the people. This
radical change in the principles, opinions, sentiments and
affections of the people was the real American Revolution.

—JOHN ADAMS

THROUGHOUT MY TIME IN CONGRESS I argued that careerists in Washington were largely responsible for stalling the Republican revolution. However, other short-term members of the Class of 1994 and I also made our fair share of mistakes. One criticism against us that was largely accurate was that we overestimated the level of support among the public for some of our more grand gestures like shutting down the government. While I am convinced that the public did want us to decrease the size of government, it did not fully support and understand our tactics.

In the years after 1994, my classmates often debated whether the public had voted *for* us or *against* the people who were currently in office. Many of my colleagues came to believe we were swept into office in what was largely a protest vote. From this basis, they defended a less risky approach to governing that would prevent us from overplaying our hand. After all, the argument went, the public was not really with us; they were only against the other guy—Clinton and the Democrats.

I thought too many members hid behind this argument as they found it increasingly comfortable to govern like the regime we had replaced. I always believed that if the 1994 elections were only a protest vote, that vote still amounted to a reform mandate. In my mind, the real argument boiled down to a question not of whether we were handed a mandate but of whether that mandate was a *reform* mandate or an *ideological* mandate. In either case, the voters wanted us to fundamentally realign government, which gave us more than enough justification to govern boldly.

Yet I do believe that what the public wanted in 1994 was not so much a Republican—or partisan—revolution, but a revival of the revolution our founders started in 1776. Had my class and my party done a better job of continually reminding the public that we were trying to realign the federal government according to the founders' vision of limited government, we would have been much more successful. The implication of John Adams's statement that the American Revolution was won before the first shot was fired is that, in a democracy, no revolutionary or sudden changes can be thrust upon an unwilling public.

> THE AMERICAN REVOLUTION OCCURRED WHEN SMALL GROUPS OF MOTIVATED CITIZENS WORKED WITH PRINCIPLED LEADERS TO CREATE A SYNERGY FOR CHANGE.

As I look back on my time in Congress, I'm convinced that change only occurs when groups of concerned citizens, which can be quite small, summon the courage to challenge the status quo. As anthropologist Margaret Mead said, "Never doubt that a small group of thoughtful, committed people can change the world. Indeed, it is the only thing that ever has." Organizations like Americans for Limited Government and the Heritage Foundation can play a critical role in educating relatively small groups of concerned citizens who can then convince the broader public of the founders' wisdom about the need for limited government.

What is also critical to the task of making the dramatic changes necessary to keep our nation strong beyond one or two generations is the coura-geous and inspired leadership of principled politicians. The American Revolution occurred when small groups of motivated citizens worked with principled leaders to create a synergy for change. Remember, a majority of colonists initially did not support breaking away from England and needed to be led, inspired, and motivated by principled leaders. Yet at the same time, leaders like Adams and Madison benefited from a citizenry in which a relatively small number of highly committed people were educating others and laying the groundwork for the revolution. Eventually, small bands of concerned citizens working in concert with principled leaders persuaded a majority of colonists to support change.

It is no coincidence, therefore, that two of the major impediments to change in our system are an apathetic and uninformed electorate and an incumbent protection system that blocks principled people from entering politics. I will outline three myths that dissuade the public from electing politicians who will truly represent their interests and govern within the confines of the Constitution.

MYTH #1: *MY REPRESENTATIVE IS GREAT; IT'S "WASHINGTON" THAT'S THE PROBLEM.*

Polls consistently show that voters tend to trust their individual repre-sentative much more than Congress as a whole. One reason for this is that members of Congress teach voters to blame the problems with government on "Washington" instead of their colleagues. For example, in 1994, the seventy-three freshman Republicans who were elected had seventy-three different opponents, but the one opponent we all had in common was "Washington." No one railed against "Washington" more ferociously than I did. I defined "Washington" as a city dominated by deceit, corruption, and the arrogance of power. Because the public held largely the same view about "Washington," we were extremely successful in 1994. We were also helped by the fact that an enemy as amorphous as "Washington" could not respond.

However, near the end of my time in Congress, as I saw more and more of my colleagues become part of "Washington" without being punished by voters back home, I realized my own rhetoric was partly misguided. The truth is, individual voters and the person who is elected to represent them are as much a part of the problem with government as "Washington." After all, those voters and their representatives *are* Washington. In our democracy, the government is a reflection of the people's wishes and desires. On one level, if the people did not want government to be a certain size and play certain roles, they would elect people who wanted to change the size and roles of government. I will deal with the question of whether voters actually have a choice later.

MYTH #2: *A GOOD REPRESENTATIVE IS ONE WHO SENDS AS MUCH MONEY AS POSSIBLE BACK TO THEIR DISTRICT.*

As I traveled throughout northeast Oklahoma, I would occasionally run into a constituent who thought I wasn't doing enough to help the second district get its "fair share" of federal funds. This was a frequent occurrence in 1998 after I turned down $15 million in highway funds. For overtaxed voters living in one of the poorest congressional districts in the country, it was natural to expect some of their money back from Washington. Yet in any congressional district, pork is hardly a good return on our tax dollars.

When I explained that the costs of spending money on new projects would be translated into higher taxes and debt for their children and grandchildren, I never had a constituent disagree with me. When I promised to fight to get their money back through tax cuts and reducing the size of a government that confiscates their money, they were even more agreeable.

The truth is, a representative who secures as much money as possible for their district also tends to be a representative who is in favor of fiscal responsibility in every district but their own. If they are unwilling to say "no" to their own constituents, how can they tell another member to say "no" to theirs? A single representative who governs this way is not a diabolical or corrupt person. Such a representative is, in most cases, an honorable person who is trying to do what he or she believes is in the best interests of his or her constituents. The problem, again, is the cumulative effect of this approach among many members. **(See "good congressman" graph on page 111.)**

Pork politics cannibalizes our institutions and economy while pretending to enrich voters back home. Pork politics is costly enough in its own right, but it also carries with it the hidden cost of perpetuating a culture of fiscal irresponsibility. When politicians fund pork projects they sacrifice the authority to seek cuts in any other program. Another factor that keeps government big and bloated is the implied threat from appropriators that members who try to cut too much of anything will not receive any money for legitimate projects in their districts.

One solution to this problem is for voters to reward politicians who refuse to play this game and to punish politicians who do play this game, even when it is done in the name of helping the district. The next time a politician sends out a press release congratulating themselves for securing funding for a road or museum in their name, tell them you would rather have your money back in the form of a tax cut or spending cut, and vote for someone else in the next election.

MYTH #3: *A GOOD REPRESENTATIVE IS ONE WITH SENIORITY.*

This myth is based, in part, on the previous myth. Members with seniority, it is assumed, have an easier time sending money back to the district, which is what every "good congressman" does. One of the most common arguments against term limits is that cutting a representative's career short would deprive Congress of members with valuable experience. In most areas of life—business, the family, church—wisdom is associated with seniority. The opposite is usually true in Congress. Seniority tends to erode sound judgment and character, not enhance it; the more experience a member attains, the less effective the majority becomes at following our founders' vision of limited government.

Several studies show how a member becomes less representative of their districts over time. The National Taxpayers Union Foundation found in a 2000 study that "[b]etween the 104th and 106th Congresses, the number of non-self-limiters whose overall agendas would cut federal spending plummeted. Whereas in the 104th Congress almost 3/4 (72%) of the Members of the Class of 1994 had agendas to cut spending, now fewer than half (48%) do." In other words, the longer a member stays in Washington, the less likely they are to cut spending and the more likely they are to walk away from an agenda that cuts spending. As NTUF President John Berthoud said, "For lawmakers, growing in office can often lead to growing Washington's waistline."

Term-limited members, on the other hand, tend to stick by their guns. NTUF's report stated, "Members first elected in 1994 who did promise to limit their tenure in office ended their first term in Congress with an agenda that would, if enacted in its entirety, cut spending by $17.3 billion annually. By the current 106th Congress, the average agenda of these would-be cutters improved, to $27.2 billion (in cuts) per year."

Berthoud said, "Critics may blame self-imposed term limits for encouraging fiscally conscientious Members of Congress to leave, but they fail to give term limits credit for developing that conscience."

Nevertheless, the problem of entrenched incumbency is not likely to be solved by term limits any time soon, which is why it is critically important for voters to take matters into their own hands and elect members who will truly represent the long-term interests of the country (i.e. noncareerists). Elect a police officer. Elect a fireman. Elect a schoolteacher. Don't elect someone who has been in politics all of his or her life.

THE INCUMBENT PROTECTION SYSTEM

When our founders established a system of checks and balances to contain the power of the three branches of government, the one check on power that undergirded the others was elections. If any branch of government seemed to be veering off course the public could always throw the bums out, so to speak. Sadly, this most important check and balance against corrupt government has been severely eroded.

While representatives typically served one or two terms in the early days of our republic, the average reelection rate for incumbents over the past ten years is more than 98 percent. In any given election cycle only a handful of incumbents lose to their challengers. In several election cycles in recent history, more incumbents died in office than lost reelection bids. An election process our founders intended to be a formidable mountain is now a speed bump on an incumbent's road to reelection.

Career politicians have gone to great lengths to expand the incumbent protection system that exists in Congress while working hard to create the impression they desire reform. Aside from the overwhelming power of simply being in office, which affords an incumbent politician tremendous opportunities for media exposure and fund-raising, career politicians have worked to limit the already dim hopes of challengers in four ways.

First, incumbents have the power to use the *frank*. "Franked" mail pieces are "informational" mailings that are almost always thinly veiled campaign pieces paid for at taxpayer expense. Every member office has a large budget to send mailings to the district to inform voters about important congressional business. On its face, this practice seems harmless enough. However, the campaign committees of both parties see the frank as a free source of campaign funds. Potential challengers simply do not have this opportunity and have to raise huge sums of money to over-come the advantage of the frank.

The second part of the incumbent protection system is our campaign finance system that limits challengers to an unreasonably low limit of $2,000 per individual contribution. Incumbents also have to abide by this limit, but the power of incumbency itself provides ample opportunities to raise sufficient funds. Challengers, on the other hand, have to scrape for every dollar in donations. Eric O'Keefe, author of *Who Rules America: The People vs. the Political Class*, believes the $2,000 limit should be raised substantially. He argues that limiting potential challengers to the $2,000 limit would be like outlawing venture capital investments in excess of $2,000. Major corporations would love it because no one could get funding to run startups and compete with them. "Rich candidates are not silenced by contribution limits," O'Keefe says, "but the non-rich candidate, the principled person who cannot be heard because he is denied the right to raise large sums of money to get his point across."

O'Keefe writes,

> Campaign finance reform, as defined by the elite media and their partners in seats of power, is a sham that uses high-sounding rhetoric in the service of incumbency protection. . . . It is ingenious, we must grant its sponsors that: they have made a skillful play to grab the banner of reform. It is as if the most ravenous wolves caucused and produced a "Sheep Protection Act."

The third aspect of the incumbent protection system is an issue close to my heart: the ridiculous and inconsistent limits placed on the income one can earn while serving in Congress.

In the early days of our Republic the political class generally believed it was inappropriate for a member to serve more than one or two terms. Today, the political class wants members to serve as long as possible so they can hold seats for their party. Congress's ethics laws make it extremely difficult for a representative to be anything but a career politician.

My plan when I came to Washington was to serve no more than three terms before returning full-time to my permanent job as a physician. However, to do this I would have to continue to practice medicine, so I could maintain my skills. Medicine isn't something you can totally walk away from for six years then come back to, so I continued to treat patients and deliver babies in my medical practice during weekends and congressional breaks while serving in Congress.

I wanted to do this in a completely above-board fashion, so I wrote a letter to the House Ethics Committee shortly after I was elected, told them what I planned to do, and asked if there would be any problems. The committee said that as long as my profit didn't exceed the $20,000 outside earned income limit that applies to all members I would be in the clear. I lived under this arrangement for three years when to my utter surprise the committee reversed its decision and said I could no longer practice medicine while serving in Congress. The committee ruled that doctors are subject to strict ethics rules that prohibit members from practicing professions that involve a "fiduciary relationship"—a position of trust such as a lawyer has for a client.

Needless to say, I was shocked and outraged by this decision. I tried to keep this battle out of the press as long as possible because I knew in my heart that if I could not continue to practice medicine I would leave Congress immediately. Yet before long, Washington was soon speculating whether I would resign over this dispute. The press attention, however, helped my case as reporters highlighted the absurdity of the Ethics Committee position. In his story on ABC's "World News Tonight," Sam Donaldson featured my battle with the committee. In his segment Donaldson asked sarcastically, "Did the parents of babies Dr. Coburn delivered choose him hoping to sway his vote?" He concluded by quoting Charles Dickens, "Sometimes the law is like a donkey, an ass."

The negative press attention and my very real resignation threat led the committee to attempt to appease me by saying I could continue to practice medicine as long as I didn't use my name in my practice. I found this position only slightly less asinine than their previous position. My staff joked that I should follow in the steps of the pop star Prince and change my name to a symbol, such as a stethoscope, and informally refer to myself as "The Doctor formerly known as Tom Coburn." In response to their proposal I said, "You guys are too modern." I just wanted to practice medicine and keep my skills sharp.

I prepared the following radio spot in response to this ruling:

This is doctor and congressman Tom Coburn. Many of you have heard that the House Ethics Committee has issued a ruling that could destroy my medical practice. I wanted to take a moment to explain this situation.

The Ethics Committee attempted to allow me to practice medicine, but they instead made a ruling that would do the opposite. Under the ruling I won't be able to see any patients because my name can't be used in association with my practice in any way. This ruling forces me to either abandon my ethical responsibility to care for my patients or my ethical responsibility as a congressman.

I want to be clear that I am not practicing medicine to make money. This is a matter of principle. If I lose this battle, America loses because all we'll have in Washington are career politicians. This ruling sends a message to thousands of potential citizen legislators in this country that you can't serve in Congress unless you're willing to trash your career and become a career politician. The Washington establishment is trying to kill the ideal of citizen legislators. . . . [O]ur founders would be outraged. . . .

In my opinion, the House ethics rules that limit the practice of professions that involve a "fiduciary relationship," or a position of trust, such as lawyers, should not be applied to family doctors.

It is ludicrous to assert that delivering a baby or treating a sore throat is influence peddling. Parents of babies I deliver don't choose me hoping to sway my vote. It's okay for me to accept a $500 campaign contribution, but I can't accept $25 for caring for a Medicare patient if my name appears on the bill. Go figure.

The $20,000 limit on outside earned income is another example of a "reform" that benefits entrenched incumbents more than any other group. Once again, under the guise of reform, Congress has told people that if they want to serve in Congress they have to trash their careers, which is fine for an aspiring career politician but terrible for the legions of qualified potential citizen legislators across America.

This episode demonstrated how difficult it is for a citizen legislator to serve in today's Congress. Our ethics rules discourage the type of representation our founders envisioned—ordinary people coming to Washington for a short time to make a difference for their country before going home and resuming their lives and careers. Many current and prospective politicians would take this path if it were open to them. During the midst of this battle I had several career politicians approach me and admit that they would have left Congress long ago had the ethics rules allowed them to maintain their previous careers.

It is also interesting to note that the ethics rules on outside income are arbitrary. Members who own farm assets are not subject to the same strict income limits as doctors even though such members might have a much clearer potential conflict of interest, especially if they serve on an Agriculture Committee.

Finally, the widespread practice of gerrymandering—drawing congressional districts to favor incumbents by including certain constituencies—is a powerful tool career politicians use, mostly at the state level, to prolong the careers of incumbents.

The incumbent protection system is blocking thousands of outstanding, qualified, and principled people from running for

Congress. Combating this system should be a top priority for any citizen group that wants to see fewer career politicians in Congress. Voters and citizen groups made tremendous strides toward dismantling this system in the 1990s with the term limits debate. It is not surprising, therefore, that something career politicians in Washington have accomplished with their reformist, anti-corruption posturing is turning the subject away from term limits—the one reform that would guarantee more turnover and genuine competition than we presently have. In today's political climate, I recognize that term limits have little chance of being enacted by a Congress that considers the policy to be a form of self-mutilation.

What gives me more hope than anything else that the incumbent protection system in Congress can be undermined is the powerful current for change in the electorate. The public does respond to courageous, principled leadership or, at least, leadership that seems interested in challenging the status quo. The unlikely election of Jesse Ventura as governor of Minnesota and the unexpected early success of Senator John McCain (R-Arizona) in the 2000 Republican presidential primaries is evidence that this trend is at work. I would submit that my own election and subsequent reelection campaigns also support this conclusion. I represented a district in which registered Democrats outnumbered registered Republicans by more than three to one. When I retired, the district went back to Democratic control and is the only district in Oklahoma that is represented by a Democrat. Had I been just another careerist Republican versus a careerist Democrat, I never would have won. It was precisely my independence and desire to challenge the status quo that enabled me to win and keep winning a seat that never would have otherwise been held by a Republican.

The fact that the public does respond to bold, principled leadership gives me tremendous encouragement that the system can be improved. With only one or two cracks in the incumbent protection system, the powerful current for change in the electorate could seep in, undermine the system, and clear it away with surprising speed. No one saw the results of the 1994 elections coming until the last moment. Bigger surprises have happened in politics. It is a business in which the rule is to expect the unexpected.

11

IN SEARCH OF
STATESMEN

Cowardice asks the question, is it expedient? And vanity asks the question, is it popular? But conscience asks the question, is it right?

—MARTIN LUTHER KING JR.

WHAT SURPRISED ME MORE THAN ANYTHING ELSE in Washington was the degree to which every decision was run through a political equation. During meetings of the Republican conference it often seemed that the sole purpose for our existence was our own self-preservation. With almost every issue, the overriding question was not, "Does this policy position make sense?" but, "How will this position affect us in the next election?"

Perhaps I was naïve, but it seemed absurd to me that any human being or political party could shape and predict voter decisions in the next election to a degree of certainty that justified the time we spent obsessing about political equations. The laws of politics were not like the predictable laws of gravity; no political equation could produce a reliable result. Even President Clinton, who was considered the most astute political operator to ever serve in the White House, was astonished when his refined political calculations helped his party lose control of the Congress in 1994. Besides, our job as representatives was to pursue the interests of the public in our *current* term, not plot our path to our *next* term.

The best example of our political calculations backfiring was the 1998 elections. Most top Republican consultants and members assumed we would capitalize on Clinton's foibles and pick up several seats. As I mentioned earlier, when a few restless members suggested during a meeting of the Republican conference prior to the 1998 elections that our agenda might not be bold enough to motivate our base, Newt Gingrich responded dismissively, "Clinton has already taken care of that."

Instead of doing what was right for the country in the months leading up to the 1998 elections by respecting the budget caps and combating pork, we put our faith in the tenuous predictions of pollsters and consultants. The result was a nearly catastrophic defeat instigating a leadership shakeup, which cost Gingrich his job.

As I worked with and observed a wide variety of leaders in Congress, I noticed that those who behaved as statesman exhibited five key commitments in their lives: 1) a commitment to principles above politics; 2) an ability to compromise without abandoning principle; 3) a commitment to truth over spin; 4) a commitment to courage over cowardice; and 5) a commitment, or willingness, to give up power.

A COMMITMENT TO PRINCIPLES ABOVE POLITICS

The tension between principles and politics is a clash of paradigms in Washington. The principled member is working for the next generation. The political member is working for the next election so they can do "good things" for the next generation, but that perfect political moment is a mirage always beckoning on the horizon.

The choice between these two approaches is not an either/or proposition. Being principled does not mean a politician should rush into every crusade without analyzing the political environment any more than a general should send his troops into battle before studying the battlefield. Likewise, members who tend to be highly political can still hold principled positions. The question is, which tendency will rule over the other? Will the very useful political tactics of framing a debate and staying on message, for example, be employed to obtain a principled end, or merely used to obtain or retain power?

The daily choices politicians make between a principled or political approach determine what kind of members they will be. As Aristotle said, "We are what we repeatedly do." Unfortunately, many members of Congress govern according to what they believe will position them best in the next election. They believe that being principled is still fine and well, as long as you don't take any principled stands that could endanger your political position.

The preferable approach, I believe, is always to do what is in the best interest of the country while, at the same time, making wise political calculations about how to proceed, just as a general conducts reconnaissance before committing troops to battle. The challenge, of course, is not to allow political calculations, which always reveal risk, to cause you to abandon your principles and the will to fight for the right thing. The paralysis that afflicts most career politicians is reminiscent of the hesitancy of early Civil War northern generals to confront General Robert E. Lee's southern forces—a failure seen as one of the great blunders of the war. Still, the number of politicians on both sides who govern with true courage most of the time is larger than voters might expect, though they are a minority in a hyper-political, poll-driven Washington culture.

One member with whom I served who demonstrated real courage was Democrat Tony Hall of Ohio, currently the United States Ambassador to the United Nation's World Food Program. Hall was deeply committed to the cause of feeding the hungry and held views about the role and scope of government that differed from mine, but I never heard him utter a partisan word or engage in the shameless self-promotion that is so common in Congress. Hall's commitment to principles higher than himself and his own reelection led him to make many courageous stands. He once took an enormous political risk by going on a fast after the House eliminated the Select Committee on Hunger. Hall thought the move would end his career because he would be viewed as a nut. Hall was also a strongly pro-life Democrat. He recalls that after he made his position known, previous pro-choice supporters in his home-town would cross the street when they saw him coming. Hall's bold, but humble, stands defied the "play it safe" logic of career politicians and propelled his career, earning him the universal respect and admiration of his colleagues as well as a nomination to his current position from the Republican Bush administration.

Another Democrat I particularly enjoyed working with was John Baldacci of Maine. During my final term we co-authored a plan to allow seniors to re-import prescription drugs from Canada and Mexico. I thought John's decision to partner with me took real guts. While we debated the plan on the floor of the House, several Democrats sitting in the front row derided John for working with a "right-winger" like me. Our amendment passed by an overwhelming margin but was watered down in committee and killed by the Clinton administration. John and I worked so well together on this important issue that I was his guest at a town hall meeting where he was discussing the issue with his constituents. Some of my Republican colleagues grumbled that I was helping a Democrat in an election year, but I thought their rigid parti-sanship was harmful for the country and our party. John and I were both committed to helping seniors obtain less-expensive prescription drugs and were not terribly concerned with the political implications. What were voters on either side going to do? Punish us for attacking drug companies who were engaging in price-fixing and charging exorbitant prices for prescription drugs?

The criticism career politicians make against this approach is that trying too hard to be principled is naïve and idealistic. Plus, they say, you simply cannot win if you try too hard to be principled, and if you are not in power you cannot "do good" and pursue your principled objectives. I never accepted this argument. I believed that you could win on a policy and political front by staying true to your principles. The primary reason I won three consecutive elections with larger and larger margins of victory in a district in which Democrats outnumber Republicans three to one was because I took principled positions.

THE ART OF PRINCIPLED COMPROMISE

Another criticism that was frequently leveled at the Class of 1994 was that we refused to accept the reality of compromise as a way of life in a legislative body. We simply did not understand the "process," as defined by careerists. In one of his final acts as Speaker, Newt Gingrich derided us for being a "perfectionist caucus" of "petty dictators" who refused to accept any way but our own way.

Gingrich's tirade, however, covered over the real debate that was occurring in the Republican conference. Many in the Class of 1994 believed that after the government shutdown the Republican leadership routinely chose capitulation over compromise during budget negotiations with the White House. Every year, the bills ballooned and contained even more amounts of pork than in the previous year. This trend culminated in the ghastly 1998 omnibus bill.

The question in our minds was not whether we knew how to compromise but whether our leadership had the will to fight for the principles that had made us the majority. As our leadership became increasingly gripped with the fear of losing the majority after the shutdown scare, they refused to risk their position to fight for the principles the Republican party supposedly believed in—and on which we had all campaigned.

I believe the first step toward victory in a debate is knowing that it is okay to lose if you maintain your principles. If you lose, at least two positive things happen that make you stronger for the next round of debate. First, you can define the issue on your terms. For example, the debate on the agriculture appropriations bill in 1999 gave me an opportunity to shine a spotlight on Congress's plans to abandon the caps. By being willing to risk the scorn of my colleagues and defeat for my numerous cutting amendments, I was able to control how the issue was framed and discussed. My opponents could no longer hide behind their budget tricks as they used Social Security to pay for bigger government. While I hardly won the overall budget battle, I do believe the small group of House budget hawks of which I was a part was largely responsible for making the term "Social Security lockbox" part of our political vocabulary. After battles like my filibusters, fewer members wanted to be accused of stealing from Social Security.

Second, standing on principle even while enduring a short-term loss can enhance your credibility and demonstrate your integrity, which are vital during tense negotiations. When people know you believe what you say and will act on those beliefs, they will eventually stop asking you to compromise in ways that violate your principles. For instance, for five years I stood on the principle that we should treat HIV/AIDS like any other infectious disease instead of a civil rights issue and employ common sense prevention methods. I failed five years in a row. Then, in my final year in Congress, I won almost everything I had been fighting for, as well as the support of groups who had routinely opposed me in the past. I believe this long-fought victory came about because I never abandoned my principles and never stopped arguing my case. I was able to secure the support of some untraditional allies because I had demonstrated integrity, honesty, and an eagerness to hear ideas and concerns from all sides. It was clear to everyone involved—from my traditional pro-family conservative allies in groups like the Family Research Council to homosexual activists in groups like ACT-UP D.C. and the Log Cabin Republicans—that I meant what I said. I was a doctor who wanted to help HIV/AIDS patients and prevent new infections, and I couldn't have cared less how my position impacted my political standing.

Winning by sacrificing principles, on the other hand, shows the public that there is no difference between either party in their pursuit of power. The ultimate rationalization in Congress is that to do good tomorrow we first have to maintain control today. Yet this tomorrow never arrives. As a result, the American people lose hope that either party is working for their best interests.

One of my favorite films, *Braveheart,* includes a classic scene that captures this struggle. In this scene, Robert the Bruce, a Scottish nobleman, is despondent over betraying his friend William Wallace, who is waging a brilliant campaign against English tyranny.

Robert the Bruce:	Lands, titles, men, power . . . nothing.
Robert's father:	Nothing!
Robert the Bruce:	I have nothing. Men fight for me because if they do not, I throw them off my land and I starve their wives and children. Those men who bled the ground red at Falkirk fought for William Wallace. He fights for something I never had. And I took it from him, when I betrayed him. I saw it in his face on the battlefield and it's tearing me apart.
Robert's father:	All men betray! All lose heart.
Robert the Bruce:	I don't want to lose heart. I want to believe as he does!

Compromise is a way of life in a legislative body, but compromise does not mean you have to betray your principles and lose heart. Ultimately, the only politician I can define principled compromise for is Tom Coburn—there is no rigid formula I can use to judge the motives of others. The line that divides compromises achieved after hard-fought principled battles from compromises primarily designed to enhance a politician's chances in their election lies deep within each politician's heart, known only by that politician and God. What I do know, however, from my own experience is that the longer a politician is exposed to the corrosive nature of power the harder it is to stand on principle and the easier it is to make the deal that seems most likely to lead to electoral success.

> THE LONGER A POLITICIAN IS EXPOSED TO THE CORROSIVE NATURE OF POWER THE HARDER IT IS TO STAND ON PRINCIPLE AND THE EASIER IT IS TO MAKE THE DEAL THAT SEEMS MOST LIKELY TO LEAD TO ELECTORAL SUCCESS.

I do believe that by practicing the art of principled compromise—compromising only after a fight in which you are willing to lose your political life for a principle—you can be principled and be rewarded from both a policy and political perspective. Political compromise—compromising on the basis of positioning yourself for the next election—sometimes yields a short-term victory but tends to stop good policy and progress (in the equations of careerists, good policy = change = risk = risk avoidance). In the long-term, political compromise too often reinforces the status quo and undermines the public's trust in its elected representatives as agents of change. Change does involve risk, but courage should lead us to action, not risk avoidance.

A COMMITMENT TO TRUTH OVER SPIN

In 1995, during the height of the Democrats' demagoguery over the GOP's Medicare plan, Frank Pallone of New Jersey delivered a special order speech every night on the floor of the House claiming we were cutting Medicare when we were, in fact, increasing Medicare's budget while slowing its rate of growth. Pallone had been sent out by the Democratic leadership as a campaign tool to spread fear among seniors that the Republicans in the House were trying to cut Medicare when, in fact, we were trying to slow the rate of growth in Medicare to prevent its imminent collapse.

After one of his speeches I decided to confront him as we were walking back from the floor. "Why would you stand up there and be untruthful?" I asked. I was treating Medicare patients every weekend in my medical practice in Muskogee. I knew what impact the Medicare "debate" was having, and Pallone knew I knew. I looked my senior patients in the face every week and watched when tears would well up in their eyes because they heard we were cutting their Medicare. Pallone answered, "Coburn, you just don't understand the game." He said flatly that the Democrats' goal was to take back the House and implied that the rules of the "game" permitted them to say or do whatever was necessary to achieve that goal.

His answer was typical of incumbents desirous of power at any cost. A seventy-five-year-old widow who lived by herself and didn't have any other source of news besides the television probably believed Pallone's speeches, though there was no truth in what he was saying. According to Pallone's convoluted reasoning, what his speeches did to an elderly and sick person's peace of mind was irrelevant if it helped his party win so they could do "good things" for that person. An honest debate on Medicare, or any issue, should lead to an informed electorate, not a terrorized electorate.

While Pallone and others were distorting our position on Medicare I was continually asked at town hall meetings why Republicans wanted to cut Medicare. When I explained to audiences of seniors and their families the fact that we were increasing Medicare spending but slowing the rate of the growth in spending, people trusted my explanation and became even more resentful of those in Washington who were using scare tactics to try to score political points. I had credibility on the issue because I was a practicing physician. Other Republican members only had their word. Unfortunately, that was not always enough to convince skeptical audiences that had grown accustomed to both sides spinning the facts. The public has a hard time believing any politician today, even when a politician is speaking the truth.

The Democrats achieved short-term success in demagoging Medicare when they regained several seats in the 1996 elections. Republicans, of course, were outraged by the Democrats' spin and distortion on Medicare. However, rather than jamming a rod of truth in Clinton and the Democrats' spin machine, they adopted their tactics of trying to out-spin their opponents.

Republican spin was most prevalent in discussions about the budget and the surplus. Every budget outcome, no matter how much it violated the caps or stole money from Social Security, was spun as a great victory for America thanks to the Republican Congress.

For example, when the House violated the budget caps and approved record levels of domestic spending in the fiscal year 2000 budget, Tom DeLay (R-Texas) boasted, "The Republican party is charging into the election year after a season of overwhelming success. From education and taxes to Social Security and the military, Republicans in Congress have reformed the way government works. This year's budget will prove to be a milestone on the road to good government far into the future." DeLay tended to be one of the more fiscally responsible members of leadership, but he sometimes shared leadership's tendency to go overboard in congratulating themselves for nonexistent victories. The fiscal year 2000 budget was another budget that led to a busting of the budget caps.

The Republicans were also guilty of spinning the numbers about the surplus. From 1998 to 2000, for example, the so-called surplus actually came from the Social Security and Medicare trust funds, as well as more than a hundred other trust funds supposedly walled off from the general budget. Only in 2001 did the government finally run a genuine surplus, three years after the surplus was first announced. The hype about the surplus made it even more difficult for Congress to restrain spending. After the onset of a recession and the September 11 attacks, the much-celebrated surpluses that had once stretched "as far as the eye could see" mysteriously vanished. The Democrats claim President Bush's tax cut eroded the surplus, but the real culprit is a Congress that has refused to restrain spending and is funding activities far beyond the scope of the Constitution.

The truth that no one in either party or in the media was willing to tell was that the surplus as described by politicians in Washington did not exist in any objective reality. Again, I was one of only a handful of members, such as John Shadegg and Mark Sanford, who thought it was foolish for Republicans to try to compete with the Democrats in taking credit for a surplus that probably would never materialize because of Congress's insatiable appetite for new spending.

Another important fact neither party bothered to mention was that as we supposedly achieved a surplus, total federal debt was still rising. The press and the entire country seemed oblivious to this ongoing problem. In fact, the hoopla surrounding the surplus convinced the owners of the National Debt Clock in New York City's Times Square to announce in the spring of 2000 that they were retiring the clock.

I released a statement on May 19, 2000, urging the owners of the clock to not pull the plug:

> The national debt is still increasing, it has not decreased one dime. This year, the national debt is expected to increase by $59 billion, according to Congress's own budget office. The propaganda machine in Washington has been working overtime to convince the American people that we have a surplus when, in fact, we do not have a true surplus. It is impossible to

have a true surplus when total debt is rising. Few politicians in Washington want to admit the truth: the surplus is a lie.

To see how Congress chronically underestimates bad economic news because of Congress's tendency to spend more and more money, examine the following graph:

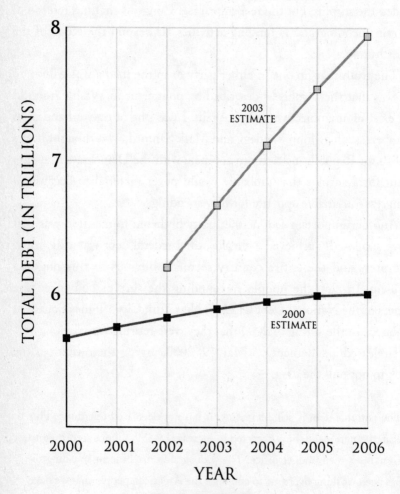

Figure 6. Debt Estimate

The graph on the preceding page shows how the Congressional Budget Office's 2000 estimate of the gross federal debt in 2006, for example, is almost $2 trillion less than the CBO's 2003 estimate of gross federal debt for that year. By the time we reach 2006, it would not be surprising to see our actual gross federal debt soar well above $8 trillion.

I explained in my statement that the so-called surplus was actually the work of politicians arbitrarily ignoring numbers they did not like while borrowing money from trust fund surpluses to mask deficits in the government's operating budget. The federal government, like most businesses, keeps two accounts. The trust fund account includes items like the Social Security Trust Fund and the Medicare Trust Fund, while the operations account covers all regular appropriations.

If I ran my medical practice like the federal government I could call a deficit year a profit year by stealing from my employee's retirement and health care funds to cover my losses. Doing so would be a federal offense, and this is precisely what the federal government is guilty of doing.

I added that for the past thirty years the federal government has been robbing the Social Security Trust Fund to mask the severity of annual deficits. What the American people did not understand, however, was that the federal government now was using the same trick to claim that we had a surplus.

That same week (May 16, 2000) I sent a letter to the *Wall Street Journal* urging them to unmask the surplus charade in Washington:

I have always appreciated the *Wall Street Journal* for its balanced, fair and thorough reporting. However, I was disappointed by your May 15 article about the Congressional Budget Office's higher than expected budget surplus estimate that reinforced several widespread misconceptions about the so-called budget surplus.

Your article reported that members of spending committees are "licking their lips" at the growing surplus. I can assure you that this is an understatement. Lusting would be a better description. Unfortunately, the problem is compounded by the false perception among the public that the surplus actually exists. Politicians have a much harder time spending money that isn't there, and the money isn't there.

The reality that few politicians in Washington want to admit is that we do not have a true surplus. In recent years, both parties have decided that it is in their interest to essentially deceive the American public about the surplus rather than risk losing a fight over the true numbers. . . . [C]onsultants on both sides of the aisle have convinced members of Congress that it is futile to discuss the real numbers because, as one consultant put it, "people's eyes will glaze over."

One number that few politicians care to repeat is that total government debt is expected to increase by $22 billion this year from roughly $5,606,100,000,000 to $5,628,300,000,000. Perhaps my math is rusty but I have yet to understand how we can have a true surplus when total debt continues to rise. . . .

Of course, nothing is so simple in Washington where a decrease in the rate of increased spending is a cut in spending. However, surplus logic is even more exotic than spending cut logic. . . .

Surplus celebrations aside, for the federal government to run a surplus this year we will need about $250 billion in after-expense funds to cover what we owe to trust funds and have a little extra to reduce total debt.

If any publication can correct these misconceptions and explain when a surplus is a surplus, it is the *Wall Street Journal*. Fairness and accuracy in the media is not merely reporting what both political parties say, but reporting whether what they say is true. In the future, I hope the *Wall Street Journal* will be the one publication that confronts the politicians in Washington who are successfully spinning a negative number into a positive number.

Unfortunately, the *Wall Street Journal* never published my letter and continued to reinforce the surplus myth until the unrestrained growth of government, a recession, and the aftermath of September 11 exposed the surplus farce perpetuated by both parties. Two of those three events—the unrestrained growth of government and a recession—were events that any person of common sense could see as a threat to rosy surplus projections, regardless of which party attained the presidency in 2000. On July 11, 2002, my concerns were vindicated when the Associated Press posted a story, "National 'Debt Clock' Restarted."

The overconfidence in the surplus estimates caused Congress to spend more money than it otherwise would have between 1998 and 2001, which harmed Congress's ability to respond to the recession and September 11. The surplus spin game is a classic example of how spin can yield short-term benefits while causing long-term damage.

The consequences of Washington's obsession with spin were obvious not only in the economy but also in the everyday real world experiences I had with patients in my medical office. As a practicing physician who had delivered more than three thousand babies, I had seen and treated almost every sexually transmitted disease imaginable. In many cases, young men and women had contracted an STD while practicing what they thought was "safe sex"—a myth created by the fusion of liberal ideology and junk science.

Study after study showed that condom use—the foundation of the safe-sex regime—did not provide adequate protection against a host of STDs. Among teenagers, encouraging condom use created a false sense of security that increased their risk of contracting an STD or becoming pregnant. Most teenagers have trouble remembering to brush their teeth at night. Why should we expect them to remember to wear a condom or take a birth control pill?

The best way to protect against STDs and unplanned pregnancy is abstinence or monogamy. As the September 10, 1997 issue of *Journal of the American Medical Association* (JAMA) reported, the factor most strongly associated with a delay in the onset of sexual activity was a pledge of abstinence. Nevertheless, few politicians in Washington were willing to question the dogma of the safe-sex establishment.

In our country we have pursued a policy of risk avoidance for young people when it comes to drugs, alcohol, tobacco, and violence. Unfortunately, we have not used that same policy when it comes to sexual activity at a very great cost both in terms of the immediate health of our children and in terms of their long-term future. We have sent our children a confused message: They have the capability of controlling their emotions and desires in every area except sexual activity. We have underestimated their capacity for self-control and have set them up to fail, compounding the problems of STDs and teen pregnancy.

Our teens deserve to hear the best medical advice, not messages that encourage them to take risks that lead to broken hearts and shattered lives. Abstinence education empowers our teens to make responsible decisions that will prepare them for true sexual fulfillment and freedom in the context of a monogamous relationship. Messages that assume our teens will make the wrong decisions will only encourage them to behave accordingly.

The problem of spin, however, is hardly confined to the Beltway. It is part of a much broader movement in our society toward the belief that truth is not absolute but varies from person to person. If there is no objective truth, the Democrats' "truth" is equal to the Republicans' "truth" and the victory goes to the side that has the better spin machine.

Our founders had a radically different view of truth. They believed in an objective, absolute truth that was not subject to the whims of individuals or political parties but existed outside human perspectives. Everyone had a right to his or her own opinion, but not everyone's opinion was right. We did not define truth for ourselves; truth defined us.

Our founders believed that truth was essential for freedom. The biblical principle "the truth will set you free" was their motto. Without truth, one person or party could control the minds of the people. The

First Amendment, which established, among other things, the freedoms of speech and the press, was drafted to prevent the American people from ever living under this kind of tyranny. The founders subscribed to the thinking of John Milton who believed that in a free and open exchange truth would always prevail over falsity. In a society in which ideas could be exchanged freely, the lies and distortions of tyrants could be exposed and discredited before they could rob people of their freedom.

In recent decades, however, the First Amendment has been perverted from a tool to protect liberty to a tool to promote license. Many of today's most outspoken defenders of the First Amendment care little for truth or the free exchange of ideas and are intent only on expanding their license to continually push the bounds of what is acceptable in society.

What politicians do not see, however, is how their own tendency to spin fosters the cultural trends they abhor. Many members of Congress, including me, have been forceful about condemning the smut and violence in the entertainment industry. Yet if the Republicans and Democrats have their own "truth" and standards, why can't Hollywood also have its own "truth" and standards? If Hollywood's "truth" says gratuitous sex and violence is acceptable and harmless, who are the Republicans or Democrats to impose their "truth" on Hollywood? Only by appealing to a higher truth than either party's spin machines can politicians have any moral authority to condemn movies or music that glorify the base and abhorrent. When politicians do attempt to appeal to a higher authority in these debates, yet persist in spinning the public on every issue from the budget to health care, the public perceives these condemnations as nothing more than political posturing or an attempt to "impose" their personal morality on each free individual's personal, relative truth.

Adlai Stevenson once warned, "Those who corrupt the public mind are just as evil as those who steal from the public purse." When politicians spin to gain a political advantage over their opponent, they corrupt the public mind. If politicians in Washington hope to regain their moral authority they must forsake the tactics of spin for truth.

Every politician needs strong communication skills. These tools, however, should be employed in service of the truth, not solely in the quest for power. Furthermore, the best communication strategy is to develop your character and your mind so that you can say the right thing at the right time without having to refer to your talking points. As Jesus Christ said in Matthew's Gospel, the mouth speaks from the overflow of the heart. If politicians would devote the time they spend making political calculations in service of their spin machines to the hard work of cultivating a wise and tempered character, the public would hang on their every word.

In his book, *Time for Truth*, which assails the culture of spin, Os Guinness quotes Joseph Goebbels, who once declared, "We do not talk to say something but to obtain a certain effect." It is chilling that today's spinmeisters have more in common with the intellectual heritage of Hitler's propaganda minister than our founders. The spin machines in Washington are not designed to illuminate the public mind to truth but to obtain a certain effect: political victory.

The culture of spin inside and outside of Washington is undermining the very foundations of our free society. As Walter Lippmann said, "There can be no liberty for a community that lacks the means by which to detect lies." In the power centers of our culture—politics, the media, business, academia, and the arts—the ability to detect lies is a lost art. The media shares a special responsibility in this area but has long since abrogated that role. Ask yourself when was the last time you read a news article that was free of bias and included a balanced presentation of the facts, whether from a conservative or liberal source.

Sadly, the press often is not concerned with reporting the truth but rather various perspectives. As a consequence, media "truth" has nothing to do with what is really happening but with what the two sides or more say and feel about what is happening. The reason the press fails to unmask untruths like the surplus charade is because they are preoccupied with covering both sides' inflated statements about the surplus. To them, whether a surplus does or does not exist is academic. The only "truth" that matters is what people are saying about it.

Even in the media's debate shows such as "Crossfire" and "Hardball," the aim often is to highlight two perspectives, not reveal the truth of an issue. For some hosts, the goal is also to produce more heat than light because conflict produces higher ratings. I agree with my conservative friends that there is a liberal bias in the media, though I believe this bias is often unconscious and a reflection of human nature—if conservatives dominated the press, the press would be conservative. However, a form of media bias that is more damaging than the liberal bias is a conflict bias. This form of bias prevents the public from knowing the truth and reality of its government's actions. A shouting match garners more readers and viewers than a revelation of truth about budget games. For example, when I held up the Agriculture Appropriations Bill in 1999 because its violation of the caps would lead to the plundering of Social Security, the stories written in the press said little about Congress's grand deception about the budget caps and instead focused on the sensational angle of a maverick Republican congressman fighting against the leadership of his own party. The press was much more interested in covering the fight than in the underlying reasons for the fight, which had much more serious implications for the public. I understand the media's need to make its stories interesting, but this need must be balanced by an ethical obligation to truly inform the public.

One thing that gives me hope that America will reject the culture of spin is the level of suspicion with which many Americans view Washington. The American people have an uncanny ability to detect spin and, if they choose, to reject the persons who revel in it. All the public needs to do is realize that their personal instincts that help them pick good friends and neighbors can also help them pick good lawmakers. The public should get to know candidates for office and use their common sense instincts to send more straight-talkers to Washington.

Aleksandr Solzhenitsyn once said, "The simple step of a courageous individual is not to take part in the lie. One word of truth outweighs the world." Truth can outweigh the culture of spin in Washington.

A COMMITMENT TO COURAGE OVER COWARDICE

A few days after my filibuster on the agriculture bill, Frank Wolf (R-Virginia) approached me on the floor and said, "You're one of the few members of Congress I've met since I've been here who has courage. I've been thinking about you, and I wanted you to have this." He handed me a speech Robert F. Kennedy delivered at the University of Capetown, South Africa, in 1966.

In Washington, there is no lack of brilliant ideas or innovative solutions to vexing problems. What is lacking is the courage to risk one's position to implement those ideas. Robert Kennedy outlined four attitudes that block a politician's desire to act with courage.

1. *The danger of futility.* The belief that there is nothing one person can do against the enormous array of the world's ills—misery and ignorance, injustice and violence, and the status quo—paralyzes many leaders. As Kennedy said, "Idealism, deeply held convictions, and high aspirations are not incompatible with practical and effective leadership. . . . Each time a man stands up for an ideal, or acts to improve the lot of others, or strikes out against injustice, he sends forth a tiny ripple of hope, and crossing each other from a million different centers of energy and daring those ripples build a current which can sweep down the mightiest walls of oppression and resistance."

2. *The danger of expediency.* The fear that one's hopes and beliefs for a

solution will not yield immediate and short-term goals prevents leaders from embarking on long-term missions that could achieve success. Kennedy said famously, "But we also know that only those who dare to fail greatly, can ever achieve greatly."

3. *The danger of timidity.* The belief that an action won't be popular has aborted many great ideas. As Kennedy said, "Few men are willing to brave the disapproval of their fellows, the censure of their colleagues, the wrath of their society. Moral courage is a rarer commodity than bravery in battle or great intelligence. Yet it is the one essential, vital quality for those who seek to change the world which yields most painfully to change."

4. *The danger of comfort.* Kennedy called this "the temptation to follow the easy and familiar path of personal ambition and financial success so grandly spread before those who have the privilege of an education."

Three specific issue areas in which there are wonderful solutions but few with the courage to implement them are government waste, Medicare, and Social Security reform. When the Republicans lost the shutdown battle of 1995/1996 the reams of information about programs that needed to be cut or downsized did not disappear. The simple problem was that no one had the guts to continue the task. As I said earlier, we were like an army that had successfully stormed the castle, but when faced with tough resistance from those defending the keep inside, we surrendered.

In the case of Social Security, every member of Congress is aware of the fact that the program is going bankrupt and faces a day of reckoning when baby boomers start retiring. The problem is simply that no one wants to do anything about it because both parties can use it as an election issue. On the Social Security battlefield each party is like a group of soldiers that has stumbled across another enemy unit only to be locked in a stalemate. Both sides want to lay down their arms and make peace, but whenever someone steps forward in a gesture of goodwill, he or she is gunned down by the opposition.

In Dick Armey's last formal address to the National Press Club in December 2002, he said that we had passed the last election cycle "in which the old Social Security demagoguery will work against Republicans. . . . Social Security as a political debate is over. Now is the time for us to start treating retirement security reform as a serious, adult, policy debate. [It's time] we respect what the American people can and do for themselves." It was commendable for Armey to issue a bold call for Social Security reform during his final press conference. I believe his interest in reforming Social Security came out of a heartfelt commitment. Yet he was helped along by a particular decision—a decision that also made it easier for me to take the stands I did in Congress: a decision to leave.

A COMMITMENT TO GIVE UP POWER

Few things infuse a member of Congress with more courage than self-imposed term limits or an imminent retirement. The issues they choose to focus on in their final months say a great deal about what are really the most important issues in the country. Dick Armey's last minute push to reform Social Security is one example.

Mark Sanford tells a fascinating story in his book, *The Trust Committed to Me,* about a conversation with a former Armey aide at a Subway sandwich shop near the Capitol:

> "I've become a huge fan of term limits," the former aide said, "because Armey and the others in leadership used to be just like you and your crew in their approach to spending. They have changed over the years."
>
> Armey's sentiment reflects the root problem in Washington: the perversity of good intentions. Nearly everyone elected has them. The problem is that before long, Congressmen and Senators think Western

civilization depends upon their being around indefinitely to act on those intentions. And that's the beginning of the end.

During my time in Congress the press often cited my term limits pledge as the reason I took so many chances in office. *Roll Call* wrote, "Of course, it's easy for Coburn to rebel. His six-year, self-imposed term limit ends in 2000, so there are no threats leadership can make to dissuade him." Mark Shields on "The NewsHour with Jim Lehrer" said, "Tom Coburn took the term limits pledge when he got elected, and he's leaving. What are you going to do? Are you going to threaten him? Are you going to tell him he's not going to have a good office next time? He's not going to be here next time!" The *Washington Post* wrote, "Coburn has little to fear in challenging the leaders because he came to Congress promising to stay no more than three terms, and his time is almost up." And columnist Debra Saunders opined, "Term limits set him free. Having kept his word on term limits, Coburn also is more inclined than House careerists to make Congress keep its word."

I would like to believe I would not have behaved differently had I not made a term limits pledge, but my own frailties and human desire for prestige and position tell me my term limits pledge did make a difference in how I approached my job in Congress.

One of the most inspiring stories in history of a politician voluntarily giving up enormous power is the story of the Roman emperor Cincinnatus. In the year 458 B.C., the Roman Empire was threatened by a sophisticated and powerful enemy, the Aequians. With the very survival of the empire at stake, the Roman senate decided to bestow upon the one man who could save Rome, the retired general Cincinnatus, the power of dictator. A delegation from the Senate was sent to summon Cincinnatus tending the fields of his small, three-acre farm. After hearing the request from Rome, a surprised Cincinnatus reportedly told his wife that if he abandoned his fields they might not have enough to live on through the winter. Yet being a great patriot, Cincinnatus retrieved his toga and assumed the title of dictator. Within sixteen days he vanquished the enemy at Rome's gate, relinquished the role of dictator, and returned to his fields.

The ease with which Cincinnatus gave up his awesome powers made him a legend. His story resonates today because the American people are longing for leaders who are not enamored with power and position but are free to govern according to their conscience.

I believe our founders expected Congress to be filled with representatives who would voluntarily give up power. The norm in our early history was for a member to serve a couple terms at most and go home. Being a congressman truly was a public service. Farmers, business people, and other citizens had to make significant sacrifices of time and money to serve in Congress.

The reason the American people have to search far and wide for statesmen today can be attributed to the condition of our institutions and the nature of man. As the power of elected office has grown, so has its power over the hearts and minds of the men and women who hold those offices. Elected office can be used to do great good, but the power it exercises over its holders is inherently corrupting. Only those rare individuals who are term-limited or who possess unshakable principles and indomitable courage manage to avoid being consumed by its trappings, which become more elaborate and difficult to avoid as the size and scope of government expands.

Tolkien's *Lord of the Rings* contains a wonderful illustration of this principle. In the story our heroes are on a quest to destroy the One Ring that gives its wearer ultimate power. The problem with the ring is that it inevitably corrupts its user. Even those with the purest of intentions to use the power of the ring to do good fall under its spell, and those who refuse to acknowledge the corrupting power of the ring become enslaved to it and are destroyed. The power of elected office in the legislature of the most powerful government in the history of the world can cast a similar spell on those within it.

Our founders understood the true nature of political power quite well, which inspired them to establish an elaborate system of checks and balances to keep this power in check.

12

FAITH: THE INTERNAL
CHECK AND BALANCE

Though one may be overpowered, two can defend themselves.
A cord of three strands is not quickly broken.

—KING SOLOMON (Ecclesiastes 4:12)

I N PREVIOUS CHAPTERS I have attempted to describe the extreme
tension that develops between the egos and core principles of people
in high elected office, and how this tension grows exponentially the
longer a person is in office. Like the hero in the *Lord of the Rings* stories,
the longer a politician bears power, the more he is controlled by that
power.

Many of the reforms I support, such as term limits, are designed to
address the *external* effects of this struggle. However, changes in institutional and political structures can at best contain, but not correct or
reform, the human tendency to abandon principle for short-term gain.
The real battle is won or lost in the hearts and minds of politicians. For
me, I believed a system of *internal* checks and balances would, more than
anything else, determine the outcome of this battle in my own life.

My faith in Jesus Christ led me to take certain positions in
Washington, such as working to protect the lives of the unborn,
promoting policies that facilitate reconciliation, and working on behalf
of the poor and the oppressed. Yet my faith was equally important in

213

determining *how* I should govern. People of faith in Washington and the U.S. are generally good about challenging politicians to think about how their faith impacts their positions on issues, but fewer talk about how faith should affect the way they govern. While my term limits pledge certainly helped give me the freedom to take political risks, it was primarily my faith, my wife, and a small band of trusted friends in Congress that gave me the security and confidence I needed to stand up for what I knew was right.

Though few members discuss the temptations of ego and prestige publicly, it is at the center of most leaders' lives. The battle between ego and principle is illustrated in a variety of ways, but it is evidenced most starkly, and tragically, by the high divorce rate in Congress. I saw colleague after colleague lose their bearings, and sometimes their wives and families, as they were unable to cope with the weight of power. A very sad example for me was to watch a great and capable congressman go through a transition in which he divorced his wife and eventually married a staff member. Having been a champion of family values, he ultimately lost his ability to influence the country in a positive way. He was a great man who campaigned on values of commitment to family and to a higher calling. Yet when the choice came, he thought he could maintain power and abandon core principles. His choice does not make him any less a person than you or I, but it is a reminder of how easily great people can be ripped from their moorings and be swept away by the currents of power, causing great pain not only to themselves but also to those close to them as well.

Another subtler illustration of ego triumphing over principles in decision-making are the rationalizations that spew out of members and their press offices. Decisions and votes that were made primarily to extend the political careers of parties and individuals were promoted as great accomplishments when, in reality, many acts promoted balanced budgets that didn't exist, mythical surpluses that would never materialize, and bold solutions that were, in the end, only ways to put off problems for yet another day. The traits in career politicians the public detests most—excessive self-promotion, irrational aversion to risk, careless deci-sion-making, and severed commitments—are produced when ego triumphs over principle.

I was hardly immune from this tension. While I was fortunate to have avoided making any catastrophic mistakes in my personal life in Congress, I did make several decisions that were a direct result of my own ego triumphing over my principles.

> THE TRAITS IN CAREER POLITICIANS THE PUBLIC DETESTS MOST ARE PRODUCED WHEN EGO TRIUMPHS OVER PRINCIPLE.

Not long after my second term began, NBC aired a movie, *Schindler's List*, which I had admired and thought was an excellent reminder of the tragedies of the Holocaust, as well as the heroism of someone who risked it all to do what was right in the face of terrible evil. My wife Carolyn and I watched the film that Sunday evening in prime time with an introduction by Steven Spielberg about the film's graphic nature and violent portrayal of injus-tices and cruelty carried out by the Germans. What was different, however, was the fact that for the first time on broadcast television, images of extreme violence and, in some places, nudity would be uncen-sored and aired at a time when many unsupervised children would be viewing without the appropriate guidance and nurturing of an adult.

I would have said then and now that, without a doubt, every human being should see *Schindler's List* and learn from its telling portrayal of brutality, hatred, and racism. However, I also feel that NBC used such a movie to break new ground, knowing that no one in his or her right mind would be critical of its broadcast because of the connotation that any critic would automatically be viewed as an anti-Semite. They forgot about one yokel from Oklahoma named Tom Coburn who blasted NBC for taking television "to an all-time low, with full-frontal nudity, violence, and profanity."

What I said, and how I said it, played directly into that strategy and created for me the worst experience in my life save the death of my father. My lack of sensitivity to the issue and my lack of insight into the still-hurting families made me seem uncaring, unsympathetic, and like someone out in left field. I became the butt of jokes and ridicule across America. Ted Koppel of ABC's "Nightline" and Jay Leno with NBC's "Tonight Show" reminded me and millions of other Americans that my comments were anything but thoughtful. In case I didn't get the point, the phones in my office rang off the hook for a week and I received a steady call from conservative luminaries like Bill Bennett who wanted to make sure I understood how foolish and insensitive my comments were.

The biggest aspect of that mistake was not in challenging the network's decision but in not carefully thinking through what I wanted to say and how to say it in a kind, compassionate, and caring manner. Perhaps my own exposure to power in Washington had impaired my judgment. In 1997, I felt like I was coming into my own as a congressman. I was into my second term, having recently defeated a career politician and former speaker of the Oklahoma House of Representatives to retain my seat. I had also started the Family Caucus, a group of members concerned about family issues, of which I was the chair. My work on these and other budget and health care issues were beginning to earn me national attention, something I had not received up until then. Because I was an expert on family issues, perhaps I assumed subconsciously that anything I said on the topic would come across as thoughtful.

My Jewish friends know without a doubt that any charge leveled against me that suggested any fault beyond carelessness and thoughtlessness was baseless, and that because of my own faith I have a deep admiration and respect for their place as God's chosen people. However, not taking the time to review a press release and contemplate its hurtful nature taught me a great lesson in communications. The whole ordeal was a profoundly humbling experience and solidified my belief that no one in Washington, especially myself, was above being compromised in some way by the trappings of power.

Another instance in which I made a decision that was hardly motivated by pure or noble motives was Congress's 1999 vote on a historic credit union bill. The bill would expand the functions of federal credit unions and give them advantages that were unavailable to commercial banks. I had worked very close with both sides and had made a commitment to support the banking industry from a standpoint of fairness. The credit unions had no federal tax obligations, paid no real estate or income taxes, and yet were expanding to compete with banks at almost every level. I had been approached about banking at a federal credit union before I ran for office solely because I did business with the federal government as a supplier of Medicare.

I walked onto the house floor, and the vote was so lopsided I failed to have the courage to vote for what I knew was right. Instead, I voted for the side that would give me the least grief after the vote. In other words, I compromised my own principles for expediency. It was a huge mistake for me personally because I was more disappointed in myself than anyone else. I succumbed to the pressure of the moment and thought in the short-term rather than according to the long-term health of the nation. Banks should not have government-subsidized competition nor should anyone else. It is unconstitutional as well as unfair. I knew those things but still voted the wrong way. When my staffer, Andrea Miles, a bright and energetic young woman from Norman, Oklahoma, who had accompanied me on the walk, asked me why I had changed my mind I failed again to admit my own cowardice. Instead, I gave her some lame excuse which she knew full well was a poor substitute for what I was trying to model for my staff.

What these failures illustrate is that no one in Washington has a monopoly on purity of purpose or motive, which, in my opinion, is all the more reason to believe that we can achieve much greater representation through term-limited members. I do believe that the term-limited member will be trapped by expediency much less often than a careerist.

Still, the kind of security and boldness I felt while in Congress often was mistaken for arrogance because I was not afraid to challenge, at any level, those whom I thought were pursuing policies that were either disloyal to the Constitution or purely political for the benefit of the party or someone's political career. One member called me "a self-promoting purist" in a profile piece *USA Today* wrote about me after I brought Congress to a halt during consideration of the agricultural spending bill. I must say that at times I took some pride in standing alone on issues. Under the guise of principled statesmanship perhaps, at times, I did enjoy a bit too much the power that came from being in the limelight after a bold stand. I believe the Scriptures teach that the motives of man are always mixed and that we are made pure, not by our own works, but by grace. While my own pride was something I always fought to keep in check, I do believe that my faith had as much or more to do with my stands as my term limits pledge.

I elaborated on this idea in a speech I prepared in the summer of 2000 for a dinner benefiting Patrick Henry College. I began by quoting Martin Luther King's speech at the National Cathedral in Washington, where he said, "Cowardice asks the question, is it expedient? And vanity asks the question, is it popular? But conscience asks the question, is it right?" I continued with Lewis's Inner Ring illustration:

> I know of no better commentary on the culture of Washington where many good people come here to do good things, only to be distracted by the quest for power and popularity. C.S. Lewis called this the quest for the Inner Ring—the place where decisions are made, the place where one is In-The-Know, the place where, once inside, one can feel delight when

those on the outside feel excluded. Lewis said that of all passions the passion for the Inner Ring is most skillful in making a man who is not yet a very bad man, do very bad things. "As long as you are governed by that desire you will never get what you want," Lewis said. "You are trying to peel an onion; if you succeed there will be nothing left. Until you conquer the fear of being an outsider, an outsider you will remain." Such a person will always be looking for another Inner Ring.

The secret of overcoming the quest for the Inner Ring is also the secret of helping conscience triumph over cowardice and vanity. The secret is in knowing that we are first citizens of the Kingdom of Heaven. If our self-esteem and security comes from something other than that we will be seekers of the Inner Ring. Throughout history those who did the most to transform their societies for the better were those who longed for a place in the next world more than a place in this world. As Lewis said, "It is since Christians have largely ceased to think of the other world that they have become so ineffective in this world. Aim at Heaven and you will get earth 'thrown in': aim at earth and you will get neither."

I was fortunate during my service in Washington to have been reminded of my true source of security by those closest to me. My greatest leveling came from my wife who has known me for greater than forty-five years and also knew me before I was a congressman, doctor, or anything else for that matter. I was also very fortunate that during my time in Congress I met each Tuesday night with a group of men, all of whom, with the exception of one, were members of the House. This time was spent pursuing friendships with one another, studying the teachings of Jesus of Nazareth, and challenging one another as we dealt with the stresses and pride that holding office entails. We took the biblical command to "walk in the light" to heart and spoke openly about the challenges of serving in public office. These weekly gatherings were the best investment of my time in Washington. Not only did I develop life-long friends (three Democrats and two Republicans), but also I grew in my ability to see the importance of pursuing unseen things like relationships and the value of service without recognition.

The transition of pursing politics ahead of principle, of course, does not happen all at once but rather surreptitiously as one starts to feel and actually believe that a different set of standards applies to those in positions of power. The transition is not a conscious decision but takes place when someone is not brought back to reality by those who care most about them. Staff members inadvertently tend to make the problem worse by convincing their congressman or senator to feel at every turn that they are superior to others.

Meeting with this small band of men helped me feel that I could stand for what I believed in even when the press, public opinion, and politicians disagreed. Experiencing the courageous and unconditional love and acceptance of six men here on earth who were also attempting to pattern their lives after the teachings of Jesus continually reminded me of the truth of what Jesus taught—that I am acceptable to him in spite of my failings, ego, and humanness.

One of the models for our time together was William Wilberforce, the British Parliamentarian who abolished slavery and reformed the morals of his nation in the nineteenth century. Wilberforce met continually with a small group of friends who shared a common faith and held one another accountable. Some in his group included Prime Minister William Pitt and John Newton, the former slave trader who wrote "Amazing Grace." Wilberforce and his group were called "the Saints," a term his colleagues in Parliament used with a mix of admiration and derision. A young man who observed Wilberforce and his colleagues said, "These wise men never endeavored to mold our uninformed opinions into any particular mold. Indeed, it was needless for them to preach to us. Their lives spoke far more plainly and convincingly than any words. We saw their patience, cheerfulness, generosity, wisdom, and activity daily before us, and we knew and felt that all this was only the natural expression of hearts given to the service of God."

One of the habits of our group that occasionally captured the attention of our colleagues was our practice of casually grabbing lunch together—both Democrats and Republicans—in the members' dining room. Members would sometimes scratch their heads to see the likes of me, Steve Largent, or Zach Wamp (R-Tennessee) sitting with Mike Doyle (D-Pennsylvania), John Baldacci (D-Maine), or Bart Stupak (D-Michigan). Our friendship did not stop us from disagreeing on major issues, such as President Clinton's impeachment, but our genuine friendship endured because it was based on a reality that transcends politics. I often found it ironic that many of my colleagues from the Class of 1994 who were accused of being partisan ideologues were far more willing to work with members from the other side of aisle than some career politicians.

The combination of these elements—my own faith, a loving wife, and a community of friends who constantly reminded me of what was real—provided a system of internal checks and balances that helped me thrive in my duties and responsibilities as a congressman. Washington can be an incredibly lonely place. The old adage among politicos is, "If you want a friend in Washington, get a dog." I am blessed and thankful to have had true friends in Congress who kept me centered and grounded in the things that matter most.

CONCLUSION

CONTINUING THE AMERICAN REVOLUTION

Politics is the art of the possible.

—OTTO VON BISMARCK

I N AN AGE WHEN A MASSIVE FEDERAL GOVERNMENT touches nearly every aspect of our daily lives as Americans, the idea that we can restore our founders' vision of limited government seems unachievable to many people. Clearly, this is a Herculan task, but it is no less possible than the initial founding of our country. Even in our increasingly complex world we can bring our government more in line with our founders' intent. I am convinced that the long-term viability of the American experiment hinges on our response to this challenge.

One blessing that has come from the tragedy of September 11 is that it has caused Americans to reflect on the vulnerability of our nation—and the concept of civilization itself—like never before. In one morning, so much that seemed secure and permanent suddenly seemed fragile. Understanding our vulnerability—without surrendering to fear—is helping our nation see our true priorities more clearly. The barbarians are not only at our gates, they have breeched our walls in dramatic fashion— and will keep coming if we do nothing to stem the tide.

While international terrorism poses a grave risk to the United States, it is not capable, by itself, of destroying our country. The greatest threat to the continuance of our government is government itself. Only by our blindly continuing our unsustainable course can terrorists succeed in their dual goal of curtailing American's freedom at home while thwarting our ability to defend freedom abroad.

America, like Rome and Athens before us, truly is tempting fate by allowing the runaway expansion of government. The potentially grave consequences of this expansion can be clearly seen in the Social Security and Medicare programs, both of which are facing a day of reckoning unless they are substantially reformed.

If Medicare and Social Security are not reformed, in approximately thirty years both programs will be running a combined debt of about $2 trillion, roughly the same amount as the annual federal budget. In forty years, the cumulative debt of those two programs will be $7 trillion. In seventy-five years, the combined debt will be a staggering $100 trillion dollars, three times the amount of money Congress has appropriated in our entire history.

The problem with Social Security and Medicare is that, as more and more Americans retire, the number of people paying taxes to support those retirees will decline. In 1950, each Social Security recipient was supported by sixteen workers. Today, each recipient is supported by only three workers. In thirty years, two workers will support each recipient. As the ratio of workers to recipients shrinks, the life spans of older Americans will increase, perhaps dramatically, depending on medical breakthroughs.

The Social Security and Medicare trustees factored in these and other variables in their 2003 report. The trustees concluded that in 2018, Social Security will not be able to make payments to seniors without a major tax increase or cut in benefits. By 2042, Social Security will be completely bankrupt when all possible trust fund assets will be exhausted.

The future of Medicare is bleaker still. In 2013 (three years earlier than last year's report), the Medicare system will not be able to keep up payments, and in 2026 (four years earlier than last year's report), the system will be completely bankrupt.[7] Also, by 2035, Medicare's share of our gross domestic product will double, forcing either massive cuts in benefits or a doubling of our Medicare tax rate. In fact, the trustees recommend an immediate increase in payroll taxes to 5.3 percent or a 5.3 percent cut in expenditures, or an immediate 42 percent cut in benefits to keep Medicare sustainable. These estimates are not the predictions of doomsday conservatives but sober conclusions reached by dispassionate economists from all sides of the political spectrum.

John C. Goodman, president of the National Center for Policy Analysis, describes the problem this way:

> Some suggest we should just ignore the problem and hope increased economic growth will make it vanish. But that's just wishful thinking. There are dark days ahead. For instance, when today's 19-year-olds become eligible for retirement in 2050, their children and grandchildren will face a payroll tax of 17 percent to pay Social Security and disability benefits, currently funded by a 12.4 percent tax. If Medicare Part A and B are included, as well as the other programs that pay medical bills for the elderly (Medicaid, the Veterans Administration, etc.) the total burden rises to 32 percent of payroll! That means almost one-third of future workers' incomes will be needed just to pay benefits to today's teenagers.

---

[7] While the trustees declare that Social Security and Medicare will not be completely bankrupt until 2042 and 2026, respectively, the public must understand that the so-called trust funds do not contain any real dollars. The trust funds are nothing more than a theoretical budgetary obligation. While technically legal, the trust funds are an Enron-style accounting gimmick. The real bankruptcy date—when Social Security and Medicare will be required to pay more in benefits than they receive in taxes—is 2013 for Medicare and 2018 for Social Security.

And that comes on top of all other services taxpayers will be expected to fund—from roads and bridges to salaries for teachers and police officers.

The public agrees that Social Security is going bankrupt, which is why polls show Americans ages eighteen to thirty-four are more confident in the existence of UFOs than their future Social Security checks.

It is important to remember that Social Security and Medicare could go bankrupt sooner than anyone expects. Future terrorist attacks or unforeseen economic downturns could hasten this impending day of reckoning. What is certain is that the federal government chronically underestimates the long-term costs of large programs. For example, as Robert B. Helms of the American Enterprise Institute points out, in 1964 the Johnson administration projected that in 1990 Medicare would cost about $12 billion in inflation adjusted dollars. The actual cost was $110 billion, almost ten times the original estimate.

One major reason I believe Americans can be persuaded to accept massive Social Security reform is that it is a terrible investment for all Americans including current retirees, future retirees, the rich, the poor, and minorities. One aspect of Social Security that is not often mentioned is how it exploits minorities, particularly African-Americans. Because the average lifespan of blacks is significantly less than non-blacks, blacks in this country receive fewer Social Security dollars while they subsidize the retirement plans of non-African-Americans who are living longer. In essence, African-Americans are pouring into the system millions of dollars that they are never going to get back. The same dynamic applies to Hispanics, who also have shorter life spans than the average American.

Another critical failure of Social Security is that the group that depends on Social Security the most—low-income elderly Americans—cannot depend on the program to meet its needs or even be a reasonable return on its investment. Older Americans have paid into Social Security for most of their working years but receive an average annual Social Security payment of only $9,078. Many of the seniors I treat in my medical practice tell me that with this payment they have to choose between buying food and medicine. The high costs of utilities, groceries, and medicine are pushing many of my senior patients into poverty, in part because Congress has lacked the courage to make Social Security truly viable.

For Social Security to be a worthwhile investment in the future many Americans will have to live far beyond their expected life spans to get back what they paid into the system. By 2010, for example, a 34-year-old worker who earns $27,000—the average salary in America—will not recover what he or she paid in Social Security taxes until their 101st birthday. The current life expectancy for that worker is only 84 years, so he or she will have to live an extra 17 years just to break even. Higher income earners will have to outlive some biblical characters to recover what they paid in Social Security taxes.

To deal with this problem Congress could either increase taxes, borrow money, or reduce benefits. Raising taxes enough to cover the future costs of Social Security would cause Social Security taxes to be doubled or tripled, according to the Citizens for a Sound Economy Foundation. The American people would revolt before paying 30 to 40 percent of their earnings into a hopelessly inefficient retirement system.

Borrowing money, and therefore increasing the federal debt, to pay for Social Security is no more desirable. The effect would also cause a doubling or tripling of payroll taxes. Every year, roughly 15 percent of our tax dollars goes toward paying off interest on the national debt. Borrowing more money to keep Social Security afloat could eventually cause 40 or 50 percent of our tax dollars to go to interest payments on the national debt. Reducing or eliminating benefits enough to shore up the program is not likely to happen. No member of Congress wants to slash Social Security benefits on their watch.

The other option open to Congress, however, is to give Americans true ownership of their retirement, an option favored by President Bush, Representative Jim DeMint (R-South Carolina), a self-term-limited citizen legislator, and championed for six years by Mark Sanford, another term-limited citizen legislator. Congress can protect the benefits of current retirees and increase benefits for future retirees by allowing individuals to invest a small portion of their Social Security taxes in individual retirement accounts. What would make this approach so effective is what Albert Einstein called the most powerful force in the universe: *compound interest.* Imagine two workers who make $24,000 a year from age twenty to sixty-five. During this time, the first worker earns 1.2 percent interest under the current Social Security system, while the second worker earns 8 percent from a small private account. The first worker ends up with about $175,000 at retirement; the second has a retirement package worth about $975,000.

If defenders of the status quo want to continue to breed fear about Social Security reform they should at least let workers put their Social Security tax dollars in a regular interest-bearing checking account, which would be a better return on their investment. If that is not an option, some workers would be better off burying their Social Security tax dollars in their backyard where it would not be squandered in an inefficient system. Americans do want to save for their retirement, and they want to choose how to invest in their retirement. What they do *not* want to do is fund the coercive and wasteful bureaucratic administration of their retirement.

It should be maddening to the American people that Congress cannot make basic and common sense reforms to Social Security and Medicare. What is lacking in Congress is not the solution to the problem but the courage to implement solutions. Because the philosophy of careerism is more potent than liberalism or conservatism, neither party wants to step out, take a political risk, and get the job done. The fear is that if one side sticks its neck out, the other side will chop it off. Both sides prefer to achieve a short-term political victory than take the necessary risks to provide financial security for our children and grandchildren.

Yet Social Security and Medicare are only two issues that represent the unsustainable trajectory of government. At all levels, the federal government has grown far beyond the founders' intent and is imperiling the long-term viability of our country. Both the Congress and voters can take a number of concrete steps to right our course.

HOW ELECTED LEADERS

CAN CORRECT OUR COURSE

1)   *Reform Social Security and Medicare today.*

For the reasons explained above, Congress must act now to reform these programs before they go bankrupt. As the trustees concluded in their 2003 report: "Though highly challenging, the financial difficulties facing Social Security and Medicare are not insurmountable. But we must take action to address them in a timely manner. The sooner they are addressed the more varied and less disruptive can be their solutions."

2)   *Reform the budget process.*

The reason why budget reform is so important was also aptly stated in President Bush's fiscal year 2002 budget:

> *A budget is not just about numbers. Far more it is about priorities—and integrity.* One great test is whether a budget legitimately supports the initiatives it purports to advance. A budget not only says a lot about how much we will spend, but it will inevitably reveal how we do the people's business. In other words, it is time to restore accountability and responsibility to Federal budget making. (emphasis added)

229

First, Congress should make the annual budget resolution binding. One of the most ridiculous exercises Congress goes through every year is passing a budget resolution it has no intention of fulfilling. The only purpose of the exercise is to give members an opportunity to send out self-aggrandizing press releases. Congress should make the budget resolutions binding or not pass them at all. The commentary in President Bush's fiscal year 2002 said it well: "The annual budget process increasingly has become a spectacle of missed deadlines, legislative pileups, cliffhanger finishes, and ill-considered last minute decisions. . . . Congressionally adopted overall spending limits have become hurdles to be cleared, not ceilings to be honored."

Second, Congress should reduce its appetite for pork. Individual members of Congress should not be given the de facto authority to direct X number of dollars to their districts. This practice is inherently wasteful and corrupting. Congress should develop a system to increase accountability in this area. For example, individual pork projects should not be lumped into much larger appropriations bills few members will vote against. Instead, individual earmarked items should be subject to a "yea" or "nay" vote on the floor of the House. The best way to limit pork is for Congress to follow the Constitution and send as much money back to the states as possible.

Third, Congress should abandon the practice of emergency spending. Using the emergency-spending provision to pay for items like the census (an event that occurs every ten years and should hardly catch Congress off-guard) and pork projects is irresponsible and dishonest. When a true emergency arises, such as the war on terrorism, Congress should pay for it by making reductions in other areas.

Fourth, Congress should end the practice of baseline budgeting. Appropriators love to figure in so-called one-time emergencies when determining the starting point of the budget every year. As I said earlier, baseline budgeting is like upping your son's or daughter's allowance every month because he or she had a one-time emergency.

Fifth, Congress should pass a budget and appropriation bills every other year. There is no reason why Congress has to revisit funding levels for every program every year. Biannual budgeting would allow Congress to appropriate money one year while conducting aggressive oversight the next year. The hard work of oversight is not being done in Congress today and is a major reason why atrocious amounts of waste in government continue to persist.

Sixth, Congress should establish a bipartisan commission composed of business leaders, ordinary citizens, our states' governors, and federal officials to scour and rethink every activity of the federal government, from top to bottom. Even as I suggest the creation of a commission, I must admit my deep distrust in such endeavors. Congress typically establishes a commission when it wants to create the appearance of working toward a solution but, in reality, does not want to take the risks necessary to force change. Commissions are often called on to do what Congress gets paid to do but will not do. Ultimately, we need more courage, not commissions. However, a commission can create the momentum for change if politicians are serious about enacting its recommendations. During the Reagan administration, a similar commission was formed called the Grace Commission, which laid out a detailed plan for reducing the size of the federal government by one-third while preserving vital services. Unfortunately, the commission's recommendations were not implemented, but it does present one blueprint for a similar effort today.

A commission could also be effective because the task of embarking on major reforms in our system will require a broader coalition. One potential ally could be our states' governors, both Republican and Democrat, who are growing increasingly resentful of the federal government's heavy-handed intrusion into the affairs of their states. Unlike the years following the Civil War, we have less of a need for a strong central government to assert national unity and cohesion. Today, tremendous advances in technology unite our geographically large and increasingly diverse nation in a way that was not possible at our founding. Advances in communications and transportation mean that people in Seattle, Washington, and Washington, D.C. are closer today than were people in Richmond, Virginia, and Washington, D.C. at our founding, or, one could even argue, during the advent of the "New Deal." Our shared popular culture, economic interdependence, and mobility are infinitely more powerful agents for cohesion than a behemoth federal government in Washington. From a political standpoint, embarking on a massive shift of power from Washington, D.C. to the states has tremendous potential. For example, if more parents can be convinced that the closing of their rural schools were, in part, caused by the fact that their scarce tax dollars were being wasted in the federal Department of Education bureaucracy, a powerful constituency for change would be formed.

3) Expand "oversight."

One of the few areas in which Congress does not spend enough money is *oversight*. Congress has a basic duty to make sure the intentions and laws that Congress has passed are carried out in a proper manner and eventually amended if unintended consequences are discovered. In essence, Congress needs to spend less time legislating and more time making sure those laws on the books are truly working for the American people.

If Congress fully devoted itself to making sure our tax dollars were being spent wisely during the year it was not budgeting, government would be vastly more efficient and sensible. We would see reined-in bureaucrats, greater efficiency in federal programs, and a return of the freedoms that have been lost by bureaucratic fiat. Unfortunately, what we mostly see instead is time and dollars wasted on hearings that have good political appeal but little impact on the lives of the average American. When one considers the encroachment on our freedoms in the last thirty-five years that came about simply by legislative bodies who, with good intentions, passed laws but failed to recognize their imperfections at the time, the need for oversight is clear.

I can recall only one example during my entire time in Congress when oversight was used effectively. In the Senate hearings on the Internal Revenue Service, the abuses were clearly displayed, and effective corrective legislation was passed and signed into law. I would make the claim that there are just as many abuses in every other branch of the federal government. In most cases these abuses are not malicious, yet they are still having disastrous consequences on freedom, innovation, efficiency, and productivity.

Congress often likes to pass off the hard work of oversight to the agencies they are supposed to be overseeing. The people conducting oversight in their own agencies may be honest and well intentioned, but one has to recognize human nature. In the club of bureaucrats the first rule is to always do what will most protect one's job. This principle of self-preservation leads to no risk-taking and a great deal of inefficiency and waste. I saw this problem extensively in the U.S. Army Corps of Engineers, the Environmental Protection Agency, the Department of Agriculture, the U.S. Fish and Wildlife Service, the Food and Drug Administration, and the National Institute of Health.

> UNFORTUNATELY, WHAT WE MOSTLY SEE INSTEAD IS TIME AND DOLLARS WASTED ON HEARINGS THAT HAVE GOOD POLITICAL APPEAL BUT LITTLE IMPACT ON THE LIVES OF THE AVERAGE AMERICAN.

If Congress took its oversight job more seriously, it would uncover an enormous amount of waste and build tremendous momentum and support among voters for streamlining and reforming government. In the very narrow slice of the federal budget pie I studied most extensively—how we spend money to combat HIV/AIDS—I found a staggering amount of waste and mismanagement. If more Americans knew that their tax dollars that were intended to combat HIV/AIDS were instead being used for activities like flirting classes and bowling nights, they would demand reform.

The one area of the federal budget that is the proverbial elephant in the room when it comes to waste is the defense budget. I fully support spending whatever is necessary to support our soldiers who are risking their lives in defense of our freedom, but I do not support the wasteful expenditure of defense funds that could be redirected, for example, to higher wages for our overworked and underpaid military personnel, many of whom are on food stamps.

In the scheme of what was the more than $300 billion annual defense budget, I barely scratched the surface, but what I found was shocking. First, I learned that the Department of Defense's accounting systems are so atrocious they cannot even be audited. The Department of Defense (DOD) possesses the most sophisticated technology developed in human history, but its accounting system is in the dark ages. In many offices within DOD, pen and paper are still the preferred tools of record keeping.

During testimony before the House Government Reform Committee in the spring of 2000, the head of the United States General Accounting Office (GAO), David M. Walker, sounded an alarm about the financial systems weaknesses within DOD. He said the federal government and, in particular, DOD is "unable to determine the full extent of improper payments—estimated to total billions of dollars annually—and therefore cannot develop effective strategies to reduce them." Walker also noted that DOD is "not yet able to produce auditable financial statements on a consistent basis."

The precise scope of the waste within DOD has never been determined because its books cannot be audited, but the evidence suggests a staggering total. DOD holds the largest share of government assets, which total nearly $500 billion. Of those assets, a majority cannot be supported by proper financial records. DOD's inability to keep track of its assets has, quite naturally, led to an enormous amount of waste. A 1998 GAO report said, "DOD reported an estimated $22 billion in disbursements that it was unable to match with corresponding obligations." In other words, DOD spent $22 billion on something but doesn't know what that something is.

If the waste within DOD totals only 10 percent of its more than $300 billion annual budget, it would amount to three-fourths of our annual education budget, three times the amount spent to combat the spread of HIV/AIDS every year, and would exceed the combined budgets of the Departments of Commerce *and* Energy.

DOD's accounting failures not only increase the likelihood of misuse of funds, they pose a serious and immediate risk to our national security. The GAO has reported that poor financial and computer systems increase the risk of theft of valuable assets and places "sensitive information at risk of inappropriate disclosure."

DOD's success in addressing the Y2K computer problem shows that it is capable of overcoming its severe management and accounting problems in a short period of time when pressed by Congress. Unfortunately, most members of Congress prefer to pretend this elephant is not really in the room. It is also difficult for congressional leaders to lead a fight against waste when they are diverting millions of defense dollars into their districts for special projects the Pentagon didn't ask for and doesn't need. In 1999, House and Senate leaders authorized $8.9 billion for defense pork. The worst offenders were former Senate Majority Leader Trent Lott, who added $375 million for a non-requested Amphibious Assault Ship to be built in his state, and House Minority Leader Richard Gephardt, who ordered DOD to build five non-requested F-15s in his district at a cost of $275 million.

If members of Congress would only tackle problems like waste within DOD, they could easily cut the federal discretionary budget by 10 percent, or $70 billion, which is far more than the gross national products of many countries. Yet these potential savings cannot be seen by most career politicians because they never take the time to look, nor do they have the experience to know that things can be done cheaper. Most members of Congress have very little private sector experience. If you have never had to be responsible for raising the money to fund an organization, you will never be responsible in the way you spend the money of that organization. The people who best fit into this category are long-term career politicians.

A factor that compounds this problem is that senior members are also reluctant to ask tough questions for fear of burning bridges. It is human nature to want to be liked, and there is something innate in holding political office that exacerbates our natural "people-pleaser" tendencies. I noticed this emotion in myself many times as I dealt with both sides of the aisle in many of the controversies during my time in Washington. This tendency in the area of oversight results in a reticence to attack forthrightly many of the problems within the bureaucracies in Washington and throughout the country. I know this to be true because of the many times when I was aggressively trying to accomplish legislative goals. Those who fully supported my goals also expressed their desire not to alienate through rigorous and pointed inquiry the very people over whom they were supposed to exercise oversight responsibility.

The sheer lack of time and money that are directed to oversight—combined with members' natural reluctance to exercise tough oversight—is a formula for absolute inefficiency in government.

4)   *Dismantle the Incumbent Protection System.*

In Chapter Ten, I suggested several reforms that would make it easier for qualified, nonpolitical people to enter the political process. Some of those reforms included reforming ethics laws to let people serve in Congress while keeping their real jobs, ending the practice of franked mail, enacting term limits, lifting campaign contribution limits that favor incumbents, and ending gerrymandering. All of these reforms would give challengers a much better chance of defeating entrenched incumbents.

5)   *Reduce the National Debt.*

The politics and the economics of the national debt and deficits are two of the most confusing aspects of our modern government. In Congress, there are essentially two camps that hold diametrically opposed views: one camp believes that the national debt is no big deal, while the other side says it will cause the collapse of our economy. The reality is somewhere in between. Economists and politicians from all sides should acknowledge that it is not healthy that one out of every seven tax dollars annually goes to pay off interest on the national debt and that those tax dollars would be much more productive if they could circulate in the economy.

Some debt in everyday life is not the end of the world (college loans, mortgages, and so forth), but the current debt level in Washington is out of control. The way to decrease debt in real life *and* in Washington is to reduce spending. Tax cuts do not make the deficit worse, although many in Washington like to blame the Reagan and Bush tax cuts for today's deficits. The Reagan deficits were caused not by tax cuts but by his determination to spend the Soviet Union into oblivion—which was worth the cost—as well as the combined refusal of Republicans and Democrats in the 1980s to reduce spending. David Stockman, Reagan's director of the Office of Management of Budget wrote a landmark book in 1986 called *The Triumph of Politics: Why the Reagan Revolution Failed* that supported the position of those who thought Reagan's economic policies were simply disastrous. In reality, the Reagan and Bush tax cuts have caused our economy to grow at a rate such that the percent of economy devoted to debt payments has not increased. Still, the real solution is not tax cuts but spending cuts. Stockman's book was half right; the triumph of careerism prevented both parties from taking serious steps to curtail spending—just like today.

BREACH OF TRUST

RESPONSIBILITIES OF CONCERNED CITIZENS

When visitors stand at the center of the rotunda in the U.S. Capitol, they are standing not only at the geographic center of our nation's capital but also at a point artfully designed to prompt them to reflect on events and values central to our republic. When one looks directly overhead high on the ceiling in the rotunda, for example, there is a mural with George Washington surrounded by figures from Greek and Roman mythology that symbolize the enormous influence both of those civilizations had on our founders.

One of the core principles passed down to us from those civilizations is that a concerned and active citizenry that practices the "civic virtues" is essential to a healthy democracy. The beauty of America is that our nation is still, despite all our institutional problems, what we the people make of it. "We the People" is still the most potent force in American politics, but only when the people act.

One of the reasons it seems Washington represents itself and special interests ahead of the real long-term interests of the people is that we the people let this happen. The reality is that no improvements in our system will be made unless the public demands those changes and holds politicians accountable if they break their promises.

The bright spot in this state of affairs is that a relatively small number of people who do get engaged in politics and policy can dramatically alter the course of our nation. Throughout history, pivotal changes that have saved civilization almost always have been initiated by small groups of highly motivated people. In the Middle Ages, a handful of forward-thinking Irish monks saved western civilization from the barbarian hordes by preserving countless works from antiquity. In the eighteenth century, a handful of American colonists decided to break away from the British Empire, creating the United States. In the same century, a small number of visionary politicians and abolitionist activists in the British

Empire ended the slave trade. In the twentieth century, a small group of visionary and decisive leaders in the Truman administration created the Marshall Plan that saved European civilization.

The Marshall Plan is a terrific example of political leaders mobilizing public opinion around a bold course of action. In his June 5, 1947 Harvard University speech outlining what would become the Marshall Plan, General Marshall explained,

> The world situation is very serious. That must be apparent to all intelligent people. I think one difficulty is that the problem is one of such enormous complexity that the very mass of facts presented to the public by press and radio make it exceedingly difficult for the man in the street to reach a clear appraisement of the situation. . . . Our policy is directed not against any country or doctrine but against hunger, poverty, desperation and chaos. . . . An essential part of any successful action on the part of the United States is an understanding on the part of the people of America of the character of the problem and the remedies to be applied. Political passion and prejudice should have no part. With foresight, and a willingness on the part of our people to face up to the vast responsibility which history has clearly placed upon our country, the difficulties I have outlined can and will be overcome.

Today, we need a Marshall Plan mentality not only on the front on which we are engaged overseas but also on the front on which we are engaged at home where dramatic steps are required to hold back the chaos and dependency that has arisen from an out-of-control federal government. When it comes to the government, we do not need more aid; we need a massive shift in aid from the federal government back to the states. Throughout our history, American citizens and their leaders have risen to the challenges that have threatened civilization, and we can do so today with a proper understanding of the dangers before us, both foreign *and* domestic.

A major part of this effort will require the public to embrace civic virtues, like personal responsibility, that reject the notion that we are entitled to free money from the public treasury. Our dependency on programs like Social Security and Medicare are literally undermining the foundations of our nation. We can find a way to care for those who are truly needy and give citizens more control over their health care and retirement dollars without bankrupting our nation.

As we practice these civic virtues we must also remember that, in America, the civic virtues are built on a more permanent foundation—a belief that our Creator has endowed us with certain unalienable rights. A recent book by Michael Novak, *On Two Wings*, argues that in order for America to soar, both wings have to be working together, according to their design. One wing represents our institutions and system of government—which I have examined in this book. The other wing represents a people guided by a belief in God and a desire to live by certain transcendent moral and spiritual truths. One such truth is that every human being created by a loving God has infinite and intrinsic worth. This belief forms the foundation of our entire concept of freedom and rights. As Thomas Jefferson asked, "Can the liberties of a nation be secure when we have removed from them the conviction that these liberties are a gift from God?"

Concerned citizens emboldened by these civic virtues can take four concrete steps to address the long-term challenges facing our country.

1) *Vote.*

The suggestion to vote sounds simplistic, and it is. But it is astonishing that in these perilous times only 50 percent of Americans vote. The issues before us do affect every single American, and it is unfortunate that so many Americans let their voting neighbors make their decisions for them. Even though our system of government is deeply dysfunctional, it is still the best in the world, and every vote does count. Anyone who wonders if his or her vote matters needs only to remember the 2000 presidential election fiasco in Florida.

While the Florida example is a dramatic illustration of the power of one vote, many elections today are decided by a few thousand votes. We live in a time when special interest groups and campaign consultants have mastered the art of campaigning for the margins. In any election the percentage of votes that is considered up for grabs is very small, sometimes as low as 2 to 4 percent. When 2 or 3 percent of the public decides to vote, the impact on elections can be enormous. For example, in the 2002 elections, Republican efforts to get out the vote resulted in as much as a 3 percent increase in voter turnout, which was more than enough to make the difference in many close races. Voters should not underestimate the impact they can have when they simply vote, but voters must be willing to vote out of office those incumbents who have grown too comfortable in Washington.

2) *Volunteer.*

For most of America's history up until the "New Deal," families, churches, and private charitable groups did most of the work of caring for the needs of the most vulnerable members of society. Marvin Olasky's book, *The Tragedy of American Compassion,* does an excellent job of explaining how the government slowly took over many of the service activities families and communities used to do for themselves. The devolution of federal power I am advocating must be accompanied by a much more determined effort on the part of the church, in particular, to care for the needs of the poor and the elderly. In some cases, church elders might want to divert part of their construction budgets to caring for the spiritual and material needs of the poor in their communities. The best way to drive out the culture of dependency and entitlement in America is through the relentless love and compassion of caring neighbors.

3) *Express your concerns.*

From my experience in Washington, I noticed that the individual constituent almost always underestimated the power of his or her lone voice. In reality, constituents who take the time to write or call their elected representatives have a tremendous impact. Many members who receive a handful of calls or letters advocating a course of action will respond and either introduce or cosponsor a bill relating to the concern raised by those few constituents. In this case, the problem of careerism can be used to the public's advantage. Even though incumbents' seats are usually safe, they are terrified of losing their next election and will take notice when constituents call or write. Another way to have an impact is through letters to the editor, which have a tremendous impact on the psyche of elected officials. Politicians assume that for every person who writes a letter there are at least one hundred people who feel the same way. From my own experience, reading two or three letters that made the same point was a sign to me that there was a deep sentiment among the public on that particular issue, and I paid attention. Being that one person in a hundred who expresses a position does make a difference in our system.

4) *Mobilize other concerned citizens.*

One of the best ways to encourage more voting, volunteerism, and the voicing of concerns is to create working groups of citizens dedicated to those tasks. Grassroots organizations are a powerful force in American politics today, and many models exist for their successful implementation. I am admittedly biased in favor of a new organization, Americans for Limited Government (of which I am the chair), that will provide a way for citizens to be engaged on these issues from their local communities.

One person in our system can still make a difference, and our future depends on each individual's willingness to act. As Edmund Burke warned, "The only thing necessary for the triumph of evil is for good men to do nothing."

CHOOSE FREEDOM, THEN SECURITY

In 1994, I was part of a band of freshman representatives who believed our country was failing to heed the warnings of history and that we were approaching the end of the cycle other great nations have gone through: from bondage to spiritual faith, from spiritual faith to liberty, from liberty to abundance, from abundance to selfishness, from selfishness to complacency, from complacency to apathy, from apathy to dependency, from dependency back to bondage.

Looking back through this cycle, I believe our nation was founded by men and women of deep faith who laid a foundation that allowed Americans to enjoy a level of liberty and prosperity that has been unparalleled in human history. In this age of abundance our strength has been impressive at home and abroad. We stood up to the cruelty and aggression of Nazi Germany, rolled back the tyranny of the Soviet Empire in Europe, and sowed the seeds of freedom and democratic reform around the world. Yet now, even as our preeminent position as the world's lone superpower has never seemed more secure, our eventual collapse seems ever more likely.

Through the "New Deal" programs of the 1930s and the "Great Society" programs of the 1960s, the public has learned that it can vote money for itself from the treasury. The career politicians who cater to these desires are nearly intractable. They happily preside over a federal government that is out of control and self-indulgent even when controlled by the party that advertises itself as the more conservative alternative. As a consequence, two of the largest government programs, Social Security and Medicare, are headed toward a collapse even a prosperous economy cannot prevent. And, despite a serious effort to reform welfare in 1995, the public continues to look to the federal government to provide services private individuals, places of worship, and local communities used to take care of themselves.

If America fails to heed these warnings and allows the federal government to grow unabated, the result may not be a sudden crashing down or collapse, but a gradual contraction of our power at home and around the world will inevitably occur. With our relative power diminished we will find it increasingly difficult to compete with regimes and nations who do not share our basic values. As a result, America and the rest of the world will be less secure, less prosperous, and more susceptible to tyranny.

America is still free, but it will cease to be free if we look to the government as the primary provider of our material security. America is at the height of its power and is the sole superpower in the world. We must leverage that power to defend liberty abroad and at home. In doing so, we can avoid the fate of other great civilizations that were crushed under the weight of their own excesses. America has strayed from the vision of our founders, but if we recapture their spirit of courage and sacrifice and heed the warnings of history, America's best days can be not buried in our past, but spread out before us.

EPILOGUE

SINCE LEAVING CONGRESS I have been actively engaged full-time back in my medical practice delivering babies (216 last year) and enjoying the privilege afforded me to have the responsibility of caring for entire families—from great-grandmothers to their great-grandbabies, and everything in between.

I find myself more and more distraught over the decline in the quality of medicine, which, in my mind, can be attributed to the federal government's many mandates and bureaucratic hurdles, as well as an overly litigious society that is suffocating my profession. We have Sovietized our health care system and taken efficiency out of care. Our command and control system is also removing the art from medicine, forcing physicians to spend their time and energy navigating a Byzantine system of rules and reimbursement schemes that do not reflect market realities. When it comes to health care, I could go on and on—perhaps for another book.

Returning to what I call the "real world" outside the Beltway has caused me to lower my expectations about what government can and cannot do. Going from the modest avenues of Muskogee, Oklahoma, to the corridors of power in Washington and back again has made me realize more than ever that the future of our country is shaped more by the daily lives and choices of ordinary citizens than by politicians in Washington. I'd like to believe I never lost this perspective while serving in Congress, yet I can recall times when my perceived importance probably eclipsed my actual importance. Returning home has made me see that much of the political maneuvering and machinations in Congress is little more than sport, a never-ending game of one-upping a political opponent. Don't get me wrong; what Congress decides matters very much, but the public ultimately decides the course of our nation.

The task of convincing the Congress to tackle issues that are so critical to our future—the impending bankruptcy of Social Security and Medicare, the unsustainable expansion of government and the federal debt, and the necessary aggressive and intelligent execution of the war on terror—ultimately is the responsibility of the public. While the focus of this book has been on the culture of Washington and how that culture is blocking much-needed reform, the culture of America is the ultimate battleground. As commentator Cal Thomas says, "The government is a reflection of the heart of the people." Thomas also says we will never see trickle-down morality from Washington, but that bubble-up morality among the people can affect Washington.

The principles that form our foundation as a country, including the principle of limited government, are only effective if we adhere to a certain minimum, basic set of moral values that include valuing human life, hard work, honesty, and integrity. It is very easy for us to see the problems in front of us and desire a time past in which crime, laziness, drug addiction, dependency, and debauchery were far less common. Yet longing for the past does nothing to change the future. What you and I do today and tomorrow will have the most impact on our future. A large part of what that means is that if we see things as less than what we would desire, we must put forth the hard effort to change things.

EPILOGUE

This may sound trite, but we can only do that one day at a time with one person at a time. There are no quick fixes in life, especially not in the affairs of nations. The model that I believe is most likely to effect such a change is the leadership model demonstrated by Jesus of Nazareth. He led by serving, putting others first, loving first and chiding last. One of my favorite quotes that capture this idea comes from Martin Luther King Jr. who said that if you want to change someone, you must love them and they must *know* you love them.

One way I have chosen to stay involved in public service is by serving on several boards. I am the co-chairman of the President's Advisory Council on HIV/AIDS. I believe historians will no doubt wonder with amazement at how the wealthiest nation in the world could allow an epidemic of death and illness to run uncontrolled while spending billions of taxpayer dollars in failed political strategies that ignored proven public health strategies. The number of new HIV cases continues to rise in spite of the massive ($16 billion) federal expenditures each year. This tragedy, I believe, is another result of careerists responding to political pressure rather than taking the courageous and proper steps of limiting an epidemic through sound and proven public health policies.

I am also embarking on a new path with a group known as Americans for Limited Government, which I hope will be a catalyst for encouraging nonpoliticians to get involved in the political process and for educating and informing the electorate about ways they can affect the political process.

I still believe that term limits is the best way to ensure that the next generation, not the next election, is the central concern in our elected bodies. Unfortunately, the needs of the next generation too often take a back seat to the careers of those inside the system. Yet it is still my belief that when you and I are well informed concerning the real voting records and positions of politicians, we can and will change how things work in Washington and in our state capitols.

EPILOGUE

The Political Climate from 2001 to 2003: Same Song, Different Verse

One of the most significant developments since I left Congress has been the collapse of large corporations like Enron. It was amusing to me to hear so many friends and associates express shock and outrage about the deceit at Enron when the same patterns of deceit have been present in Congress, and other parts of our society, for decades. In the Enron debacle, executives literally created a reality for themselves, not unlike Congress and President Clinton's surplus celebration that ultimately collapsed. What was unique about the Enron situation was that a philosophy of relativism that is usually relegated to matters of lifestyle choices—"Don't impose your values on me"—was applied to accounting—"Don't impose your numbers on me." Yet the spin and deceit at Enron was the same kind of spin and deceit Republicans and Democrats in Congress have practiced for years.

Another common denominator between the Enron fiasco and the state of our government is one of the few but important flaws in the modern American dream. We are so focused on material advancement and the accumulation of wealth that we fail to see the pitfalls of that approach. In the Enron case, many bright professional people failed to see how their accounting lies were destined to unravel. In the case of our government, too many politicians and citizens fail to see how our desire for government to take care of us is driving our nation toward an economic cliff.

The 2002 elections were heralded as a great victory for Republicans, and, to a certain degree, this is true. Still, in the 2002 elections the debates deciding elections rarely had anything to do with pertinent long-term issues facing our country. When was the last time you heard someone forcefully say that his or her main objective in Congress was to reform Social Security, reform Medicare, and spend less of our money so that our children will have a more secure future? And while few of the important issues for our security were debated, well-endowed incumbents won 99 percent of all races.

EPILOGUE

What you hear from Republicans is a litany of ideas, some of which are good but, nevertheless, largely ignore the real and pressing long-term problems we face. Tax cuts, prescription drug coverage for Medicare patients, and homeland security are all important issues, but they mean little to voters when not placed in the context of a coherent vision that is about something bigger than Republican victories.

Too often what we hear from the left is rhetoric about division. Today many liberals seek to obtain power by castigating those who call for reform. Those who want to pull our country out of an economic nosedive are portrayed as wanting to shatter a system of services that is stable and sustainable only in the minds of liberals and Western European socialists. Reformers are cast as uncaring, mean-spirited tax cutters for only the rich and extremists for desiring a more moral and decent society. Demagoguery indeed is the preferred tool for careerists with a microphone. Encouraging the public to form opinions about the future of our country based on half-truths, fear, and distrust is manipulation masquerading as leadership. As my father taught me, "A half-truth is a whole lie."

The polarization in our country at this present time is a great risk to our country, greater than even the threat of terrorism. This polarization, and the paralysis it causes in the face of challenges, is enhanced daily by a lazy press, self-serving and hyperpartisan career politicians, and those of us who tend to believe what we are told coming from the television or news media without digging any deeper.

I was continually amazed in Washington at the number of stories the press did not tell. Congress today is full of fascinating stories and manipulations waiting to be told by the curious reporter. There are some exceptions in the press. Reporters like Alan Fram with the Associated Press, Mike Grunwald with the *Washington Post*, Tom Shine, Dean Norland with ABC News, and Julie Rovner with National Public Radio were some of the reporters with whom I worked who seemed genuinely interested in getting to the heart of the matter and did more than write sophomoric "he said, she said" stories that pit one side against another without informing the reader of the broader context.

The fact that we have a political system run by careerists who use divisiveness to advance themselves and their party is a sign that we have very few statesmen left in Washington. The disunity caused by the insincere manipulations of both political parties in Washington is putting our very freedoms at risk because they have created a climate that makes common sense discussion and principled compromise almost impossible.

Virtually any group of Americans would agree that it would be wise to determine as a nation that it is in our interest for Social Security and Medicare to survive and at the same time not bankrupt the next generation. Americans would also agree that it is foolish to let the national debt grow unchecked, especially while we are struggling to pay for enhanced homeland security and overseas operations. These are not partisan positions, just basic economic facts. If people can agree about these goals, then why can't our elected representatives make changes instead of, by default, forcing us to choose between massive tax increases and a massive reduction in promised benefits?

In the case of Medicare, its present doomsday is about 2026, according to the trustees' report. And we know if something is not done soon to either slow down the costs or increase the revenue, Medicare will not be available for those who are in their forties today. Let us also agree that there is not a true market rationing of health care today, but rather a price-controlled system that is terribly inefficient and contributes to the increase in costs. Let us also agree that having parents in our homes instead of nursing homes is probably preferable in terms of quality of life at the sunset of our lives. Given that fact, let us have a public debate that is designed to recognize the reality of the situation, and let us censure anyone who uses the debate to demagogue or instill fear by suggesting that those who have a different view want to harm those who are most dependent on us.

Let us also realize that the debate of adding a drug benefit to Medicare at a time when it is fiscally unsound is nothing more than a failing by our elected representatives to address the real issue—the extremely high cost of prescription drugs (prescription drugs in the U.S. are 40 percent higher than anywhere else in the world). When was the last hearing in Congress on the competitive nature of the pharmaceutical industry and a real investigation into product price-fixing? Does any politician wonder why all the new drugs that come out in the same category cost the same?

I see the problem of a lack of consensus on Social Security and Medicare reform as one of a lack of information coming to the public. How many grandparents would like for their Social Security and Medicare to come from the decreased standard of living of their grandchildren? Exactly 12.4 percent of everything we earn today is taken up by a payroll tax for Social Security and Medicare (employers, component included). That tax will need to rise to approximately 18 to 20 percent in the next twenty years to generate minimal stability in the Social Security and Medicare systems. Taking an additional 8 percent of your children's and grandchildren's earnings to keep Social Security and Medicare at their present level is like telling them not to count on owning a home or sending their children to college.

I have presented these facts to hundreds of seniors in my district and medical practice, and not one senior has expressed a desire to increase their federal benefits on the backs of their children and grandchildren. When the American people understand the facts, they will demand action, but I fear they will never trust the spin from either party in Washington.

Not long ago I spoke to a group of doctors, and I followed a sitting congressman whose last statement to the group was, "The most important thing to a congressman is getting reelected." He was honest and offered sound advice to those seeking to lobby in Washington, but that is the problem. Because if getting reelected is the most important thing on the politician's radar screen, then our children, our future, and our nation is not the most important thing on his or her radar screen. The consequence of this pursuit places our nation at extreme risk.

> IF GETTING ELECTED IS THE MOST IMPORTANT THING ON THE POLITICIAN'S RADAR SCREEN THEN OUR CHILDREN, OUR FUTURE, AND OUR NATION IS NOT THE MOST IMPORTANT THING ON HIS OR HER RADAR SCREEN. THE CONSEQUENCE OF THIS PURSUIT PLACES OUR NATION AT EXTREME RISK.

The events in Congress since I left office tell me little has changed. Careerism—the importance of reelection above all else—is still the governing philosophy in Washington and is still blocking honest moves for reform. The Senate's decision in March 2003 to "pay for" the Iraq war by cutting President Bush's $726 billion tax cut in half is the latest classic example of Congress avoiding the real problem. Privately, many Republicans believe tax cuts are not only sound economic policy but also a way to deprive oxygen to the out-of-control fires of a government that is raging outside of its constitutional confines. Tax cuts are, in part, a way for Republicans to fight defensively a battle they lack the political will to fight offensively—reducing the unsustainable scope and size of government.

Democrats, on the other hand, believe in their heart of hearts that tax cuts do make good economic sense (JFK was a tax-cutter and sounded like a "personal responsibility" conservative when he said famously, "Ask not what your country can do for you, but what you can do for your country"). However, Democrats also understand that tax cuts will deprive the fires of big government of oxygen. Their problem is they believe the fires of big government create warmth, not wanton economic and cultural destruction as our founders warned.

The real debate and the real issue behind all the maneuvering on tax cuts, prescription drugs, and Social Security is the size and scope of government itself. The debate about today's tax cuts is not framed by either President Bush or Tom Daschle, but by the legacy of the secessionist South, the "New Deal," and the "Great Society." Attempting to blame President Bush's tax cut proposal for deficits is asinine. The trajectory of today's federal government that is creating huge deficits was set 40, 70, or even 140 years ago, not in 2000 or 2002.

Even in a time of war, it is doubtful the force of careerism will restrain Congress from doing what it knows it should not do but cannot help itself from doing because of the intoxicant of power. As Edmund Burke warned, "Those who have once been intoxicated with power . . . can never willingly abandon it." Yet this time of war and peril is the best time for the public to force Congress to confront some of the long-term challenges facing our country. Of course, mobilizing the public to force Congress to address these issues is difficult because CNN will never air alongside a "Showdown with Saddam" segment a "Showdown with Unsustainable Government" segment. This makes the task of educating the public all the more difficult for leaders and concerned citizens, but we should be motivated by the knowledge that the issues on the home front are no less threatening, and are arguably more threatening, than any threat from abroad.

I was amused by President Bush's March 25, 2003 speech requesting $75 billion for the Iraq war in which he took Congress to task. "One thing is for certain," the president said, "business as usual on Capitol Hill can't go on during this time of war, and by that I mean this supplemental should not be viewed as an opportunity to add spending that is unrelated, unwise, and unnecessary. Every dollar we spend must serve the interest of our nation, and the interest of our nation in this supplemental is to win this war and to be able to keep the peace."

As we sacrifice blood and treasure to fight tyranny abroad, we should remember that our founders emerged from an era of tyranny to establish our nation. Just past the FDR memorial in Washington, D.C. is the Jefferson Memorial. A statement from Jefferson that rings the inside of that memorial is a fitting motto for the challenges America faces today, both foreign and domestic: "I have sworn upon the altar of God eternal vigilance over every form of tyranny over the mind of man." Our founders lived through tyranny and from it emerged with a passionate but simple message: as government increases, liberty decreases. We would be wise to remember their warning as we continue this great experiment in representative democracy, an idea called America.